Common Planet

COMMON PLANET

A New Game of Life

an evolution of economics

Remzi Bajrami

ADDRESSED TO THE

INHABITANTS

OF

EARTH

On the following interesting

SUBJECTS

Of Universal Human Rights

Of the Security of Life

Thoughts on Universal & Contributory Value

Of the present ability of Humanity,

with Collective Production & Commons Resources

"Man knows no Master save creating Heaven,
Or those whom choice and common good ordain."
- Thomson

Common Planet: A New Game of Life

ISBN# 978-0-578-38108-4

Contact via website: http://www.Common-Planet.org. Cover design by Remzi Bajrami.

Version 1.1.0, February 22, 2022.

This manuscript may be periodically updated with corrections and small improvements. Revised versions may be posted to the Common Planet website. If you find errors or have a suggested improvement, please contact us through our website.

Warning and Disclaimer

Every effort has been made to make this book as accurate as possible, but information is provided on an "as is" basis with no warranty implied. Common Planet holds no responsibility for the persistence, accuracy or appropriateness of URL links or the content of linked websites.

Bulk Sales

Common Planet offers favorable discounts on this title when ordered in quantity. We invite small book sellers, nonprofits, social entrepreneurs and others to use this book as part of their fundraising programs. And we invite instructors to use it in schools. For information, contact us through the Common Planet website.

To my family, friends

and to all species

past and present.

And to those crazy dreamers and the ones who set out daily to establish a brighter future for all, especially those I hope to meet online and who'd do me the honor of making *my little community*

Community.Common-Planet.org

more habitable.

In memory of David Graeber.

"Perhaps the sentiments contained in the following pages are not yet sufficiently fashionable to procure them general favor; a long habit of not thinking a thing wrong, gives it a superficial appearance of being right, and raises at first a formidable outcry in defense of custom. But the tumult soon subsides. Time makes more converts than reason.

As a long and violent abuse of power, the (**Corporations**) support and corrupt all the (**Nations**) in what (**both**) call Theirs, and as the good people of this world are grievously oppressed by the combination, they have an undoubted privilege to inquire into the pretensions of both, and equally to reject the usurpation of either.

The cause of (**Earth**) is in a great measure the cause of all mankind. Many circumstances hath, and will arise, which are not local, but universal, and through which the principles of all Lovers of Mankind are affected, and in the Event of which, their Affections are interested. The laying a (**Planet**) desolate with Fire and Sword, declaring War against the natural rights of all Mankind, and extirpating the Defenders thereof from the Face of the Earth, is the Concern of every Man to whom Nature hath given the Power of feeling."[1]

---

[1] Thomas Paine, *Common Sense* (London: Publishers, 1776) pp. 12-14, (altered text in **bold**)

CONTENTS

	Acknowledgements	x
	Introduction by Adelina Bajrami	xii
1	What Kind of World Do You Want To Live In?	1
2	A Brief History of Game A	42
	• The Realm of Governance	57
	• The Realm of Economics	66
3	Common Planet	124
	• Circulatory Currency: Money	145
	• Banks	152
	• Flow Currency: Credit	166
4	Sovereignty	178
	• Community & Community Credit	182
	• Housing	184
5	Opportunity	188
	• Proof of Value (POV)	194
	• A Vision of Life on Common Planet, a story	196
	• Clubs & Enterprises	202
6	Liberty	214
	• Democracy	219
	• Law, Police & Military	225
7	Transition	231
	• Technology & Tactics	241

ACKNOWLEDGEMENTS

As the author, I wish to thank every person with whom I've ever connected with in this world. My contribution was made possible entirely because of your influence and from the vast wealth of information and knowledge produced by our ancestors and the billions alive today. To this human experiment, I wish to reciprocate and share what I've learned, in hopes that we may prosper on our journey together in this universe.

First, I'd like to thank my incredible parents: Mesude and Bajram Bajrami for their self-sacrificing support and patience for this work. Their struggle formed the foundation on which my life was built. We're all perched atop the proverbial 'shoulders of giants.' And in my case, my father is my giant.

Next, a debt of incredible gratitude to my love Ardijana, my life partner and best friend. With all of my love in dedication also to: my adult kids, brother, cousins, uncles, aunts, nephews, nieces and friends. Thank you all.

A special thank you to Lisa Bloniarz for the hundreds of hours of conversations exploring the territory with me. I learned a lot from you. You must know how much I benefited from the confidence you built in me.

Lastly, I'd like to thank people from the past and present that have had some influence in this work (listed in no particular order): Isni Bajrami

Terrance McKenna, Yuval Harari, Ezra Bowen, John K. Galbraith

Joan Robinson, Buckminster Fuller, Jacque Fresco, Martin Luther King Jr.

Thorstein Veblen, James Baldwin, David Graeber, Rutger Bregman

Jason Hickel, Richard Wolff, David Harvey, Dan Ariely, John Perkins

Naomi Klein, Colin Turner, Nick Chugg, David Campbell, Alastair Lord

Tony Seba, Paul Ehrlich, Kate Raworth, Steve Keen, Mariana Mazzucato

Stephanie Kelton, Guy Standing, Yanis Varoufakis, William McDonough

Troy Wiley, Jim O'Reilly, Gar Alperavitz, Elinor Ostrom, Chris Hedges

Daniel Christian Wahl, Ralph Nader, Aldous Huxley, Bertrand Russell
Thomas Paine, Daniel Quinn, Cornel West, Bret Weinstein, Eric Weinstein
Peter Schurman, David Korten, Bill McKibben, George Monbiot
Shimshon Bichler, Jonathan Nitzan, Thomas Greco Jr., Robert Schram
Blair Fix, Arash Kolahi, Oshan Jarow, Norm Kurland, Russell Roberts
Anand Giridharadas, Malcolm Gladwell, Marianne Williamson, Peter Joseph
Caitlin Johnstone, Arthur Brock, Fernanda Ibarra, Giorgos Kallis
Tyler Patterson, Vinay Gupta, Kylie Stedman, Jubilee Briscoe, Anton Wilson
Raymond Powell, Daniel Schmachtenberger, Jordan Hall, John Vervaeke
Hanzi Freinacht, Douglas Rushkoff, Gregory Rawlins, Michael Linton
Asatar Bair, Brent Cooper, Jim Rutt, Wayne Lewis, Paul Mason
David Fuller, Nora Bateson, Bonnitta Roy, Michel Bauwens, Ken Wilber
Charles Eisenstein, Vandana Shiva, David Bollier, George Pór, Stef Kuypers
Nathan Waters, John Ash, Orkun Baysal, Guillermo Martin, Nils Semmler
Bentley Davis, David Roviks, Mark Nadal, Spencer Winans, Perry Gruber
"John" (JEWL), Brett Scott, Rob Konrad, Scott Santens, Todd McKissick
George Mekhail, Gary Chartier, Charles Johnson, Nathan Robinson
Jeffrey Anthony, Nick Estes, Michael Kubler, Joe Brewer, Michael Hudson
Oshan Jarow, Warren Mosler, John Boik, Steve Grumbine, Henry George
Daniel Pinchbeck, Aaron Bastoni, Nick Srnicek

INTRODUCTION

by Adelina Bajrami

Early 2016 email from Remzi: "Write a two page introduction to our plan."

My reply: So I still don't really know what you're asking me to write about. What do you mean by "plan"?

I have some questions: (sidenote: When I say "we," I refer to a general we, we as in the people)

- So, what's going to happen to government? Who's going to govern the people? Will we have any formal leadership? How is that all going to work? What does "real" democracy look like?
- The basis of EarthVote is to actually get the entire Earth to vote, but how?
- This might be too far into the future, but if we are able to accomplish our goal- you know, giving the power back to the people, revolutionizing the system, etc.- what are we to do with existing landfills, polluted waters/soil, destroyed habitats, and other difficulties relating to the environment? We could revitalize forests and the like by planting trees, but trees take a long time to grow. The necessity for vegetation is great, so there is always nothing wrong with planting stuff, but that's definitely not a quick solution. There are also existing ways to purify water, so we shouldn't be having a water predicament either. Everyone should have access to clean, safe water; it is unjust to deprive people of the most vital component of survival, and it is just as criminal to purposely contaminate good water. But landfills, though? What do you propose we do about that? How can we eliminate the billions of accumulated waste without further damaging the planet? How about restoring habitats?
- What would a transition look like? How long would it take? How could we get everyone to contribute to a switch?
- Side thought: Imagine how cool the world would be with new technology. Like 3D printers- those things are my favorite. At this point, we can create almost anything with a 3D printer; this is one of many inventions that are changing the way we do stuff in society.
- Okay, so this isn't a question either, but a thought to consider: Right now we have a food crisis, but I feel as if I shouldn't be too worried about

supplying food to people in the future with all these advancements in science and- don't bash-the genetic modification of food to thrive in different conditions. Genetically altering a food item isn't BAD, like many people claim it is. The only thing bad about adding science experimentation to our food (in our current situation) is that a lot of it is under corporate control, so we are completely unsure of what the frick is being put in our food.

Late 2016: My Introduction

There are problems in this world: greed, war, ecological destruction, crime, oppression, abuse, addiction, mental illness, suicide; that list is too long.

We all know what is needed: an alternative system. But they say there is no alternative. That is a lie. Here's a plan to solve all problems.

Utopia. I actually hesitate to say this. Utopia is certainly not the right word, is it? Maybe not, but what we've got on our hands is a good start— a great start— that will surely inspire people out there to rise up and get their voice heard. Our glorious plan will light a spark that will rapidly spread and grow to a flame, and then transform into a bigger and bigger fire, sweeping the planet until it has reached the span of the entire population, igniting within every human being a flare of emotions, whether it be hope, fear, or rage. People are going to feel something, and that is what we want. We need people to at least be aware of what is going on before we can really begin impacting change. So, what is our so-called glorious plan?

Well, first something we need to recognize and understand is our current situation. Let's just focus on housing for a moment. Right now, we have an abundance of housing, but we continue to build more and more living spaces. We tear down trees and habitats to make space for houses that will remain vacant until a person or people come along with the sufficient means to purchase or rent the house. Not to mention, there are plenty of existing apartments that are permanently empty and will doubtably be used by anyone anytime soon. What I am getting at is we have enough living space for pretty much every human on this planet, really There isn't any reason why we should have a homeless population when we could easily provide these people with a safer place to live. The issue at hand is money, of course; that is the only thing holding us back.

Housing is just one aspect of our messed up system, but I want to highlight the last thing I just mentioned: money. Money is essentially the root of our problems; and not-so coincidentally the root of our plan. Before I begin on laying out this plan, there are a couple things to keep in mind. For one, our plan neutralises money's power. Secondly, our plan is a great deal to take in, so it will sound crazy upon the initial reading. But I assure you, it is anything but.

So, money. The current system is powered by money. It is well known that money leads to greed and greed leads to other evil things and in turn creates a whole spiral of crap in which we fall into and can't get out of. We spend a lot of time avoiding stepping into dog waste, but why is it we've never used the same precaution with the crap money constantly pumps out? Do we really want to live in a world where we are perpetually stuck in the center of a pile of crap? Ew, no way, that's gross, unsanitary. Yuck. No, we want to get away from this system. How? Simple: get rid of money. That's blasphemy, you say? Well, I say that's genius!

So now we just got rid of money. In our plan, we present the idea of Credit. Okay, so the name isn't perfect, but it's an idea- just focus on the concept and then we can deal with the name if the need arises. Credit is currency everyone gets automatically every month and something everyone earns more of simply by contributing in their community. To ease any confusion, I must mention something I failed to do earlier on: the plan consists of a completely remodeled society, so everything you understand of how the world works now you must forget, throw out the window or into a fire. For in our plan, people don't work countless hours in useless jobs, they work whenever they want in circumstances they will enjoy. For in our plan, we can share and learn information with each other freely and collectively. And for everything we contribute, we will earn an amount of Credit we can use to obtain something of necessity or pleasure.

Let's go back to housing again for a moment. Previously I stated that we have an abundance of houses and apartments and other living spaces for anyone who wants or needs to use them. Since we've gotten rid of money, everyone now has the opportunity to live wherever they please for however long they please. In this new society, we do not have debts either, so you will be the caretaker of your living space free and clear. That's how it should be, correct? Everyone deserves the right to a comfortable, safe shelter, yes? This is what we want to see in our plan.

To summarize thus far, we've destroyed money, replaced it with Credit, and offered guaranteed housing. Some other free things include school, information, food and water. Some things you might still be confused about:

travel, government, global warming, and technology, and maybe Credit. Well, I only have two pages, so it is impossible to outline every single detail of our plan; I am only speaking in general terms for now. To appease a few lingering questions, climate change will be much easier to address with the abandonment of money because corporations will no longer be drilling into earth or releasing poison into our water or our air for their own private gain. We can finally begin the transition into a society less dependent on fossil fuel because it will no longer require bucket loads of money We will finally be able to live in a peaceful world because war will no longer be "necessary." What will there be to fight over? We will finally be able to recognize everyone's basic human rights and honor everyone's status as a human being. Although not blood related, you are my brother (or sister) and so is everyone else around you. We were all born on this planet and deserve the same amount of basic respect. Since the planet is our home, it is our responsibility to protect and take care of it. It is also our duty to live in harmony with other species and wildlife for they are a part of the wonder that is Earth. We live in a world where we are always competing for everything, and it's only hurting us more than anything. It is time to change.

The plan isn't perfect, and there is always room for improvement; but it is a start- and a good one I might add. Too often in revolutions do we see failure as the people did not have a clear picture of what they truly desired. Now it is time to begin and finish a revolution across the globe and ultimately succeed. No more capitalism, no more communism, no more dictatorships, no more socialism, no more fascism- we need something new and we need it now or else we really are screwed. I'm sick of always being stuck in this crap pile: I want out. And so do you, most likely. I just want to live a life where I can read and write and travel in peace without having to worry about working for nothing for some old white dudes. Enough is enough. I'm done.

So there you have it: your gosh darn two pages. I honestly wrote and rewrote the beginning so many times so that's whatever. Anyway, I still feel as if I did not say everything I wanted to say but like I said in those two pages I was just speaking generally. And my audience is anyone unfamiliar with what we were doing.

Chapter 1

What Kind of World Do You Want To Live In?

"Create a place for people to live like human beings, instead of slaves to some bullshit concept of progress that is driving us all mad." - Hunter S. Thompson

This is a book of hope. It is about a vision of a new game of life conceived in 2015 during the most depressing and challenging period of my life. Driven out of desperation to find an alternative to the incessant inequality and instability of our economic system led to questions which led to answers which lead to solutions.

The purpose of this book and the primary objective of Common Planet is to introduce to the world an alternative global economic protocol designed to meet the basic needs and maximum desires of all people within a sustainable biosphere. It's basically a foundational economic blueprint for how we can work together to solve all of our problems without killing each other: to begin real Civilization.

We do this by changing the game of money and property, resulting in Sovereignty, Opportunity and Liberty for each person on the planet.

So this is a new socio-economic innovation of the monetary system which enables economic fairness leading to social cohesion, democratic participation and environmental sustainability. We call it a Flow currency system, in contrast to the traditional Circulatory currency system now in play. It's an evolution of economics which ends poverty, homelessness and war by eliminating the need for banks, debt and taxes forever!

Indeed, these are some bold and seemingly ridiculous claims, notwithstanding, you'll soon read about how.

How money is created and directed is the crux of our problems. Money is the most powerful tool in the history of the world and yet is also the least understood. How money works is concealed behind a veil of complexity, muddled by disinformation and covered in secrecy. In the comprehensive classic 1973 book *Money: Whence It Came, Where It Went*, John Kenneth Galbraith exposes how "The study of money, above all other fields in economics, is one in which complexity is used to disguise truth or to evade truth, not to reveal it." Money was purposely shaped to become the ultimate tool of power that it is today and now it's time for us to reshape it into a tool for peace and prosperity.

The economic system we've inherited evolved from an expanding industrial system and it is no longer fit for purpose. It never really was. It is based on a primitive notion of ownership, that of private enclosure, and uses the simple equation of profit through trade. It's justified based on the childish premise of 'finders keepers, losers weepers', which itself evolved into the equally childish premise of the 'divine right of Kings.' Today, money is our master. The divine right of capital is the law of the land everywhere.

What we think of as economics is based on the concept of trade, which is based on the concept of ownership of things that can be traded. In the game of life today, it is <u>only</u> through trade that value can be realized. Over time, financial tools, like currency, emerged to measure value and to command all the resources of the planet, including human activity, toward the perpetual production of material goods from the physical world because the drive for profit fuels the race to produce more stuff for trade. That is the equation of today's economics.

What is traded? Property. What is Property? At its most basic, Property is any *thing* of value.[1] It can be physical or abstract. Land, buildings, houses, equipment, cars, plants, animals, people (labor), money, stocks, bonds, jewelry, art, patents, copyrights, intellectual property, crypto currencies and non-fungible tokens (NFT) are all examples of Property: any *thing* of value.

Throughout this book, I will make reference to **'<u>Game A</u>'[2]: to own Property for value extraction or value appreciation.** Essentially, the game is to acquire as much Property as possible for its value.

---

[1] The word 'value' is synonymous with 'money' or 'currency' throughout this book.

[2] In 2017 we referred to Common Planet as "a new game of life." In this 2018 interview, Tyler Patterson & Remzi Bajrami use Game A/B terminology, https://www.youtube.com/watch?v=euWFP1GzuEc&t

There are three different kinds of players: People, Corporations and Nations and they are all perpetually in pursuit of more Property. The value of any player is something called net worth, which is exactly the sum total value of all Property they own. All the players compete with one another over Property and are ranked by net worth.

Leo Tolstoy's remarks on Property sums up the Game A world perfectly:

> States and governments intrigue and go to war for property. Bankers, traders, manufacturers, and landowners work, scheme, and torment themselves and others for property; officials and artisans struggle, cheat, oppress and suffer for the sake of property; our Law Courts and police defend property; our penal settlements and prisons and all the horrors of our so-called repression of crime, exist on account of property.
>
> Property is the root of all evil, and the division and safeguarding of property occupies the whole world.[3]

Adam Smith, the so-called 'father of economics', described the right to trade Property as the defining feature of capitalism. Innovations in science and technology made trade a more valuable part of the economy and thus capitalism advanced first by navigation at sea then by the harnessing of steam and electric power in the late eighteenth and nineteenth centuries which fueled a massive expansion in trade. Today, trade is still the giant global game and "the division and safeguarding of property occupies the whole world."

Humans have throughout recent history mostly been playing variations of this same game: to trade Property for maximum value (profit). Much of it has to do with natural laws and biology, however, the role of humans is continually obscured to hide the truth. But it should be no mystery that people have designed and continue to shape many of its rules. One of my favorite authors, the late David Graeber, reminds us that "the ultimate, hidden truth of the world is that it's something that we make, and could just as easily make differently."

Change is inevitable. The world is constantly transforming, but while change is constant, the rate at which things change is not. Our population and technological advances are expanding exponentially, and the adjustments we absolutely need to make won't come for a while, or maybe even not at all, if we continue to live the way we do. In fact, if we keep going on this way, we will continue to see more harmful happenings occur rather than positive

---

[3] Leo Tolstoy, *What then Must We Do?,* (1942), Translated by A. Maude, online, https://arvindguptatoys.com/arvindgupta/whatthenmustwedo.pdf

ones.[4] So this is our task: to fashion an entirely new game of life in which all humans on Earth can live in an environment of opportunity and autonomy rather than oppression and domination.

All life depends on Property and economics is the study of the management of Property. **Property *is* life**. How Property continues to be managed today can be said to be evil. What else do you call increasing inequality and perpetual poverty amidst escalating ecological destruction? Property is a necessity for life, for continuation of game play, but what is private vs common is misunderstood, misidentified and misallocated all because we've confused prices for value. The value of a person should never have been measured by the prices of trading Property. In the beginning Property was scarce, but that is no longer a major concern. Today, our problems are inefficiency, corruption and intentional bad policy.

Common Planet is a new global economic game where every person gets access to housing for life, monthly UBI of Flow Credit currency and more Credit every time they learn, play or work. All commercial land, properties and resources become the commons, accounted for and listed in networked, Holochain databases. Corporations and government agencies transform operations into co-ops with free lease to their equipment and properties. Workers are paid directly with Credit as mentioned. Bonus Credit is awarded to workers in Enterprises based on new 'profit' measures oriented toward producing the best possible products in the best possible ways that benefit the real stakeholders: workers, consumers and society. Credit flows to all and all use it to acquire goods produced from the commons which then turn into private personal possessions. Credit is a Flow currency, not circulatory like money, so it is created when earned and deleted when used.

That's just a broad overview to give you a sense of what this is all about. It may sound fantastic and unbelievable right now but after chapter six you'll have a clear understanding of how all this relates to real life.

"We live in capitalism," said the great Ursula K. Le Guin, "Its power seems inescapable. So did the divine right of kings. Any human power can be resisted and changed by human beings. Resistance and change often begin in art, and very often in our art, the art of words."[5] It will take a lot of words and a lot of voices. This new global canvas will require artists of all kinds to

---

[4] CNN, "Vanishing: The extinction crisis is far worse than you think", https://www.cnn.com/interactive/2016/12/specials/vanishing/index.html

[5] https://www.ursulakleguin.com/nbf-medal

spread the message, to build the new world. So that soon we may all dance in a world of our choosing. I'm looking forward to others' contributions.

Game A: Trade. All value comes from trading.
To extract value by trading Property. It is a rivalrous, win/lose game using money that is created by banks who get it as free credit but issue it as interest-bearing debt (Property) to Nations, Corporations and people, who then use it to value and exchange all the Property on Earth. Only Property is valuable.

Common Planet: Contribute. All value comes from contributions.
To create value by managing Property as stewards, not owners. Credit flows directly to all people, who then use it to satisfy their needs and desires in the open market of goods produced from the Commons. People are valuable.

According to all economic theory, 'there is no alternative' (TINA) to economic growth. Unfortunately, economic growth means continued ecological destruction. Author Naomi Klein writes a lot about the practices of business and how "our economy is at war with the many forms of life on earth, including human life. What the climate needs to avoid collapse is a contraction in humanity's use of resources; what our economic model demands to avoid collapse is unfettered expansion. Only one of these sets of rules can be changed, and it's not the laws of nature."

"Whether we and our politicians know it or not, Nature is party to all our deals and decisions, and she has more votes, a longer memory, and a sterner sense of justice than we do," cautions Wendell Berry.

Over 15,000 scientists from 184 countries issued a second dire warning to humanity in 2017. They show how the overconsumption of the world's resources is leading us to "widespread misery and catastrophic biodiversity loss." Time is running out, they warned: "Soon it will be too late to shift course away from our failing trajectory."[6]

More recently, the Intergovernmental Panel on Climate Change (IPCC) just released its sixth report in August 2021 using words like "unequivocal", "unprecedented" and "irreversible."[7] Things are not going well. On August 14, 2021, at Summit Station, the highest point in elevation (3,216m or 10,551 ft), on the Greenland Ice Sheet which is basically the coldest location in the Northern Hemisphere, it rained for the first time ever![8]

Not all economic growth is inherently destructive. However, the current metric we use, Gross Domestic Product (GDP), makes no distinctions on which production processes are sustainable and which are harmful. It's all considered 'economic growth.' Even Simon Kuznets, the inventor of GDP, testified before US Congress in 1934, "Goals for more growth should specify more growth of what and for what." We cannot continue to be willfully ignorant and allow ecological destruction to continue because of old economic thinking and entrenched power.

"Anyone who believes exponential growth can go on forever in a finite world is either a madman or an economist," remarked Kenneth Boulding, co-founder of General Systems Theory.

In March 1968, Robert (Bobby) Kennedy, while running for President, gave this speech highly critical of measuring value based on prices of goods:

> If we judge the United States of America by that— that Gross National Product counts air pollution and cigarette advertising, and ambulances to clear our highways of carnage. It counts special locks for our doors and the jails for the people who break them. It counts the destruction of the redwood and the loss of our natural wonder in chaotic sprawl. It counts napalm and counts nuclear warheads and armored cars for the police to fight the riots in our cities. It counts Whitman's rifle and Speck's knife, and the television programs which glorify violence in order to sell toys to our children. Yet the gross national product does not allow for the health of our children, the quality of their education or the joy of their play. It does not include the beauty of our poetry or the strength of our marriages, the

---

[6] William J. Ripple and 15,371 scientists, *World Scientists' Warning to Humanity: A Second Notice*, BioScience, Vol. 67, No. 12 (December 2017), pp. 1026-1028, online, https://academic.oup.com/bioscience/article/67/12/1026/460522

[7] IPCC, Sixth Assessment Report, online, https://www.ipcc.ch/report/ar6/wg1/#SPM

[8] National Snow & Ice Data Center, online, https://nsidc.org/greenland-today/2021/08/rain-at-the-summit-of-greenland/

> intelligence of our public debate or the integrity of our public officials. It measures neither our wit nor our courage, neither our wisdom nor our learning, neither our compassion nor our devotion to our country, it measures everything in short, except that which makes life worthwhile.[9]

The solution, of course, is to build an economy that is geared toward well-being— toward economic development— rather than economic growth. Some say we've already passed the tipping point. Let's hope not. The architect, inventor and futurist Buckminster Fuller offered us this hope and warning in 1981:

> To know now what we could never have known before 1969—that we now have an option for all humanity to "make it" successfully on this planet in this lifetime—is not to be optimistic. It is only a validation of hope... Whether it is to be Utopia or Oblivion will be a touch-and-go relay race right up to the final moment. The race is between a better-informed, hopefully inspired young world versus a running-scared, misinformedly brain-conditioned, older world. Humanity is in "final exam" as to whether or not it qualifies for continuance in Universe.[10] Quite clearly, our task is predominantly metaphysical, for it is how to get all of humanity to educate itself swiftly enough to generate spontaneous social behaviors that will avoid extinction.[11]

If, for well over half a century— longer than me and most people alive today — we've had the necessary technology and scientific knowledge to provide every person with the material conditions for a prosperous and sustainable society, why all this inefficiency, suffering and waste?

The civil rights movement of the 1960s advanced the cause of racial equality in America, and while it wasn't tolerated it was ultimately accepted because they knew as long as they controlled Property with the laws, the police and the courts, power would be maintained. Just like John Daniel Ehrlichman, counsel and Assistant to the President for Domestic Affairs under President Richard Nixon told us: "The Nixon campaign in 1968, and the Nixon White House after that, had two enemies: the antiwar left and black people. You understand what I'm saying? We knew we couldn't make it

---

[9] Robert F. Kennedy, University of Kansas speech, March 18, 1968, online, https://www.jfklibrary.org/learn/about-jfk/the-kennedy-family/robert-f-kennedy/robert-f-kennedy-speeches/remarks-at-the-university-of-kansas-march-18-1968

[10] R. Buckminster Fuller, *Critical Path* (1981), p. xxxvi

[11] Wikiquote, https://en.wikiquote.org/wiki/Buckminster_Fuller

illegal to be either against the war or black, but by getting the public to associate the hippies with marijuana and blacks with heroin, and then criminalizing both heavily, we could disrupt those communities. We could arrest their leaders, raid their homes, break up their meetings, and vilify them night after night on the evening news. Did we know we were lying about the drugs? Of course we did."

Make something illegal then use force to justify the non-crime crime. This is common knowledge. Ayn Rand wrote about this in her 1957 novel *Atlas Shrugged*: "There's no way to rule innocent men. The only power any government has is the power to crack down on criminals. Well, when there aren't enough criminals one makes them. One declares so many things to be a crime that it becomes impossible for men to live without breaking laws." In this way, policing became a bigger tool for social control, and it's only gotten worse since.

> In the 1960s, the United States incarcerated its population at a rate that was comparable to other developed countries. Today, America ranks among the most punitive states in world history. Black men born between 1965 and 1969 have been more likely to go to prison than to graduate from college. American punishment is thus of unprecedented *severity* — more prisoners per capita than ever before, and more so than any comparable country in world history. It is also characterized by extreme *inequality* — some Americans are much more likely to languish in prisons than others. These are its twin features.[12]

It is only power over Property the rich have ever cared about, and so as soon as talk began about poverty, inequality and the unfairness of economics, so too did the killing. They had already killed Bobby's brother JFK in 1963, then just a few weeks after Bobby's 1968 speech, Martin Luther King Jr (MLK) was shot and killed, and two months later Bobby was shot and killed too.

In a 1967 speech titled "Beyond Vietnam: A Time to Break Silence," MLK linked poverty to the failure of capitalism: "We as a nation must undergo a radical revolution of values. We must rapidly begin the shift from a thing-oriented society to a person oriented society. When machines and computers, profit motives and property rights are considered more important than people, the giant triplets of racism, extreme materialism, and militarism are incapable of being conquered." They murdered MLK for daring to challenge

---

[12] Catalyst, "The Economic Origins of Mass Incarceration", https://catalyst-journal.com/2019/12/the-economic-origins-of-mass-incarceration

power, and every year since have continued to suppress, repress and murder thousands of people all over the world without pause.[13] All of this evil is 100% driven by our amoral economic game.

If not for a lack of tools or brains, then our failures to protect human health and the environment must stem from our dysfunctional socio-economic system. As highly social animals, above all, we value fairness and seek cooperation. Why then have we locked ourselves into this perpetual war over the resources of the planet? Make no mistake, it's a game of power and it's deep rooted in Property.

Players lie, steal and kill to compete for economic advantage. Everybody knows we have no choice but to compete for Property, that the game we are playing is unfair, rigged and built on lies and secrets to hide the theft and plunder of the past. Much of who owns what, how and how much is secret. For her role in exposing some of the truth in the 2016 release of the Panama Papers[14] they killed Daphne C. Galizia, the journalist from Malta, in a car bomb triggered via text by some paid goons who were on a boat out at sea.

Now there is another leak, called the Pandora Papers, which, unlike the Panama Papers with data drawn from just one law firm, "this new material includes records from 14 separate financial-services entities operating in countries and territories including Switzerland, Singapore, Cyprus, Belize and the British Virgin Islands. The files detail more than 29,000 offshore accounts, more than double the number identified in the Panama Papers. Among the account owners are more than 130 people listed as billionaires by Forbes magazine and more than 330 public officials in over 90 countries and territories, twice the number found in the Panama documents."[15]

Who was responsible for this latest leak? Journalist Benjamin Norton, in a Twitter thread claims it's just Game A information warfare:

> ...the so-called "leak" was likely a hack by US spy agencies. The "journalists" in Nicaragua that billionaire-funded @ICIJorg worked with on the Pandora Papers are all US govt-funded anti-Sandinista activists. The goal of these right-wing opposition activists was to show how Venezuela found ways to get

[13] The Guardian, "Murders of environment and land defenders hit record high", Sept. 12, 2021, https://www.theguardian.com/environment/2021/sep/13/murders-environment-land-defenders-record-high

[14] Panama Papers, https://panamapapers.org/

[15] Greg Miller et al, "Billions Hidden Beyond Reach", Washington Post, Oct 3, 2021, https://www.washingtonpost.com/business/interactive/2021/pandora-papers-offshore-finance/

> around illegal US sanctions, and portray that as "corruption." That's not journalism; it's US govt-sponsored information warfare to justify a murderous blockade. The message? Evading illegal US sanctions = "corruption." There are ZERO US politicians in the Pandora Papers, but there are 1200 Venezuelans. No major US assets were hurt by the Pandora Papers.[16]

I'm all for transparency but selective transparency is gamesmanship. Author Max Borders says "We're living in an information Hall of Mirrors. That means everything we consume — whether articles, memes, videos, or the nightly news — should invite our suspicion. It's hard to tell what's true anymore. Journalism has devolved from being a truth-tracking enterprise into a mechanism of behavioral control by powerful elites."[17]

Information is power so this isn't a surprise. After all, disinformation is one of the most powerful tactics in this rivalrous game.

> No matter where you live, if you are on the Internet you are in a war zone... For as long as humans have fought, military tactics have always involved propaganda, information manipulation, and deception. Today, digital communication technologies have changed the landscape... In this kind of war, the mind of every citizen is a potential target, and tactical victories could include a delegitimized election, implosions of civic discourse, and mutual hatred sparked between fellow citizens... Just as the destructive power of nuclear weapons forced humanity to reorient to the idea that mutually assured destruction exists at the extremes of physical violence, so advances in information warfare require us to face the same truth of inevitable self-destruction, and to mutually back away. The challenges before us are technological, psychological, and cultural... There are potential futures in which the technology currently being used to create information weapons of mass destruction could be used to create the most powerful educational infrastructures humans have ever experienced. We must make this choice, for that future is not the default path. There is no future for open societies otherwise.[18]

Because of the colossal information warfare escalating in our insta-connected world, nobody knows what to believe anymore. We don't even know how

---

[16] Benjamin Norton, https://twitter.com/BenjaminNorton/status/1444770698925326336

[17] Max Borders, "Sensemaking in the Era of Authoritarian Media", https://www.aier.org/article/sensemaking-in-the-era-of-authoritarian-media/

[18] The Consilience Project, "It's a MAD Information War", online, https://consilienceproject.org/its-a-mad-information-war/

much money exists in the world[19]; how can we when things like secret financial accounts exist. "The US has now become the global center for money hiding and illicit wealth storage... An estimated $24 trillion to $36 trillion in wealth, controlled by the planet's wealthiest 0.1 percent, is now hidden in various mechanisms."[20] Give me a break, how much more illegitimate can it get!

How much Property is there in the world right now? Is accounting of the values of Property real?[21] How much of the 'scientific' or 'academic' research done today is true and real? And how much is done in the pursuit of making or protecting profit? We don't even know. We are operating completely blind. Such is the corrupting power of money. We have allowed it to so completely warp our principles and morals. An embarrassing blemish on our history.

There was the Renaissance and the Enlightenment, both eras in which knowledge and new ideas were embraced and realized. Then came along the 20th Century which gave rise to Public Relations and the mass manipulation of information, destroyers of knowledge and innovation... yet it continues.

To put it into perspective: if you *own* one of the most valuable Properties in the game today— a liquid in the ground called oil— is there any limit to what you would do to extract the most value from *your* Property? There is not! And there is no shortage of people who will *help* (conspire with) you to extract value so they can get some too. We have little idea how much technology and innovation have been quashed due to rivalrousness and greed rewarded by today's economic incentives (human designed protocols). And although too many people do nasty things in justification of trying to *earn* a living, most people are not evil. The system we live under drives the evil that is happening full force... yet it continues.

American science fiction writer, Kim Stanley Robinson, in a recent interview, talked about how our current, man-made, economic incentives drive our actions, and about how those actions will lead to danger.

> So although almost every nation has signed the Paris agreement and agreed in theory to the principle of rapid emissions reduction, nations including

---

[19] Visual Capitalist, https://www.visualcapitalist.com/all-of-the-worlds-money-and-markets-in-one-visualization-2020/

[20] Chuck Collins, The Nation, "How Tax Haven States Enable Billionaires to Hide Trillions", https://www.thenation.com/article/economy/tax-haven-delaware-south-dakota/tnamp/

[21] Dave Lindorff, The Nation, "Exclusive: The Pentagon's Massive Accounting Fraud Exposed" https://www.thenation.com/article/archive/pentagon-audit-budget-fraud/

> Saudi Arabia, Russia, Canada, Brazil, Nigeria, Australia, Mexico, China, Venezuela, Norway and the US — not to mention several others — have made promises under the Paris agreement that will cost them many trillions of dollars in lost income... Naturally, there will be elected officials and civil servants in these governments doing their best to burn a few last trillions' worth of these soon-to-be-stranded assets. They will see this as their patriotic and fiduciary duty. So unless we make other arrangements, there will be a fire sale. This means that one giant aspect of the problem we face is financial. Thinking about money, and directing money, are key to getting through this crisis century successfully.[22]

This mass information manipulation could potentially doom our species if we let it continue. In 1995, Carl Sagan had an ominous vision of our future, now our present, when he wrote:

> I have a foreboding of an America in my children's or grandchildren's time - when the United States is a service and information economy; when nearly all the key manufacturing industries have slipped away to other countries; when awesome technological powers are in the hands of a very few, and no one representing the public interest can even grasp the issues; when the people have lost the ability to set their own agendas or knowledgeably question those in authority; when, clutching our crystals and nervously consulting our horoscopes, our critical faculties in decline, unable to distinguish between what feels good and what's true, we slide, almost without noticing, back into superstition and darkness.[23]

Standard global economic protocols using modern technology in a shared, open information accounting architecture can solve this problem. So why haven't we created the peaceful, prosperous and sustainable society that we all want and need so desperately now more than ever?

Many philosophers, sociologists, economists and other thinkers have examined how and why the system operates as it does. Those of us studying history and theory are blessed with access to libraries and new books perpetually fill the bookstores. Then there's the Internet[24] where practically anything ever written or recorded can be found to help us better understand our predicament.

---

[22] Kim Stanley Robinson, "a climate plan for a world in flames", Financial Times, online, https://www.ft.com/content/ff94df96-b702-4e01-addd-f4253d0eecf6

[23] Carl Sagan, The Demon-Haunted World, (1995)

[24] Pew Research Center, The negatives of digital life, https://www.pewresearch.org/internet/2018/07/03/the-negatives-of-digital-life/

But how many books promote global structural socio-economic solutions? How many proposals for actual alternatives exist? Not enough. Yet that is exactly what we need in this late hour. Karl Marx famously wrote, "Philosophers have hitherto only interpreted the world in various ways; the point is to change it."[25] Full disclosure: I had not yet read any Marx prior to this alternative vision, but have since benefited immensely by reading him.

In 2014, my new business failed and plunged me into economic ruin. There I was, broke, a publicly branded dirty rotten scoundrel whose life just derailed. I didn't know what to do, so I froze. That combination of helplessness and hopelessness is a volatile mix which so often leads either to suicide or a rebirth. I was not yet dead and I didn't want to die, but just thinking about my future and how hard and miserable it seemed had me wishing for death. And then, of course, here we are accelerating exponentially toward ecological collapse. **Everything is accelerating exponentially!**

That kind of math is terrifying. Physicist Albert A. Bartlett once said, "The greatest shortcoming of the human race is our inability to understand the exponential function." Does the term 'tipping point' mean anything to you?

I thought, "what's the point of struggling through life only to watch the world burn?" Sure, there'd be some ups and downs but in the end it doesn't even matter, or so some song says. Except I have children too and could not in good conscience abandon and let them suffer this terrible fate alone.

A year later, as my wife and I were sitting on the couch watching yet another documentary and talking about all the problems in the world, in walks our eldest daughter Adelina and yells, "I'm sick of you guys constantly talking about all the problems in the world. Why don't you search for solutions instead?" And just like that, she buried my hopelessness and redirected my life toward a purpose.

Soon after, EarthVote[26] was created in late 2015 as just a collection of solution seekers with a generic website calling for system change. In September 2016 I wrote the first intro to Common Planet and, besides some minor editing, it is what still remains on that website today.

"In order to change the world, you need to know what kind of world you want; in order to know what you want, you need to know what exists; and in order to know what exists, you need *radical, autonomous* — and therefore *non-*

---

[25] Karl Marx, *Theses On Feuerbach* (1845), online, https://www.marxists.org/archive/marx/works/1845/theses/

[26] EarthVote, website, http://earthvote.org/

academic — re-search."[27] That statement accurately reflects the approach we took. My lifetime pursuit of knowledge, both academic and non-academic, and two decades of personal and relevant professional experience had already offered me a clear view of what exists. So, we started with a simple question: "What kind of world do you want to live in?"And this was our answer:

> I want to live in a world where there is no poverty, no homelessness, no war, and no nuclear weapons. A world where people are free to live anywhere, with guaranteed housing, access to good food, clean water, clean energy, healthcare, free education for life and spiritual freedom.

The task of defining the goals and vision for a Common Planet turned out to be quite simple and universal. Imagining a better ordering of human society is as old as Plato and his *Republic.* All lovers of mankind apparently have the same dream: liberty and justice in peace. MLK had the same dream too:

> In a sense we have come to our nation's capital to cash a check. When the architects of our republic wrote the magnificent words of the Constitution and the Declaration of Independence, they were signing a promissory note to which every American was to fall heir. This note was a promise that all men, yes, black men as well as white men, would be guaranteed the unalienable rights of life, liberty, and the pursuit of happiness... It is obvious today that America has defaulted on this promissory note insofar as her citizens of color are concerned. Instead of honoring this sacred obligation, America has given the Negro people a bad check, a check which has come back marked "insufficient funds." But we refuse to believe that the bank of justice is bankrupt. We refuse to believe that there are insufficient funds in the great vaults of opportunity of this nation. So we have come to cash this check — a check that will give us upon demand the riches of freedom and the security of justice. We have also come to this hallowed spot to remind America of the fierce urgency of now. This is no time to engage in the luxury of cooling off or to take the tranquilizing drug of gradualism. Now is the time to make real the promises of democracy. Now is the time to rise from the dark and desolate valley of segregation to the sunlit path of racial justice. Now is the time to lift our nation from the quicksands of racial injustice to the solid rock of brotherhood. Now is the time to make justice a reality for all of God's children."[28]

---

[27] Nitzan and Bichler, online, https://capitalaspower.com/

[28] Dr. Martin Luther King Jr., "I have a dream", speech, August 28, 1963, Lincoln Memorial steps

Almost 50 years later and that check has still not been cashed, democracy still remains a lie and justice is still a mirage. By the way, it is no coincidence that I began to care more about the poor only after I became broke. I started life poorer than 80% globally, like a middle-ages villager, and rose quickly to the top 1% globally before I crashed back to the bottom. My instinct was to just get back on my feet, get out there and hustle to make some money again, but it was different this time. Ahead lay economic and/or ecological collapse. The existential risks now clear were too much to be ignored. Before the hope came, I was talking and thinking about becoming a prepper because all I could think and see was the world was overpopulated and we were doomed. I was a negative, miserable bastard. Can you blame me though, it's not like I had any power to do anything about anything, or even ideas about how we might change course. That is, until we started to look for solutions.

Once the clarity came, I became transfixed. Ended up sacrificing my life to this path. Renewed hope brought feelings of empathy, joy and a yearning for life at the same time as feelings of disgust and rage in having to watch Game A continuing to suck the life out of the people and the planet.

Society is like one of those patients who is being operated on, totally conscious of everything that is happening, brain firing on all cylinders and the rest of the body completely numb with eyes wide open unable to even blink. We all see what's going on while at the same time we are all individually powerless to do anything about it.

The incredibly brave, young activist Greta Thunberg points the blame directly at today's *leaders*: "Many are asking what it'll take for people in power to wake up. But let's be clear - they're already awake. They know exactly what they're doing. They know exactly what priceless values they're sacrificing to maintain business as usual."[29] While this is true, so *is* TINA, for now.

Jason Hickel explains this feeling: "We are a depressed, lonely and alienated society because we live in an economic system that is organized around artificial scarcity, exploitation and extraction. It breaks us every day."[30]

I hate the game, not the players. "It is only a few rare and exceptional men who have that kind of love towards mankind at large that makes them unable to endure patiently the general mass of evil and suffering, regardless of any relation it may have to their own lives. These few, driven by sympathetic pain, will seek, first in thought and then in action, for some way of escape, some

[29] Greta Thunberg, https://twitter.com/GretaThunberg/status/1456731487928205321

[30] Jason Hickel, https://twitter.com/jasonhickel/status/1444590724452913152

new system of society by which life may become richer more full of joy and less full of preventable evils than it is at present."[31]

This isn't about jealousy or envy. It's about replacing an unfair economics that concentrates power in the hands of amoral, flawed humans into one that distributes that power in a fair, equitable game with equality of opportunity for all.[32] Will some excel more than others in the new game? Of course, but nobody gets left behind in a fair game and that is an absolute basic principle of any game.

I'm no saint, wait, actually I was in 1991. In high school we were the Canterbury Saints, lol. So, when I was 18, and was afforded a day alone for perhaps the first time in my life, I tripped into a profound life experience. I asked myself, "What's the purpose of life?" and instinctively answered, "to help as many people as possible." And that remains my guiding principle to this day. Sounds corny but it's the truth.

How does one "help as many people as possible?" The answer I landed on pretty quickly was "to make as much money as possible." You see, I was born money poor in a Yugoslavian village that is now a part of North Macedonia. We moved to the United States when I was five and after some years of my dad working masonry construction, we became rich, or so I thought. I grew up watching my father work his ass off, sacrificing his body and his life to make money, and with it, I saw how he was able to help so many other families. I'm not the first child to worship and copy his dad.

For over two decades after college, I tried to make as much money as possible, sort of. It takes money to make money, but if you're generous and give it away, then by definition you aren't actually trying to make as much money as possible. Because I am generous both by nature and by direction, it's no surprise I failed spectacularly.

After figuring out what kind of world we wanted, we then searched for alternative proposals that could produce this glorious new world. There are no shortage of proposals claiming they are alternatives, but almost always they are merely modified, albeit usually improved, versions of Game A.

Anybody can improve the outcomes of Game A, if that is the goal, but only temporarily because there is a fundamental mathematical equation of Game A that always produces inequality, just like in the property game of

---

[31] Bertrand Russell, *Roads to Freedom*, London 1918

[32] Hanzi Freinacht, MetaModerna, "Equality, Equivalence, Equanimity", https://metamoderna.org/equality-equivalence-equanimity-towards-deeper-forms-of-equality/

Monopoly.[33] No doubt you've heard the notion that if all the Property in the world was suddenly redistributed equally (like starting a new game of Monopoly), that in due course, it becomes unequal real quick. A glance at the Forbes 500 richest people or the biggest companies— the standings or tables of Game A— should immediately be evidence of that. Along with endless warfare, the boom and bust cycles have repeated for thousands of years. It should be obvious why, because we must all compete to own as much Property as possible, but Property is scarce; meanwhile, new people enter the game at the bottom with nothing, starving and desperate for Property. "Life's not fair" they parrot, as if to suggest this is some truism rather than a result of our own making. Indeed it isn't fair by intentional human design.

"As of 2010, just 388 individuals possessed as much household wealth as the lower half of the world's population combined— about 3.5 billion people; today Oxfam estimates that number as 26. Statistics from almost all nations that measure wealth in their household surveys indicate that it is becoming increasingly concentrated."[34] That's from an article in 2019 before the 2020 Covid crisis which only increased inequality even faster.

Inequality is possibly at its worst right now than ever before.[35] "The wealthiest 10% of American households now own 89% of all U.S. stocks, a record high. The top 1% gained over $6.5 trillion in corporate equities and mutual fund wealth during the pandemic, according to the latest data from the Federal Reserve."[36] Before the pandemic, there was 1 person worth over $100 billion. Now there are 11. Before the pandemic, those 11 people were worth $650 billion. Now they are worth over $1.5 trillion.

This inequality producing effect of Game A has been known for thousands of years. Here's Pope Leo XIII in the late 1800's: "On the one side there is the party which holds the power because it holds the wealth; which has in its grasp all labor and all trade; which manipulates for its own benefit and its own purposes all the sources of supply, and which is powerfully represented in the councils of State itself. On the other side there is the needy and powerless multitude, sore and suffering. Rapacious usury, which,

---

33 The Landlord's Game, https://en.wikipedia.org/wiki/The_Landlord%27s_Game

34 Scientific American, Is Inequality Inevitable?, online, https://www.scientificamerican.com/article/is-inequality-inevitable/

35 Word Inequality Report 2022, https://wir2022.wid.world/

36 CNBC, https://www.cnbc.com/2021/10/18/the-wealthiest-10percent-of-americans-own-a-record-89percent-of-all-us-stocks.html

although more than once condemned by the Church, is nevertheless under a different form but with the same guilt, still practiced by avaricious and grasping men… so that a small number of very rich men have been able to lay upon the masses of the poor a yoke little better than slavery itself."

Here is what Pope Francis wrote about inequality in his 2013 mandate to change the world called "Apostolic Exhortation":

> Inequality is the root of social ills... as long as the problems of the poor are not radically resolved by rejecting the absolute autonomy of markets and financial speculation and by attacking the structural causes of inequality, no solution will be found for the world's problems or, for that matter, to any problems... ponder the words of one of the sages of antiquity: "Not to share one's wealth with the poor is to steal from them and to take away their livelihood. It is not our own goods which we hold, but theirs."[37] Money must serve, not rule! In this context, some people continue to defend trickle-down theories which assume that economic growth, encouraged by a free market, will inevitably succeed in bringing about greater justice and inclusiveness in the world. This opinion, which has never been confirmed by the facts, expresses a crude and naïve trust in the goodness of those wielding economic power and in the sacralized workings of the prevailing economic system. Meanwhile, the excluded are still waiting. To sustain a lifestyle which excludes others, or to sustain enthusiasm for that selfish ideal, a globalization of indifference has developed. Almost without being aware of it, we end up being incapable of feeling compassion at the outcry of the poor, weeping for other people's pain, and feeling a need to help them, as though all this were someone else's responsibility and not our own. The culture of prosperity deadens us; we are thrilled if the market offers us something new to purchase. In the meantime all those lives stunted for lack of opportunity seem a mere spectacle; they fail to move us.[38]

A new acquaintance of mine, Vinay Gupta, an enlightened Buddhist, wrote on Facebook, "Now, *all human deprivation and starvation are choices being made by the rich*. The suffering has gone from inevitable to optional, and we are all high on that karmic hog. Don't kid yourself: we are directly liable, karmically, for being rich in a world with starving children. You cannot escape that responsibility: if you believe you can, I'll see you in your next birth in a refugee camp. That's how it works."

---

[37] Saint John Chrysostom, *De Lazaro Concio*, II, 6: PG 48, 992D.

[38] Pope Francis, "Apostolic Exhortation", 2013, https://www.vatican.va/content/francesco/en/apost_exhortations/documents/papa-francesco_esortazione-ap_20131124_evangelii-gaudium.html

Deprivation was the usual condition for most of human history. Life was a never ending struggle and competition for what little there was. The economic equation has remained stuck in that same paradigm of scarcity even though we now have technological marvels producing plenty, but not efficiently and certainly not sustainably. "It is easy to dodge our responsibilities, but we cannot dodge the consequences of dodging our responsibilities," warned Josiah Charles Stamp.

There are so many experts, organizations and volunteers doing their part to solve our proliferating problems, many of which are critical and demand attention, unfortunately, much of this work addresses only the symptoms. The poverty, pollution and violence continues unabated. We need to strike at the root cause.

In his 1891 essay "The Soul of Man Under Socialism" Oscar Wilde argues that, under capitalism, "the majority of people spoil their lives by an unhealthy and exaggerated altruism—are forced, indeed, so to spoil them": instead of realizing their true talents, they waste their time solving the social problems caused by capitalism, without taking their common cause away. Thus, caring people "seriously and very sentimentally set themselves to the task of remedying the evils that they see in poverty but their remedies do not cure the disease: they merely prolong it" because, as Wilde puts it, "the proper aim is to try and reconstruct society on such a basis that poverty will be impossible."[39]

Even the winners of capitalism are saying as much. "Capitalism as we have known it is dead. This obsession we have with maximizing profits for shareholders alone has led to incredible inequality and a planetary emergency," exclaimed Marc Benioff, Chairman of SalesForce, at the 50th World Economic Forum (WEF) held in Davos in June 2020.

Ray Dalio, the famous Investment Officer of Bridgewater Associates, L.P., wrote a LinkedIn article in April 2019 titled, "Why and How Capitalism Needs to Be Reformed (Parts 1 & 2)."[40] He wrote: "I think that most capitalists don't know how to divide the economic pie well and most socialists don't know how to grow it well, yet we are now at a juncture in which either a) people of different ideological inclinations will work together to skillfully re-engineer the system so that the pie is both divided and grown well or b) we

[39] Oscar Wilde, "The Soul of Man Under Socialism", https://libcom.org/files/The%20soul%20of%20man%20under%20socialism.pdf

[40] Ray Dalio, LinkedIn, online, https://www.linkedin.com/pulse/why-how-capitalism-needs-reformed-parts-1-2-ray-dalio

will have great conflict and some form of revolution that will hurt most everyone and will shrink the pie." Of course there have been no reforms at any level whatsoever. On the same platform in November 2019 he wrote a post titled, "The World Has Gone Mad and the System is Broken"[41] which he ends with this prophetic prediction for a Common Planet, "That is why I believe that the world is approaching a big paradigm shift."

Yanis Varoufakis, co-founder of DiEM25 and Greece's Parliament and parliamentary leader of MeRA25, in this interview with Evgeny Morozov says that capitalism has in fact morphed into techno-feudalism:

> The question is this: Is capitalism undergoing one more of its many metamorphoses, thus warranting nothing more than a new epithet, e.g. rentier capitalism, platform capitalism, hyper-capitalism or xxxxx-capitalism? Or are we witnessing a qualitative transformation of capitalism into a brand new exploitative mode of production?
>
> Capitalism is everywhere we look. Capital is accumulating rapidly and beating labour over the head everywhere and in cruel new ways… My claim is that, similarly today, capitalism – like feudalism in the 1780s – is being usurped by a far more exploitative and very distinct new extractive/exploitative system (which I call techno-feudalism), one that is arriving complete with a new ruling class.
>
> What makes a system capitalist? The answer is: It is a system driven by private profits (Nb. not rents) extracted within markets. (To compare and contrast, feudalism was driven by rents extracted outside of markets.) Has that changed? I believe so. What has replaced profit on the one hand and markets on the other? My answer: Central bank money has replaced private profit (as the system's main fuel and lubricant) and digital fiefdoms/platforms have become the realm in which value and capital are extracted from the majority by a tiny oligarchy.
>
> Summing up: Capital is getting stronger but capitalism is dying. A new system is taking over in which a new ruling class owns and runs both the state money that lubricates it (instead of profits) and the new non-market realms in which the very, very few make the many work on their behalf. Capitalist profits (in the sense of the entrepreneurial profits as understood by Adam Smith and Marx) are disappearing, while new forms of rent are accumulating in the accounts of the new techno-lords in control of both the state and the digital fiefs, in which unwaged or precarious work is performed by the masses – who begin to resemble techno-peasants.[42]

---

[41] Ray Dalio, LinkedIn , online, https://www.linkedin.com/pulse/world-has-gone-mad-system-broken-ray-dalio

[42] Mėta - Centre *for* Post Capitalist Civilization, Yanis Varoufakis, Evgeny Morozov, https://metacpc.org/en/crypto-blockchain/

Billionaire entrepreneur and venture capitalist Nick Hanauer warns that the 'pitchforks' are coming if something isn't done:

> So, what is a society to do? Well, it's super clear to me what we need to do. We need a new economics. So, economics has been described as the dismal science, and for good reason, because as much as it is taught today, it isn't a science at all, in spite of all of the dazzling mathematics. In fact, a growing number of academics and practitioners have concluded that neoliberal economic theory is dangerously wrong and that today's growing crises of rising inequality and growing political instability are the direct result of decades of bad economic theory. What we now know is that the economics that made me so rich isn't just wrong, it's backwards, because it turns out it isn't capital that creates economic growth, it's people; and it isn't self interest that promotes the public good, it's reciprocity; and it isn't competition that produces our prosperity, it's cooperation. What we can now see is that an economics that is neither just nor inclusive can never sustain the high levels of social cooperation necessary to enable a modern society to thrive.[43]

How can we re-imagine the economic system so that it produces the world we want? Einstein told us "insanity is doing the same thing over and over again expecting different results." So if attempts at redistribution of the Property— modifying just the numbers of the factors within the equation— still produce the same end result: inequality, then it must be the economic equation itself that is the problem. The math is clear and irrefutable.

Our economics is nothing more than endless primitive war of extraction of Property for its value. This is called imperialism. Here's Michael Parenti in 1986 describing this for us: "The third world is not poor. You don't go to poor countries to make money. There are very few poor countries in this world. Most countries are rich. The Philippines are rich, Brazil is rich, Mexico is rich, Chile is rich. Only the people are poor, but there's billions to be made there, to be carved out and be taken. There's been billions for 400 years. The capitalist European and North American powers have carved out and taken the timber, the flax, the hemp, the cocoa, the rum, the tin, the copper, the iron, the bauxite, the slaves and the cheap labor. They have taken out of these countries. These countries are not underdeveloped, they are overexploited."[44]

---

[43] Nick Hanauer, TED, https://www.ted.com/talks/nick_hanauer_the_dirty_secret_of_capitalism_and_a_new_way_forward

[44] Michael Parenti speech, University of Colorado, April 15, 1986, https://www.youtube.com/watch?v=xP8CzlFhc14

The only righteous war is a war to end all wars over Property, once and for all. That is a war worth fighting and the war Bob Marley sang about:

> Until the philosophy which hold one race superior and another inferior is finally and permanently discredited and abandoned, everywhere is war, me say war. That until there no longer first class and second class citizens of any nation; until the color of a man's skin is of no more significance than the color of his eyes, me say war. That until the basic human rights are equally guaranteed to all without regard to race, dis a war. That until that day, the dream of lasting peace, world citizenship, rule of international morality, will remain in but a fleeting illusion to be pursued, but never attained. Now everywhere is war. War.[45]

The lyrics for Marley's song were inspired by and pulled directly from a speech addressed to the United Nations (UN) in 1963 by Haile Selassie, Emperor of Ethiopia, who spoke these eloquent words earlier in that speech:

> When we talk of the equality of man, we find, also, a challenge and an opportunity; a challenge to breathe new life into the ideals enshrined in the Charter, an opportunity to bring men closer to freedom and true equality, and thus, closer to a love of peace. The goal of the equality of man which we seek is the antithesis of the exploitation of one people by another with which the pages of history speak at such lengths... It is the sacred duty of this Organization to ensure that the dream of equality is finally realized for all men to whom it is still denied, to guarantee that exploitation is not reincarnated in other forms in places whence it has already been banished.[46]

Therefore, our task is to change the game so it doesn't produce massive inequality. "All previous revolutions have been political—in them the have-not majority has attempted revengefully to pull down the economically advantaged minority. If realized, this historically greatest design revolution will joyously elevate all humanity to unprecedented heights."[47]

You may have heard about "The Great Reset", the name of the 50th annual meeting of the WEF held in June 2020.[48] The WEF and its banking

---

[45] Bob Marley, War, https://www.youtube.com/watch?v=4XHEPoMNP0I

[46] Haile Salassie, speech to UN, Oct 6, 1963, https://www.youtube.com/watch?v=lIUTt0EmGiw

[47] Fuller, *Critical Path* (1981), p. xxxvi

[48] World Economic Forum, online, https://www.weforum.org/agenda/2020/06/now-is-the-time-for-a-great-reset/

constituents' plan is not a reset at all. It's a three part plan that calls for governments to "steer the market toward fairer outcomes", for governments to provide more funds (as debt or from taxes) toward "equality and sustainability", and "to harness the innovations of the Fourth Industrial Revolution." This is probably public relations posturing with platitudes. I mean no disrespect to the people at the WEF, in fact, I share many of their concerns. If we see support for the new economics of Common Planet from these institutions and their people then we will find out if they are genuine or not. I challenge them to 'put your money where your mouth is.'

The WEF said "you will own nothing and be happy" about their 'reset.' Many are calling their plan a New World Order (NWO), but it's not. In Conservative circles they fear a one world economy would strip away property rights and basic democratic rights. But I got news for you, that's already the situation. We have no power over the majority of the Property in the world and not much democratic rights either. We have politicians who cosplay as leaders but are really just puppets of banks and Corporations. Like John Jay Chapman said over 100 years ago, "All our politics is business and our business is politics."

The macro picture shows the world is the same now as at any other time and their 'reset' changes little. We have rights to some personal private property, sure, but we are ruled none-the-less by those who just happen to own all the common Property already with no liability, only profit.

Do you think that those who have all the power and own everything are really calling for a 'reset'? Nobody believes that. Is it possible there are some enlightened rich and powerful people out there? I'd bet there is. We'll find out. As there are both good and bad rich people, unfortunately, the bad ones consistently do whatever they can to smear and kill anyone who dares actually threaten their wealth and power. That sucks for me and you too.

Flooding our networks with misinformation and propaganda is their primary weapon. None of us are immune to its effects. I find the fact that we are so easily deceived to be profoundly disturbing.

Knowing the correct *real* information is not just important, it's critical. How can you know to question or counter falsehoods if you don't even know the truth? This year, two journalists just won the Nobel Peace Prize. Not since 1935 has a journalist won it and just like the last time it was because of the rise of fascism. The journalist who won it – Carl von Ossietzky – had revealed how Hitler was secretly rearming Germany. He couldn't pick up his prize because he was in a Nazi prison.

This years winners, Maria Ressa of the Philippines and Dmitry Muratov of Russia both believe there is no doubt that the award is symbolic not just of an existential threat to press freedom but of a world on the brink. "I think our world has stopped loving democracy and has started reaching for dictatorships," said Muratov. "Journalists are like independent media. They're the defence line between dictatorship and war."[49]

The very next day the UK government voted to extradite Julian Assange back to the US so they can continue punishing anyone who dares speak truth.

Because oligarchs own all mainstream media all over the world, they will use every instrument of power in their control to stop us from uniting. Any real alternative, like Common Planet, that actually threatens their power will be twisted and branded as stupid, dangerous or even anti-freedom.

On the Common Planet website, since 2018, we described our plan as 'a global reset', however, ours is actually more a transition into a real alternative, a Game B[50] rather than a simple reset of another round of Game A. The activist group Anonymous said, "The majority of us believe in Open Source government backed by resource based economics on a planetary level. If a computer's operating system is malfunctioning it is replaced. We view governments as global operating systems, flawed and full of bugs and crash reports. Hitting the off switch and rebooting simply won't help how corrupted these global operating systems have become. Reformatting and installing a humanitarian based open sourced government will ensure equality for all." So, a reset of an inequality producing game would produce the exact same result, specifically: concentrated power.

One can fix inequality and address poverty by simple redistribution, or resets (debt jubilees) as was often done historically, but what is needed is a remedy for the evils of power and that is rooted in the equation of economics itself. This point was made back in 1917 by Mr. G. D. H. Cole.

> What, I want to ask, is the fundamental evil in our modern Society which we should set out to abolish? There are two possible answers to that question, and I am sure that very many well-meaning people would make the wrong one. They would answer POVERTY, when they ought to answer SLAVERY. Face to face every day with the shameful contrasts of riches and destitution,

---

[49] The Guardian, https://www.theguardian.com/world/2021/dec/04/nobel-winner-we-journalists-are-the-defence-line-between-dictatorship-and-war

[50] In use since at least 2013. Bret Weinstein, Jim Rutt, Jordan Hall et al, use Game A/B, YouTube: https://www.youtube.com/watch?v=9MT0h6EQhUw By 2019, Game B proliferated on social media.

> high dividends and low wages, and painfully conscious of the futility of trying to adjust the balance by means of charity, private or public, they would answer unhesitatingly that they stand for the ABOLITION OF POVERTY. Well and good! On that issue every socialist is with them. But their answer to my question is none the less wrong. Poverty is the symptom: slavery the disease. The extremes of riches and destitution follow inevitably upon the extremes of license and bondage. The many are not enslaved because they are poor, they are poor because they are enslaved. Yet Socialists have all too often fixed their eyes upon the material misery of the poor without realizing that it rests upon the spiritual degradation of the slave.[51]

Therefore, we must also heed the advice of Paulo Freire: "In order for this struggle to have meaning, the oppressed must not, in seeking to regain their humanity (which is a way to create it), become in turn oppressors of the oppressors, but rather restorers of the humanity of both. This, then, is the great humanistic and historical task of the oppressed: to liberate themselves and their oppressors as well."[52]

So, here we are still playing the same wrong game of Property over and over again. The 2019 Edelman Trust Barometer revealed that 4 out of 5 people believe the system is broken and not working for them. 2 out of 3 people believe the future will be even worse.[53] The world is already incredibly complex and exponential change is only worsening the crisis. Everyone is trying to make sense of what is going on.

Here's how many of today's leading thinkers describe this crisis:

Tomas Björkman calls it the Meta-Crisis. John Vervaeke the Meaning Crisis. Douglas Rushkoff the Spiritual Disease. Otto Scharmer the Crisis of our Time. Deepak Chopra the Cognitive Revolution. Frédéric Laloux the New Management Paradigm. Jordan Hall Game A vs Game B. Indy Johar the Boring Revolution. Adam Gazzaley the Cognition Crisis. Peter Jones the Global Problematique. Manual Manga the Evolutionary Crisis. Joshua Cooper Ramo the Insanity Challenge.

It doesn't matter what you call it. It doesn't matter what your religion or philosophy is. You can't change the game unless you change its rule set. You can not predictably rely on appeals to the morality of humans or especially on the good will of Nations or Corporations. The game itself and its rules

---

[51] Mr. G. D. H. Cole, *Self-Government in Industry*, G. Bell and Sons, 1917, pp.110-111

[52] Paulo Freire, *Pedagogy of the Oppressed*, p. 44

[53] 2019 Edelman Trust Barometer, online, https://www.edelman.com/sites/g/files/aatuss191/files/2019-02/2019_Edelman_Trust_Barometer_Global_Report.pdf

are a bigger determinant of resulting behavior than our morals will ever be. Regardless of what -ism you call your ideology, your relationship to Property is determined by the economic protocols. For this reason, I and many others refer to current economics as Game A.

The Common Planet approach is different. We use a new currency and new accounting system. Credit is a Flow currency— not circulatory like debt money — which constantly flows to everyone then simply deletes when used. Credit is a tool to incentivize people whereas Debt is a tool to control people. All Property is essentially the commons, including finished goods, meaning nobody *owns* them per se; everything is accounted for then made available in the open market for anyone to buy with their Credit, whereby eventually things become private property. Your home, car and all your other personal possessions will still be your private property, similar to now, but you won't ever have sole ownership and control of the oil, timber, mining or any other major common resource or of a large corporation; certainly not without democratic approval and oversight from your community. The commons have stakeholders and caretakers so no longer do *owners* get to dictate how and where common resources are used. The commons are managed through local, regional and global democracy, then goods are distributed using the magic mechanism of an open market pricing system. In this way, we secure our individual rights to private property for each person, but the days of oligarchs dictating industry and pushing wars over common resources will be over, once and for all.

Here's Duane Elgin, author of "Choosing Earth: Humanity's Great Transition to a Mature Planetary Civilization", speaking in an interview:

> I don't see our situation as 'bad' as much as I see it as one of unyielding difficulty that must be addressed at a global scale. In my view, hitting an evolutionary wall is not a mistake. Reaching limits to material growth is a recurring and predictable progression for all species that seek to exploit their ecological niche. Humanity's 'niche' or operating domain is now the entire Earth—and we are exploiting it to the extreme. Overshoot and collapse are a common story in evolution... The most foundational challenge facing humanity is not devising solutions to the energy crisis or climate crisis; rather, it is bringing visions and narratives of the human journey into our collective awareness that empower us to look beyond a future of great adversity and to see a future of great opportunity.[54]

---

[54] Duane Elgin, online, https://mahb.stanford.edu/blog/mahb-dialogue-author-humanist-duane-elgin

I started by considering the first principles of money creation. By breaking down all the economic pieces separately, they could be reconstructed to see what happens when they are mixed up in different ways. For example, the ultimate Property of value that you have for trade is your labor power, which is your time, your mind and your body. For most human players it is the only Property of value they have to trade. But in order for you to collect any value from trading yourself, you must sell your labor power to another player in exchange for their Property, usually money. In the economic equation of Game A, your labor is Property purchased by other players. Since someone pays you for your labor, you are treated as their Property (commodity). That means they *own* your labor and that means they get the legal right to control ***you***. They are your boss, which is defined as the head, top, or chief and means they get to order, bully or dominate you, *legally*.

Could this be just a coincidence of our economic evolution? This hidden-in-plain-sight tradition that money, a fictional Property, gets to control all real Property in the world, including people, was by intentional clever design. Friedrich Engels said it best: "The only difference as compared with the old, outspoken slavery is this, that the worker of today seems to be free because he is not sold once and for all, but piecemeal by the day, the week, the year, and because no one owner sells him to another, but he is forced to sell himself in this way instead, being the slave of no particular person, but of the whole property-holding class." It was believed a person would only work if they are forced. Sadly, many still believe this.

Banks have the legal power to access unlimited free credit and turn that into money, issuing it as debt to any player they choose. These corporations called banks are literal creators of money, thus, the masters of all Property. There is no economic democracy. Banks seek only profit for themselves. That's why Banks own the largest buildings in every major city on the planet; and even the ones they don't *own* are financed by money they created from credit (out of thin air). Banks *own* the majority stake in most commercial and residential real estate as well as Corporations and Nations too. Real Property may be scarce, but money isn't. Today it's all just digital numbers; it can be created by banks anytime they wish to trade for damn near anything. It can buy weapons, chemicals, opinions, governments and it can buy humans into doing some nasty things like murder, rape and war.

Railroad tycoon Jay Gould, in the late 1800s, may be famously misquoted as saying "I can hire one half of the working class to kill the other half," but the sentiment stands as true.

Basically it's a game of masters and slaves[55] and I don't know about you, but I don't want to be either. I want to be equal sovereigns as God intended. We don't need masters! Karl Hess said it best, "No person is so grand or wise or perfect as to be the master of another person. Teacher, perhaps. Setter of good example, perhaps. Genius, perhaps. But master, no."

> If democracy and self-rule are the fundamentals, then why should people give up these rights when they enter their workplace? In politics we fight like tigers for freedom, for the right to elect our leaders, for freedom of movement, choice of residence, choice of what work to pursue- control of our lives, in short. And then we wake up in the morning and go to work, and all those rights disappear. We no longer insist on them. And so for most of the day we return to feudalism. That is what capitalism is— a version of feudalism in which capital replaces land, and business leaders replace kings. But the hierarchy remains. And so we still hand over our lives' labor, under duress, to feed rulers who do no real work.[56]

So I thought, "what if we remove labor as an expense from an Enterprise? Could the value of labor be paid directly as money creation itself?" This way, a person would truly own themself and choose freely when and where to contribute their time. This question led ultimately to the design of Common Planet. It wasn't overnight but we realized very quickly that by removing the factor of labor out of the profit equation, it opened the door for the development of a new value equation, hence a new game.

Here, the currency, Credit is an incentive available to anyone who chooses to do the work. Work is done by choice not by force. Giving currency directly to labor was actually the obvious and easy part; many others have historically come to this same realization but without ultimately also changing the profit equation. I was also combining it with another idea about a new housing game I had that summer of 2015. It was obvious these features together fundamentally changed the game, even though I hadn't explored all the connections and implications yet. Part of the reason for this book not being written earlier is because I wanted to make sure that what we are proposing is actually well thought out and good for the world, so that it's good in reality and not just good in theory. Modeling of the numbers and simulations are the next necessary steps along with planning the transition.

---

[55] Slavery Footprint, https://slaveryfootprint.org/

[56] Kim Stanley Robinson, *Blue Mars* (New York: Bantam, 1996), p. 116-117

Here's what I realized: **Governance**[57] (rules of behavior) **+ Economics** (rules of Property) **= Society**.[58]

This all came about because the 2008 near collapse of the financial system gave us all reason to consider just what is this thing called money and who controls its supply. Surprisingly, of all the extensive financial information I had gorged on for years, about so-called 'investing', on how to make money with money, not once did I ever read about or consider how money is actually made. Like, who creates it? But I didn't ask those questions until 2013.

I wasn't thinking about those things before then. I was too busy trading stocks and *making* money. I killed it with trading in 2008. From my personal perspective, the game was working just fine. A few years later as I was walking past the Occupy Wall Street protestors in Zuccotti Park, I looked upon them with a mixture of pity and disgust. I happily feasted on lobster around the corner without a clue as to what the heck they were complaining about. What exactly were they going on about? Were they just futilely bitching about reality? Money exists. It is what it is. What was there to do?

Little did I know, right across the street, Occupy, led by my now hero the late David Graeber, was fighting the good fight for us. They were me then. I am them now. This is one of Graeber's last pieces of writing before he died in late 2020: "After the Pandemic, We Can't Go Back To Sleep":

> There was a brief moment of questioning. (What is "finance," anyway? Isn't it just other people's debts? What is money? Is it just debt, too? What's debt? Isn't it just a promise? If money and debt are just a collection of promises we make to each other, then couldn't we just as easily make different ones?) The window was almost instantly shut by those insisting we shut up, stop thinking, and get back to work, or at least start looking for it.
> Last time, most of us fell for it. This time, it is critical that we do not.
> This time around, can we please just ignore them?[59]

After the spectacular financial shenanigans of 2008, the world realized there are actually men behind the curtains. We watched the banks get 'bailed out' without a clue what that meant really. Millions of us finally wondered about

[57] P2P Foundation Wiki, https://wiki.p2pfoundation.net/Category:Governance

[58] Remzi Bajrami, Youtube, https://www.youtube.com/watch?v=1tpNn436BJ4

[59] David Graeber, Jacobin, https://www.jacobinmag.com/2021/03/david-graeber-posthumous-essay-pandemic

where exactly does all the money come from anyway. The answer is both disgusting and awesome.

Having been intrigued in 2013 by Peter Joseph's "Zeitgeist" series of documentaries, we became instant fans of the ideas for a Resource Based Economy (RBE).[60] The Zeitgeist Movement (TZM) had lots of interesting organizations like the Venus Project and individuals pursuing and promoting visions of a better world without money. Perhaps they are right about our ultimate economic destination, except they have the wrong understanding of banking, money and currency, thus some wrong conclusions for a transition.

Most people assume incorrectly that only the government controls and issues the money supply. But it turns out that private for-profit corporations called banks create over 95% of all money in circulation. Legal charters allow banks to 'lend' credit based on their capitalization (how much Capital or Assets the bank itself owns— not customer deposits) and loan worthiness of the borrower. The rules are designed to allow banks to lend out much more money than they have. Banks 'lend' from credit, thus creating new money. They do not lend out customer deposits to non-banks. "Everyone subconsciously knows banks do not lend money. When you draw on your savings account, the bank doesn't tell you you can't do this because it has lent the money to somebody else," points out Mark Mansfield, economic author.

In one of their annual Zeitgeist Zday meetings, a Portland man, Perry Gruber, gave a presentation promoting Copiosis[61], which has an interesting new currency system but perhaps not enough of an alternative property system. Most TZM supporters reacted by ignoring, dismissing or rejecting Perry's ideas. They insist on believing a no-money system can run the RBE. I'm not sure if they make any distinctions between money and currency.

I met Perry at the end of 2015. In that first conversation, when Perry described the features of the currency called Net Benefit Reward as being for personal use only, kinda like a non-transferable token, I immediately knew that was a killer feature, a must have as part of a currency system because it solved so many of the problems that still remained in my new equation. I immediately adopted that feature and believe with every ounce of my being that it is a critical foundational requirement for any fair currency system. This is what makes it a Flow currency instead of circulatory. Later, in 2017, I learned that it was called a No-POM which is short for No Physical Object

---

[60] Resource Based Economy, https://www.resourcebasedeconomy.org/

[61] Perry Gruber, Copiosis, https://copiosis.com

Money, coined by Larry Mason decades ago in his short story called "Invisible Hand"[62], which Gruber got permission to advance.

The last thing that remained to be solved was how to change the profit equation; how to account for Enterprise production and its values. This was by far the hardest and most time consuming part. For the first six months of 2016, it was the only thing I talked about and thought about until the simple realization that if we could create Credit as direct value recognition for labor, why not also to reward best Enterprise production practices and results? In this way, the metrics of what is considered *profit* can be changed too. And that's how the last piece was *discovered.* This is outlined and referred to as opportunity in chapter 5.

So then we had to do like Steve Jobs said, "You have to work hard to get your thinking clean to make it simple." That meant we had to do a lot of research. We had to familiarize ourselves with this historical struggle, of which I knew very little about. I was a former libertarian and a former staunch supporter of capitalism. I thought of myself as a serial entrepreneur, an independent free thinker and a maverick. I'm embarrassed to admit I really had no idea what socialism or communism was at all, even though I was born in a *communist* country and spent many summers there. I can assure you, it was and remains Game A through and through. The words and labels change but the structural hierarchy of power always persists. A hierarchy is a system or organization in which people or groups are ranked one above the other according to status or authority. A hierarchy means rulers, in one form or another. Everywhere around us, hierarchies surround us.

For the remainder of the book, please do me a favor and continue reading past labels like capitalism, socialism, communism, anarchism or any other -ism mentioned. They are often either too broad, too limiting or sometimes even contradictory. If you get hung up on any of these words and attempt to equate Common Planet with any of these labels, you will be doing a disservice to others by giving them a preconceived notion without the complete picture. We are dealing here with reality, and labels can be used to either clarify or confuse. Where appropriate, I will define words, but still, just keep reading because this is a Common Planet, which means it will incorporate elements of these various -isms at different layers. Only after chapter 5 can a reader have a complete understanding of this proposal.

There is a famous parable from India, "The Blind Men and the Elephant", adapted by many religions and in story form here by James Baldwin. It is

---

62 Larry Mason, "Invisible Hand", online, https://nopomstuff.info/

about a group of six blind men who attempt to learn what an elephant is, each touching a different part, and disagreeing on their findings:

> Of course they could not see him with their eyes; but they thought that by touching him they could learn just what kind of animal he was.
>
> The first one happened to put his hand on the elephant's side. "Well, well!" he said, "now I know all about this beast. He is exactly like a wall."
>
> The second felt only of the elephant's tusk. "My brother," he said, "you are mistaken. He is not at all like a wall. He is round and smooth and sharp. He is more like a spear than anything else."
>
> The third happened to take hold of the elephant's trunk. "Both of you are wrong," he said. "Anybody who knows anything can see that this elephant is like a snake."
>
> The fourth reached out his arms, and grasped one of the elephant's legs. "Oh, how blind you are!" he said. "It is very plain to me that he is round and tall like a tree."
>
> The fifth was a very tall man, and he chanced to take hold of the elephant's ear. "The blindest man ought to know this beast is not like any of the things that you name," he said. "He is exactly like a huge fan."
>
> The sixth was very blind indeed, and it was some time before he could find the elephant at all. At last he seized the animal's tail. "O foolish fellows!" he cried. "You surely have lost your senses. This elephant is not like a wall, or a spear, or a snake, or a tree; neither is he like a fan. But any man with a particle of sense can see that he is exactly like a rope."
>
> Then the elephant moved on, and the six blind men sat by the roadside all day, and quarreled about him. Each believed that he knew just how the animal looked; and each called the others hard names because they did not agree with him. People who have eyes sometimes act as foolishly.[63]

In the Gameb Facebook group[64] where hundreds of people, now thousands, use the most deep insight and beautiful language to describe Game B which reminds me of this parable. None of us has ever *seen* Game B, so our brief descriptions can never encompass the whole of it, try as we might. With the addition of these new currency and property accounting protocols, this book

---

[63] James Baldwin, "The Blind Men and the Elephant", https://americanliterature.com/author/james-baldwin/short-story/the-blind-men-and-the-elephant

[64] Gameb Facebook group, https://www.facebook.com/groups/gamebcore

attempts to incorporate as much of their insight and wisdom in trying to describe Common Planet, which is not Game B, but a portion of a Game B, or perhaps as a generator function.

> Let's not speak anymore about capitalism, socialism. Let's just speak of using the incredible wealth of the earth for human beings. Give people what they need: food, medicine, clean air, pure water, trees and grass, pleasant homes to live in, some hours of work, more hours of leisure. Don't ask who deserves it. Every human being deserves it.[65]

It is impossible to play both American Football and Soccer at the same time on the same field. They are simply not compatible even though both have many identical features. Both have 2 teams of 11, yet you can only play one at a time. It is the same on the playing field of Earth. Game A is ubiquitous, baked in, thus seems a *natural* part of the evolution of human nature.

The US education system taught me that communism = USSR, our backwards enemy, a dictatorship, state central planning, authoritarian morons, thugs and spies, a veritable police state and the opposite of freedom. All of that is obviously bad and the reason I had never bothered to investigate further so I was shocked when I learned how much of my own thinking mirrored the philosophy of socialism and communism. Please don't be quick to judge until after you've read the details. When viewing the totality of what is Common Planet, no single -ism defines the whole. Its features are: decentralization, sustainable competition (win/win), open markets, stateless, classless, local bottom up direct democracy, individual sovereignty, security, opportunity and liberty. And I suppose you can add moneyless to that description but that's only a partial truth, because we do maintain the need for accounting of value, using a currency and markets too, but not a currency in the form of money and that is one of the key design features.

There is a reason why proponents of both communism and capitalism say that their *pure* system has never been tried, because many of their good layers became factors inserted into the Game A equation which ended up perverting their intent and philosophy. Recall, Game A is an inequality producing game, a hierarchy of power, regardless of how you tinker with the factors (to reduce inequality), the equation will still continue to produce inequality and it doesn't matter if you call those changed factors capitalism, socialism or communism if it's still actually Game A. It's still football.

---

[65] Howard Zinn, *Three Plays: Marx in Soho*, (Beacon Press: Boston), 2010, p. 141. Also as play: https://www.youtube.com/watch?v=i2baw7stI6U

While the world was playing football, some changed the rules to play flag football instead and claimed to be playing soccer without ever changing the ball or actual game play. Any team playing flag football (socialism) against teams playing actual football (capitalism) get crushed. With the creation of a new currency system (a new ball), I believe Common Planet has found a way to bridge the divide and bring these seemingly disparate philosophies into symbiosis, into something that is better, whatever it be called.

All previous and existing 'socialist' countries to date merely placed the football into the hands of the player I call a Nation, which concentrates Game A Property ownership in the hands of the State, the few people who get to rule the Nation. They called this socialism and they thought it was the only way, thus, necessary step on the way to real communism. They didn't change economics (the ball or the game), even though they said they did. They merely swapped the quarterbacks and coaches. This was their first step toward taking power, to use it to control and make sure the outcome be as equitable and fair as possible. It is said the Nation = the people, implying that the people each have equal say and power. Does a family also = the people? Of course not. The family is made up of parents and children just as a Nation is made up of rulers and subjects; they are not equals.

The State (rulers of Nations, coaches and quarterbacks) can either manage Property for the people (socialism) or for themselves (capitalism/fascism), but both are inevitably ruled by oligarchs; the old dichotomy of good ruler or bad ruler are the only options in Game A. Just like you can have a good family and a toxic family. As in Thomas Jefferson's time, so too in ours, "The issue today is the same as it has been throughout all history, whether man shall be allowed to govern himself or be ruled by a small elite."

I hope you can appreciate how hard this was for us and how powerful and evil the forces against us could be. It will take courage even though we are still burdened by fear. "Courage is not the absence of fear but fear walking," says Susan David. As dangerous as the enemy is, we have a secret weapon. Sorry to spoil some of the popular HBO TV show *The Game of Thrones* but Common Planet is dragon glass and the global banking oligarchy is the White King.

In an article calling for a global Debt Jubilee, Jordan Hall highlights the power of money and its weakness: "Money is at the center of our current system and debt is at the center of money. Money is simultaneously the core of the current institutional order and its most vulnerable achilles heel."[66]

Like the story of David and Goliath, the "classic underdog tale: David, a young shepherd armed only with a sling, beats Goliath, the mighty warrior. The story has transcended its biblical origins to become a common shorthand for unlikely victory. But, asks Malcolm Gladwell, is that really what the David and Goliath story is about?" Gladwell tells us that "Giants are not as strong and powerful as they seem, and sometimes the shepherd boy has a sling in his pocket."[67] Flow currency is our sling, and with it we will take down the Goliath debt currency system.

Currency is just a unit of measure of value of Property which enables exchange. What I learned is that all currency comes from credit, and there is no limit to credit (it's all just numbers and accounting), which means we can literally create the currency from credit directly to labor and to profit when it is earned instead of giving banks access to free credit who then issue it as interest-bearing debt money. Currency DOESN'T HAVE TO CIRCULATE!

Let me repeat that: currency is created from credit as Credit, not as Debt money. "Money and Currency are different. Currency comes from the latin word: Current or Flow. In our work at the MetaCurrency Project, currency is also defined as 'Current-See' as a way to make a current or flow visible," founder Ferananda Ibarra says. "In nature, if I observe the flow, I observe the interdependence, I observe the relationship, I observe what flows create life and what flows destroy life."

Credit is a Flow currency, not circulatory. Think of Credit like a faucet in the sky; it can be turned on anytime to create currency. That's how money is created. They turn the faucet on and money enters the world. They told you money doesn't grow on trees. No it doesn't. It's actually easier and instantaneous. It's simply requested, then accounted for and made real. When we transition from the debt money system to a Credit currency system, ***all banks and all debts will disappear forever*!** Like I said, dragon glass.

Common Planet is an economic equation that turns labor from an expense into an opportunity for value creation itself. You get to decide where and when to create value. And because all value comes as credit, we've re-

---

[66] Jordan Hall, *It is time for a global Debt Jubilee: Part I,* Medium, online, https://medium.com/emergent-culture/it-is-time-for-a-global-debt-jubilee-part-i

[67] Malcolm Gladwell, TED talks, "The unheard story of David and Goliath", online, https://www.youtube.com/watch?v=ziGD7vQOwl8

designed it so you can never run out of Credit; you will always be valuable.[68] A universal or unconditional basic income (UBI) of Credit is distributed equally to every person on Earth just for existing. Why? Because every person on the planet is valuable, that's why. It's just a matter of turning on the imaginary faucet. Plus, just by living, every time you learn, play or work, you will collect more Credit as direct value creation. Credit flows directly to people because people are the most valuable resource we have.

In Common Planet you will collect Credit currency directly just for living and contributing. It's that simple.

This new economic equation will empower you and every person on Earth, for the first time in history, to claim their God given individual sovereignty or self-rule. It will be like Kurt Vonnegut said, "The main business of humanity is to do a good job of being human beings, not to serve as appendages to machines, institutions and systems."

For all of my life I've been obsessed with the desire and search for freedom and now I can finally see the road to freedom ahead. Bertrand Russell, British philosopher and one of my favorite thinkers, wrote *Roads to Freedom: Socialism, Anarchism and Syndicalism* in 1918, which I've read more than a few times already. My favorite is the last chapter "The World as it could be made" because it so clearly outlines very much my own thinking for a Common Planet: "In the daily lives of most men and women, fear plays a greater part than hope: they are more filled with the thought of the possessions that others may take from them, than of the joy that they might create in their own lives and in the lives with which they come in contact. It is not so that life should be lived."[69]

Does the desire for freedom transcend humans? Here's Abdullah Ocalan in *Sociology of Freedom*: "I almost want to say *freedom* is *the goal of the universe*. I have often asked myself if the universe is not, in fact, in pursuit of freedom. The formulation of freedom as a profound quest unique to human society always seemed incomplete to me, and I thought there must definitely be an aspect related to the universe."

Ultimately, my aim is for this book to fill you with joy, optimism and a renewed faith in the human experience. So, if you're interested in learning about how we can change the world with a new currency system within a new

---

[68] You're thinking, "but what about inflation?" It's not a problem in a flow currency system.

[69] Bertrand Russell, *Roads to Freedom*, London 1918, p.187

economic equation, you've found the right book. Hoo-boy, wait til you read the section on banking. "You know nothing Jon Snow."[70]

The next chapter is a brief history of Game A before we lay out the path of the new game which is Common Planet. The rest of the book compares and contrasts these two different economic systems to give a more clear view of what your life would be like in the new game. Many other theories and proposals, old and new, are also discussed. The book ends with how we might transition to a Common Planet.

This is my first book, self published and meant for a general audience. I was not paid to write this. Nobody is directing or manipulating me and there were no ghost writers or editors used. I'm going to try to write using the most simple and clear language possible given the subject matter. I am not an academic, or an economist, however, I'm experienced and well read. Please don't judge the quality of the ideas presented based on what you think of me or my writing style.

On a personal level, I've always struggled with language. English being my second language and never the family language held me back. I scored a pathetic 420 on my verbal SAT as a high school sophomore. My 730 math score was excellent though. I excel in comprehension and memory but not so much in explaining to others. Once I got to college, that's when I decided to devote full time to language and gave up math entirely.

Einstein, an expert, said "we should not assume that experts are the only ones who have a right to express themselves on questions affecting the organization of society."[71]

Me not working full time in Game A these past 6+ years has been extremely difficult for my family. None of this is for money, or fame, but we are not blind to the present reality of the power that money can play in promoting and facilitating change. Which is why we will be asking for support for this project. Lots of friends and family think I'm crazy for not trying to make as much money as possible, but according to Indian philosopher Jiddu Krishnamurti, "it's no measure of health to be adjusted to a profoundly sick society." As Robert Anton Wilson observed, "Under the present brutal and primitive conditions on this planet, every person you meet should be regarded as one of the walking wounded. We have never seen a

---

[70] Memorable phrase from HBO TV series, *The Game of Thrones*

[71] Albert Einstein, "Why Socialism?", Monthly Review, 1949, online, https://archive.org/details/AlbertEinsteinWhySocialism/mode/2up

man or woman not slightly deranged by either anxiety or grief. We have never seen a totally sane human being."

> Here's to the crazy ones. The misfits. The rebels. The troublemakers. The round pegs in the square holes. The ones who see things differently. They're not fond of rules. And they have no respect for the status quo. You can quote them, disagree with them, glorify or vilify them. About the only thing you can't do is ignore them. Because they change things. They push the human race forward. And while some may see them as the crazy ones, we see genius. Because the people who are crazy enough to think they can change the world, are the ones who do.[72]

Jack Kerouac said it best, "I realized either I was crazy or the world was crazy; and I picked on the world. And of course I was right." This book is not about me but I feel readers are curious to know how this all came about so I don't want to hear any bullshit rumors about me or my family. We're just a regular family. There is nothing special about us. Please focus on the ideas. I'm just a dumb nerd who knows too much about the money game, and stubborn enough to fight for what's right. Malcolm Gladwell, in his 2002 book *The Tipping Point,* calls people like me "mavens": people who are endlessly curious and adept at gathering and retaining information on a wide variety of topics.

I was born speaking Shqip (Albanian) and continue to use it with my family everyday. I didn't learn English until we moved to Connecticut, USA when I was 5. We lived near a small town center so as kids we often walked to the public library, where I immediately fell in love with books. I read a lot in those early years before school work and playing soccer later occupied most of my life. Doing mostly assigned reading stunted my language development.

College was the best and the worst. Even though I pursued economics most of the classes were a continuation of the same subjects as high school; it was a complete waste of time. I quit after two years but went back part time, taking only classes that interested me. Just three per semester. And I was only interested in one thing at that time: writing.

One of those Fairfield University writing classes was taught by Ezra Bowen, a retired TIME magazine journalist who had spent his life traveling and interviewing the most powerful people on the planet. That's what I wanted to do because I always fancied myself as wanting to make a difference in the world. After all, I had a mission in life to help as many people as

[72] Rob Siltanen, Steve Jobs, Apple TV ad, https://www.youtube.com/watch?v=5sMBhDv4sik

possible, so maybe this was the way. Ezra inspired me to pursue journalism and so I went to him as often as I could for help on my writing. In a way, this book is very much one long piece of journalism.

In the second semester, I got a job writing for ASSEMBLY magazine, the alumni magazine (at that time, 1995) of the U.S. Military Academy at West Point. Finally, all of my undercover training paid off and it was here that I found ***all*** the secrets of the United States. I'm totally joking, I'm just being a dork. I'm not a spy and I only got that job because my ex-girlfriend's dad was the Editor. My first piece was a feature on graduate Steve Case, the co-founder of America Online Inc.

For a sociology class, I wrote my finest paper titled: "Freedom", and of course I went to Ezra for help. He let me read his writings on liberty, which I don't think were published, so if anyone alive knows or has his work, please reach out. He made me read *The Federalist Papers* and he taught me Benjamin Franklin's definition: "Liberty is freedom, with responsibility." Too many equate freedom with being able to do whatever they want without consequences, but rights come with responsibilities, so liberty is the best we can hope for in Society.

After that summer, I moved cross country to get a degree in journalism and communication at the University of Oregon with an emphasis in public relations. I took a bunch of business classes too. While there, I landed an internship with the PR Director of the Planning Division of the City of Eugene and got to see my first real inner workings of a small city.

After college I worked in data management & sales, left that for my first startup in 1999 called World Privacy Inc.[73], which lasted only 2 years, then I became a financial advisor with Northwestern Mutual, traded stocks, bought land, built and sold some new houses, started trading stocks again and failed miserably at the end. Common Planet will produce world privacy too.

Then came the twin ideas about a new currency and new property game which revealed a possible alternative. I had to pursue it and that's what ultimately led to EarthVote. I worked odd jobs and sold insurance again but the rest of my time and mind was consumed by this new economic vision. I even worked in a factory and weekend delivery driving so that I could listen to audiobooks and podcasts while *working*. The research was the real work.

In September 2016, we attributed the original intro to Common Planet on the EarthVote website to author 'iPaemer' (which means 'nameless', or 'he

---

[73] World Privacy Inc. website archive, https://web.archive.org/web/20000301164134/http://www.worldprivacy.com/

without a name' in Albanian), and we did not reveal all of our thinking and results of research, out of fear. I've been paralyzed with fear because the people in Game A are not in control of themselves. They are controlled by those with money. Money makes men mad; Money is a malady of morals. Money **is** power! And here I am, attacking the power of the most powerful group of people in the history of the world. Who am I? A nobody.

Except I'm not afraid anymore because I've discovered dragon glass. They can kill a nobody but they can never kill the idea of Common Planet. And if they do kill me, you bastards better not let me down.

Our enemies are supremely powerful at this moment. As the most powerful players, they get to create the money which they use to pay people, to control people, to command people to do and to say whatever they want. So, if you are captured or beholden to Game A power, or a paid actor, intentionally biased, have an agenda, or are being manipulated or in any way not in self-command, then I don't care about your opinion at all. Not at all. I'm going to follow the advice of Albert Einstein and "stay away from negative people, they have a problem for every solution."

However, if you read the entire book, I expect nothing but your honest judgement, whether that be excitement, concern or support. The more you understand the new game, the better your questions or critique will be. It is easy to take a sentence or a paragraph out of its context in order to discredit the ideas or the author, especially given the complexity of this topic. Because it is about a new equation your impulse will be to relate it to the existing equation. While reading, if you find yourself thinking, "but it's always been done this way", yes, it has, and that's exactly the problem!

Here's what futurist Tony Seba has to tell us:

> The bitter truth is that our industrial civilization has reached its end game, collapse is inevitable as it has been for every civilization hardwired to breach its limits. The good news is that a technology convergence is opening a window of opportunity for a whole new world to emerge with possibilities beyond our wildest imaginations. A world where economic growth and genuine prosperity are possible for all without the exploitation of people and planet. An age of freedom.[74]

We need to do like Buckminster Fuller said, "You never change things by fighting the existing reality. To change something, build a new model that makes the existing model obsolete… It is now highly feasible to take care of

---

[74] James Arbib, Tony Seba, RethinkX, https://www.youtube.com/watch?v=Rtesg8tYAu4

everybody on Earth at a higher standard of living than any have ever known. It no longer has to be you or me. Selfishness is unnecessary. War is obsolete. It is a matter of converting the high technology from weaponry to livingry."

People's actions, either freely or unwittingly, are collectively responsible for creating the enormous social and ecological problems which now threaten the future of the entire human species. We are all responsible for the situation we find ourselves in. The good news is, it is also through our collective actions— when organized by a new game of life— that we will be able to survive and thrive. Let's go, "...let us cultivate our garden."[75]

[75] Voltaire, *Candide (or Optimism)*, 1759, print, last sentence of book.

Chapter 2

A Brief History of Game A

"We have Paleolithic emotions, medieval institutions, and god-like technology."
– E.O. Wilson

God
@TheTweetOfGod

Will the owners of the blue planet between Venus and Mars please attend to your vehicle.

It is overheating.

8:29 AM · Dec 14, 2021 · TweetDeck

Life is a miracle. At this very moment there are almost 8 billion humans alive, all flying together, spinning and speeding through space on Spaceship Earth. It is just a "sphere only 8,000 miles in diameter shrouded in a thin film of air and clouds... Man was the last to come but the first to use his brain for the purpose of conquering the forces of nature."[1]

The story of all evolution is a history of ecology. The root of 'ecology' comes from Oikos, a Greek word that means 'house.' The story of all mankind is a history of economics, of how people interact with each other and their ecology. Economics at its root means the 'management of the household', so it's not just a figure of speech to say Earth is our home and it is horrifying to see how we are mismanaging it. *Man* conquered *the forces* of nature to dominate all species on Earth but we most certainly haven't conquered nature, and we never will. Manage: yes. Conquer: no.

Yuri Gagarin was the first man to orbit the Earth in 1961: "Orbiting Earth in the spaceship, I saw how beautiful our planet is. People, let us preserve and increase this beauty, not destroy it!"

[1] Hendrik Willem van Loon, *The Story of Mankind*, Washington Sq Press 1973, p. 532

> We find ourselves at an extraordinary threshold. One need not be graced with prophetic insight to recognize that we are living in one of those rare ages, like the end of classical antiquity or the beginning of the modern era, that bring forth, through great stress and struggle, a genuinely fundamental transformation in the underlying assumptions and principles of the cultural world view. Amidst the multitude of debates and controversies that fill the intellectual arena, our basic understanding of reality is in contention: the role of the human being in nature and the cosmos, the status of human knowledge, the basis of moral values, the dilemmas of pluralism, relativism, objectivity, the spiritual dimension of life, the direction and meaning—if any—of history and evolution. The outcome of this tremendous moment in our civilization's history is deeply uncertain. Something is dying, and something is being born. The stakes are high, for the future of humanity and the future of the Earth.[2]

When most people think of Darwin's theory of evolution, they might think of survival of the fittest, kill or be killed where being fast, strong and dominating are great individual survival strategies, and they are, but still, the deeper understanding reveals the true secret for species survival, for continuance in Universe, lies in adapting within a sustainable ecology, a livable Spaceship. "It is not the strongest of the species that survives, nor the most intelligent… It is the one most adaptable to change," noted Leon C. Megginson, as Professor at Louisiana State University.

The story of mankind is a history of the evolution of our big brains and what we've been able to achieve with it. Possessing a larger and better brain is the defining feature that separates us from over 8 million other species.

Homo Sapiens have been around for over 300,000 years, but it wasn't until about 50,000 years ago when we began to talk that we truly took *control* of the Spaceship. It was abstract thinking which led to language which led to advanced tool making which turned humans into apex players dominating everything on the planet.

> The technology of language— and it is a technology, it's something we've had to invent, and it took us over 100,000 years to do it— is the greatest gift we humans have ever given ourselves... It was language that gave us the ability to imagine better, grander, more world-changing ideas than we otherwise could, and most important, it gave us the ability to store an idea not just in our own heads but inside the minds of others. Shared ideas lead to communities, which are the basis of culture and civilization: Language is

[2] Richard Tarnas, *Cosmos and Psyche: Intimations of a New World View*, 2007

> the technology from which all others spread, and you've already got it for free.[3]
>
> That probably sounds crazy if you take 'technology' to mean something we made in the last half century or so—something shiny you can buy in a store. But dirt roads are technology too. So are shoes and chopsticks. So is money. So are buttons, gum, and eating oranges to prevent scurvy. Technology is on the farm as well, and not just in the tractor. Modern corn is ancient technology. So are seedless grapes. So wool, and cows, and butter. Much of how we organize ourselves is also technology. A bank is something we had to invent. So is a stock exchange. So too is an insurance company, a credit card, a bond market. Even in the wilderness we make technology. Building stones into a cairn to cover a dead body is technology. So is kindling a fire. We make all those things to serve our needs, and they wouldn't exist without us. Most things surrounding us are technology, or the result of technology. Technology is what we do.[4]

We use these technologies today to mold and manipulate nature for present advantage but not for future sustainability. As a species, we may dominate Spaceship Earth but we are still only along for the ride. And considering the ecological problems we are creating, it's a good thing we have big brains to figure it out. Not long ago, environmental hardships like the Ice Age required us to rely more on our brains for survival too. That struggle forced us to evolve, to grow and eventually to thrive.

Today's climate crisis[5] also compels us to change our ways, to evolve our economics. The President of Bolivia suggested just this at the recent annual COP26 climate summit: "The solution to the climate crisis will not be achieved with more 'green capitalism', or more global carbon markets. The solution is civilizational change, to move towards an alternative model to capitalism." Economics is a Property data management system. It's a kind of information and coordination system of collective human actions. It will take information before we can change how we manage our household. We need an open accounting of everything on the planet. We need to know and share all the information about production, distribution and consumption of

[3] Ryan North, *How To Invent Everything*, (Riverhead Books: New York, 2018) pp 6-8

[4] Gregory J. E. Rawlins, *Shoulders of Giants*, https://archive.li/rT0yq, alternate title: *The Human Swarm*, https://homes.luddy.indiana.edu/rawlins/books/shoulders/

[5] NYT, "Postcards From A World On Fire", Dec. 10, 2021, https://www.nytimes.com/interactive/2021/12/13/opinion/climate-change-effects-countries.html

resources in order to manage our way out of this crisis. We need transparency and cooperation. It's the only way.

> Only three things matter in this cosmos: matter, energy, and information. We use matter and energy to gain information. Then we use that to turn more matter and energy into infrastructure. Then we use that infrastructure to gain more information. In the long run, neither energy supplies nor raw materials constrain our lives. Our knowledge and tools do. Our homes, roads, jets, steel, machines, plastics, power plants, water filters, fertilizers all were always there. They were buried in the earth or floating in the sky, waiting for us to see through their disguises. All the atoms and energy we use today to make steel plows and breast implants and toaster ovens and heart pacemakers and protease inhibitors were ready for us 50,000 years ago. What we lacked was knowledge that those things were possible, and knowledge of how to make them cheaply. The same will be true in future. Because many things are still buried in the earth, perhaps including food replicators, human-like robots, and efficient orbitals. Things that our progenitors thought of as vital, like flint and obsidian, or that we today think of as irreplaceable, like oil and diamonds, our inheritors may think of as garbage. Conversely, they'll marvel that we lived surrounded by resources without once recognizing them for what they were. Instead we called them weeds and rocks and seawater and dirt. Even the poorest nation on earth is a wondrous garden stuffed with resources that we could use, if only we knew how.[6]

We are born with big empty brains, physically weak and defenseless creatures, literally unable to survive on our own, but once our five senses are fully formed, information is collected from the environment, sent to the brain where these signals are interpreted and causes our body to respond. This is how we perceive the world around us. But it's more complicated than that because humans are intelligent beings, equipped with memory, thought, introspection, facial expressions, self-awareness, imagination and most importantly the passing down of knowledge through generations.

The evolution of our brains is a fascinating subject, not one this book will explore, however, I do want to mention Terence McKenna, ethnobotanist and revered psychonaut, and his 1993 book *Food of the Gods* wherein he posits his 'stoned ape' theory, that our cultures, and perhaps even our brains, were affected heavily by the kinds of foods we ate, especially psychedelic foods that we came into contact with. McKenna called for an Archaic Revival, a return to our connection to the earth, and a revival of value systems that

[6] Rawlins, *Shoulders of Giants*

connect us to our niche in the ecosystem. That idea resonates deeply within me.

Sensation and perception are fundamental to nearly every aspect of our cognition, behavior and thought. "People tend to think of perception as a passive process. We see, hear, smell, taste or feel stimuli that impinge upon our senses. We think that if we are at all objective, we record what is actually there. Yet perception is demonstrably an active rather than a passive process; it constructs rather than records 'reality.' Perception implies understanding as well as awareness. It is a process of inference in which people construct their own version of reality on the basis of information provided through the five senses."[7] In other words, what we *see* (reality) and what we think we *saw* (perception) are not necessarily the same. Nikola Tesla said, "Our senses enable us to perceive only a minute portion of the outside world."

According to *The Kybalion: Hermetic Philosophy*, there are 7 laws of the universe.[8] Others claim there are 12, 20 or even more. 'The Principle of Mentalism' is the first of the 7 laws and embodies the idea that 'All is Mind - The Universe is Mental.' It tells us there is a single Universal Consciousness - the Universal Mind, from which all things manifest. Everything we experience in the physical world has its origin in the invisible, mental realm. All energy and matter at all levels is created by and is subordinate to the Omnipresent Universal Mind. Our reality is a manifestation of our mind. This is true Mind Power.

Tesla claimed "My brain is only a receiver, in the Universe there is a core from which we obtain knowledge, strength and inspiration. I have not penetrated into the secrets of this core, but I know that it exists." McKenna expressed something similar: "Half the time you think you're thinking you're actually listening."

"Realize that everything connects to everything else," said Leonardo da Vinci pointing out the obviousness that humans are totally interconnected with everything in our environment. "Knowledge is what we know. Also, what we know we do not know. We discover what we do not know essentially by what we know. Thus knowledge expands. With more knowledge we come to know more of what we do not know. Thus knowledge expands endlessly.

---

[7] Richards J. Heurer Jr., "Psychology of Intelligence Analysis", p. 7, Central Intelligence Agency, https://www.cia.gov/static/9a5f1162fd0932c29bfed1c030edf4ae/Pyschology-of-Intelligence-Analysis.pdf

[8] Three Initiates, *The Kybalion: Hermetic Philosophy*, Yogi Publication Society, Chicago, 1912, http://www.kybalion.org/TheKybalion.pdf

All knowledge is, in final analysis, history. All sciences are, in the abstract, mathematics. All judgements are, in their rationale, statistics."[9]

All that we learn comes from other people and the environment. Tool making, hunting, cooking, art, language, math, architecture, medicine, astrology... all information received by our brains came from the struggles and technologies of our ancestors. None of it is truly *ours* alone. We are 100% a product of our environment, a part of the Universal Mind as receiver and transmitter.

The ideas presented in this book formed 'in my head' because I was consciously seeking answers. I was only able to *see* because it was there already to be *seen* or because it wanted to become *seen*?

Obviously I'm not the only one with this vision. If you look for the *others*[10] you will discover they are everywhere; kinda like when you get a new car and discover that so many others have the same car too. It's everywhere. It was always everywhere, a part of reality, you just weren't looking for it so it wasn't a part of your perception. "If you are possessed by an idea, you find it expressed everywhere, you even smell it," said Thomas Mann.

One of these *others*, Frederick Scanlin, wrote this in an email to us four years ago: "It doesn't take near as much education or intelligence to come up with some very beneficial ways to utilize the knowledge & technology that originally took someone with a higher level of 'intellectual expertise' to learn, 'create' or discover in the first place. Creating anything that doesn't require any new &/or untried knowledge or technology to make it function properly is basically just an exercise in simply re-arranging whatever presently existing knowledge/technology is necessary in order to make it whatever it is meant to be." What I did is very much re-imagine existing economics and financial tools that already exist. I didn't invent anything new. I didn't have to. All I had to do was to focus and examine the existing tools and ideas 'out there' and that was enough to question and to imagine how they might be used in a different way.

Once the clarity came, I could not unsee it. It turned out, I did not want to see it actually. I did not want that responsibility. Like McKenna said, "The problem is not to find the answer, it's to face the answer." Overwhelmed by fear, I cried uncontrollably for over an hour, both in my head and out loud, repeating "why me?" Leonardo Da Vinci lied when he said, "Learning is the

---

[9] C. Radhakrishna Rao, *Statistics and Truth*, (Singapore: World Scientific, 1999)

[10] Noosphere Map, https://miro.com/app/board/o9J_kniyxiY=/?moveToWidget=3074457351086378738

only thing the mind never exhausts, never fears, and never regrets" because sometimes 'ignorance is bliss.' Meng Tzu was right: "When heaven is about to confer a great responsibility on any man, it will exercise his mind with suffering, subject his sinews and bones to hard work, expose his body to hunger, put him to poverty, place obstacles in the paths of his deeds, so as to stimulate his mind, harden his nature, and improve wherever he is incompetent."

Seeing it and describing it, or rather, getting others to *see* it has proved more difficult. Because it's basically about everything, I didn't know where to start. I built up an incredible following on Twitter and tried desperately to get more popular/famous people to see it so they could be the ones to champion it, but I just couldn't paint the complete picture. The only way would be to understand it as fully as I could first, and then try again. This is that try.

Okay, back to where we were: big brains allowed humans to dominate all the other creatures as well as nature itself.

These forces of nature, the laws of physics, first revealed themselves to us through experience and simple empirical observations. They are like God's rules which affect all beings and things in the same environment with the same force. There are dozens of *laws* of physics and many are immutable. This means they cannot change or be altered in any way. They are absolute, have always existed and will always exist. Things like gravity, the speed of light, time and space. Think of them as Earth's standard protocols. Beyond Earth, physics becomes much more complicated with relativity, dark matter, string theory and black holes. It's still a new, mostly unknown frontier.

Then there is biology. We enter this world as physical beings with limited time, destined to die, the same as all living creatures: finite beings in an infinite world. Did you know that "all different kinds of mammals here on Earth live for the same number of heart beats?... about 1.5 billion heart beats."[11] For humans, there are but two biological imperatives: to stay alive as long as possible and to procreate. The purpose of the game or the meaning of life remains a mystery, thank God, but at least we know the basic biological rules which serve as the driving force of the players. When most people say 'human nature', it is these two biological imperatives they are usually referring to. The game of life is to stay alive as long as possible. Since survival is the primary objective of each player, let us start there.

---

[11] Sean Carroll, "The Nature of Reality: A Dialogue Between a Buddhist Scholar and a Theoretical Physicist", YouTube, https://www.youtube.com/watch?v=pLbSlC0Pucw, 21:20

Earth is the playing field containing everything the players need for survival. To continue living, to play, all the humans and animals must compete for access to the resources in the game: the water, food and resources for shelter. Nobody can survive more than a few days without water or more than a week or two without food. This constant need for life energy is a daily struggle. Unfortunately, the players are either competing for the same limited resources or are themselves sometimes the food or other resource for other players. You know, the circle of life.

In order for a lion to continue living it must take the life energy by eating another animal. It's vicious and seems overly cruel, and certainly unfair, right? No, not at all, considering that interdependence is how nature is designed. Antelopes eat grass, lions eat antelopes and dead lions feed the grass. Everything is connected.

Before humans and our big brains came along, there is no doubt the game of life for all the creatures was considered as fair as can be. Where all rules apply equally to all players it is considered fair even though some players are better than others. That a lion is faster than a young gazelle or one with a broken leg is part of the game. All of them are bound to play by the exact same physical and biological laws of nature. If lions could become faster it would make it easier to catch gazelles and so through the long process of natural selection and evolution, the lion gradually becomes faster, but so too does the gazelle precisely because of the same evolutionary forces and everything stays in balance, sustainable, all within the most fair conditions possible. Competition is an essential force in evolutionary progress.

Evolution has its own pace, but on account of our large brains, advancements in knowledge and technology stack on top of one another driving change at an exponential pace. While these new technologies have enabled us to manipulate and change the physical world, our biological programming remains essentially unchanged for thousands of generations.

What if lions suddenly learned to talk, make weapons and machines to more easily kill gazelles, is that any longer a fair game? Obviously not because gazelles don't have access to the same technology, to the same tools to compete in the game. This is exactly what our big brains have allowed us to do, to create technologies to outcompete all the other *players* on Earth, to the point where, if we're being honest, we're the only players really. It's all us. All of it. We *manage* all the material on Earth. So much so that all other animals, who used to be equal players, have, for thousands of years now, been considered as part of the *material* we manage. What I call Property. Any *thing* that has use value or trade value— any Property— is certain to be taken and claimed as private, as *owned*. That's Game A in a nutshell.

There is no chance or possibility of ever making the game of life more fair among all the species ever again, unless humans go extinct. The best we can hope for is to make it fair among the human players because all the other creatures are forever at our mercy.

With big brains and incredible technologies, how are we managing our home? Here's how we're doing according to Ben See (@ClimateBen): The oceans are being killed, forests will soon be gone, fertile soil is disappearing, insects are vanishing and plastic is in our blood. The Amazon is burning, the arctic's on fire, oceans are boiling, coral reefs are dying, Greenland is melting, permafrost is collapsing, Antarctica is heating, ecosystems are crashing, Earth is turning to desert as emissions are accelerating. Extinction is now. Scientists are calling this the Anthropocene[12], a new geological epoch whereby humans influence the climate and environment.

The thing that most people don't understand about climate change is "that it's a justice issue, not a science issue. The science just proves the injustice. It's about power, not energy," wrote Mary Hegler (@maryhegler). Gus Speth, a Yale professor and US advisor on climate change says, "I used to think that top environmental problems were biodiversity loss, ecosystem collapse and climate change. I thought that thirty years of good science could address these problems. I was wrong... The top environmental problems are selfishness, greed and apathy, and to deal with these... we scientists don't know how to do that."

Indeed, *humanity* isn't causing climate change, Game A is. The majority of consumption, waste and carbon emissions are caused by a small class of corporations and people. Just 100 companies cause more than 70% of carbon emissions and the top 10% of people cause 50%.[13] By cutting down the emissions of just those top 10% of people would go a long way to reducing this pollution. This is called *degrowth*, and would look something like managed, selective reductions of specific resource usage via better, more open, democratic decision making and scientifically based prioritization. Our so-called *free markets* don't and can't do this. They are based only on profit from trade and what is first extracted. There is no global management of our

---

[12] The Royal Society of Victoria, "The Anthropocene: Where on Earth are we Going?", https://www.youtube.com/watch?v=HvD0TgE34HA

[13] Stefan Wagstyl, Financial Times, "Climate change is becoming less a battle of nations than rich vs poor", https://www.ft.com/content/4788beae-9035-4449-b5cd-200dc7b6ea9d

common resources. Game A is a global free for all race to extract the most. As Jason Hickel tweeted on February 3, 2021: "It is astonishing to think that, under capitalism, "progress" is defined as an increase in the total quantity of commodities that we produce and consume each year. That's it. That is the primary purpose we are enjoined to pursue."

So, our real predicament stems from an economic coordination problem. Ironically, a species named the homo Sapiens (wise humans) are presently so stupid as to still be competing against one another rather than coordinating cooperatively when it has been cooperation, as historian Yuval Harari revealed in his amazing book *Sapiens*, that was responsible for the survival of our species and its thriving.

> If you look at homo sapiens, at our species, what makes us really unique compared to any other animal on the planet is our ability to cooperate really in unlimited numbers. So the big question of human history, and the first question of human history, is how do you get hundreds and then thousands and finally hundreds of millions of humans to cooperate? Which is our secret of success as a species. But we ruled the world and not the Neanderthals because they couldn't cooperate in larger numbers then, again, 50 or 100. We could. And what made it possible is not intelligence, it's imagination, and in particular, the ability to invent and believe fictional stories.[14]
>
> The secret was probably the appearance of fiction. Large numbers of strangers can cooperate successfully by believing in common myths. Any large-scale human cooperation— whether a modern state, a medieval church, an ancient city or an archaic tribe— is rooted in common myths that exist only in people's collective imagination... There are no gods in the universe, no nations, no money, no human rights, no laws, and no justice outside the common imagination of human beings.[15]

That's a powerful tool, to be able "to invent and believe fictional stories" was a game changer for sure. Prior to that, for most of history, all humans were nomadic hunter-gatherers. Small tribes of equal players playing the same game of life with all the other animals. It wasn't until around 13,000 years ago that we settled down to grow food, but once we did, food became plentiful.

It was surplus food that started us down our journey to becoming the most dominant players. Surplus led to fictions of value and accounting, then

---

[14] Yuval Harari, Center for Humane Technology, interview, online, https://www.humanetech.com/podcast/28-two-million-years-in-two-hours-a-conversation-with-yuval-noah-harari

[15] Yuval Harari, *Sapiens: A Brief History of Humankind*, 2015

the need to distribute and trade— with people you knew and trusted— led to IOUs of credit and debt. Tribes turned into cities then into nations, led to trading with strangers— who you didn't trust— led to manifesting the currency (a fictional unit of value) into the form of money (a physical representation of value)— which you could trust. BOOM. Just like that, money then becomes the most valuable Property in Game A.

This is when the game between humans turns into a hierarchy and becomes unfair, perpetually producing inequality. Game A isn't really that old after all. Then came banking, with the *legal* power to access the free credit fiction and turn it into money for them and debt for you with just the flick of a pen… now just keystrokes. Today, money is mostly digital, still fiat, still comes from the credit fiction but it's used, owned and traded as physical Property in the game. This fictional property we call money has become more valuable than real property, that's how powerful our imagination is.

Money is just a story, but we all believe it, and that makes all the difference in the world. Christopher Hitchens once said, "If you're critical of religion, I've got a faith for you to go after. There's a set of beliefs—this is wacky—where they think there's an invisible hand that ensures that if you just adopt the correct economic system, justice will flow automatically."

If humans merely acquired knowledge and developed tools and technology during their lives and used those in the course of game play, then it would be fair because it was due to their unique qualities and skills that allowed them to play in the manner that emerges. But this is not the case. Knowledge and technology is handed down from generation to generation, not re-created but passed down, copied, stacked and networked so that today, we are not remotely the same human players as 1,000 years ago, or even 100. Collectively, we are human+++++, but individually we are still just human. Look around you, marvel at all the amazing technology your life depends on and realize you have absolutely no idea how most of it works, let alone how it was made or how it was sourced. In many respects, individually, we might actually be human minus minus because we've lost the knowledge of our ancestors who were intimate with the land. You can identify hundreds of corporate logos but can you recognize more than a few plants in the forest? As individuals, without each other, we're hopeless.

"Everything we call civilization was invented in the last 500 generations—way too short a time for our bodies and brains to re-optimize,"[16] says Tim

[16] Tim Urban, "Wait But Why", https://waitbutwhy.com/2019/09/thinking-ladder.html

Urban. To give you a better perspective of time, this chart below from Urban's blog shows what 500 rounds of game play looks like.

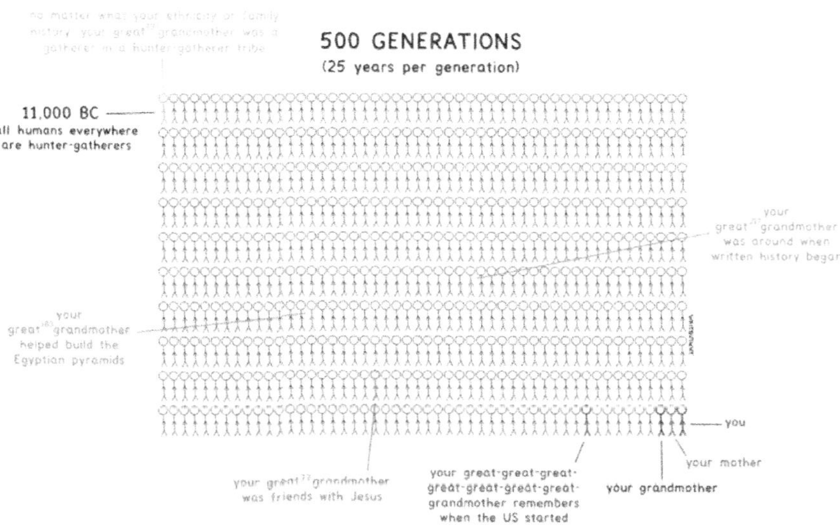

In just the last 3 generations, mankind has undergone more changes than all of human history before it combined. The spread of information led to an increase in knowledge which led to an increase in technology which led to an increase of everything else. The terrifying math of exponential growth.

Imagine if some massive loss befell humans, and we lost a majority of the population— our network composed of our knowledge stack— there is no telling if and when we would regain that lost knowledge. We are nothing without each other.

Consider a toilet. My village didn't have indoor plumbing when I was born. I didn't see a toilet until I moved to the US in 1979. Do you think all the people manufacturing, delivering and installing them have a clue about the underlying technologies that it took to make this amazing daily convenience that most of us get to enjoy? It features advanced technology of metallurgy, chemistry, physics, ceramics and fluid dynamics. If we had to start from scratch and figure out all this every generation, we'd never advance to make toilets because a toilet represents the process of thousands of years of continuous development and sharing of human knowledge.

This seems like quite a significant advantage for the human players. Remember, this advantage is still growing exponentially, adding more + to the human+++, especially now with the added benefit of computers— more and better brains— helping to develop ever more technologies and leaps in knowledge and to the size and solidity of the stack.

We are all the beneficiaries of this new ever growing stronger stack. Some famous economists make a living attributing this massive gift from our ancestors, this massive technology stack, and laying praise upon capitalism as being the source of the stack as an excuse to justify and continue this hierarchy shit show. We owe everything we have to the brains and brawn of our ancestors just as our children's' future is in our hands too. Please heed this message from Chief Seattle (1786 - 1866), Suquamish & Duwamish: "We do not inherit the earth from our ancestors, we borrow it from our children." Also the Iroquois *7 Generations* maxim: "In our every deliberation, we must consider the impact of our decisions on the next seven generations."

"Have you ever looked for the root of production? Take a look at an electric generator and dare tell yourself that it was created by the muscular effort of unthinking brutes. Try to grow a seed of wheat without the knowledge left to you by men who had to discover it for the first time. Try to obtain your food by means of nothing but physical motions–and you'll learn that man's mind is the root of all the goods produced and of all the wealth that has ever existed on earth."[17] Ayn Rand recognized our inherited technology stack, but used its existence to rail against *labor* in an effort to justify why most of the monetary reward should go to *owners* of production because presumably they are the brains of production, even though value is subjective. Besides, it takes lots of labor first to produce thinking owners; so which came first, the labor or the thinker, the chicken or the egg? One does not exist without the other. They are both invaluable.

Pope Francis in a video message said: "Let us not forget that today's huge fortunes are the fruit of the work, scientific research and technical innovation of thousands of men and women over generations."[18] Perched atop this existing, ever growing technology stack, Bill Gates, Jeff Bezos and Elon Musk claim credit for the majority of value of what millions of others did and are producing, none of which would even be possible without the benefit of our large technology stack. How much value would Amazon produce without the shipping routes, roads, railways and airports which serve as its distribution network, not to mention all the computer hardware and software

---

[17] Ayn Rand, *Atlas Shrugged*, 1957

[18] Pope Francis, Oct 16, 2021, https://www.vatican.va/content/francesco/en/messages/pont-messages/2021/documents/20211016-videomessaggio-movimentipopolari.html

technology? Jeff Bezos created or paid for none of that and uses it everyday to place himself as the middleman of trade to extract value for himself. Who *owns* the wealth that our ancestors built? Oligarchs. On wealth, Eugene V Debs said, "The savings of many in the hands of one."

There are those that will point to the Pareto principle or the 80/20 rule, which shows that 80% of consequences come from just 20% of causes. In other words, 80% of the work is done by just 20% of the workers and this is used as justification to explain the inequality of Game A, so as to make it seem natural and fair. The Pareto principle seems to be found in a lot of reality, but it's absolutely ridiculous to suggest that the way money is distributed in Game A is because of this principle. It is not.

Looking at player statistics of any professional sports league like basketball, soccer, or football, we would likely find the Pareto principle in action. A handful of players score most of the baskets, goals and touch-downs. What changes if instead of awarding just 3 points for a win, 1 for a tie and 0 for a loss, we award 30 points for a win, 3 for a tie and -3 for a loss? Only the points changed but it affects their ranking. Their position on the table has changed but otherwise the players' performances would still adhere to the Pareto principle. What if some players and teams were awarded more points for their goals and games? For example, every time Barcelona scores it counts 2 goals for them and victories earn 6 points instead of the usual 3, similar to how labor is paid more in some countries than others. Here again, the new point rules would affect ranking (wealth) but still the players' performances stay the same, Pareto efficient. Therefore, the points system (money) is an arbitrary human chosen value equation and can be whatever we want it to be. It is the same with real life economics. Labor productivity may be Pareto efficient but how much labor is paid and how much profit is made has nothing to do with the Pareto principle.

Please just stop with this nonsense of constantly trying to justify massive inequality. It's one thing if someone gets 5x or 10x more than others for their outsized contribution but how do you justify 100x or 1000x more? You can't. Nobody is that much more productive than others. How is wealth distributed today, is it Pareto efficient? Do 20% own 80%? Oops, looks like 1% own >50% of all wealth in the world. That's not very Pareto efficient is it?

Money too is a point system, and it too is human designed. The men who designed it are much more clever than you realize but not nearly as clever as they think they are. Over 2,000 years ago the Roman Historian Plutarch pointed out how "The abuse of buying and selling votes crept in and money began to play an important part in determining elections. Later on, this process of corruption spread to the law courts. And then to the army, and finally the Republic was subjected to the rule of emperors." Our reigning financial system is an ineffective, inefficient and unfair plutocracy. Whether by accident or deliberate intent, an oligarchic elite has captured and centralized wealth, privilege and power.

From a systems perspective, it is the system itself which determines what set of actions agents can make. The way people behave does not determine the system but rather the design of the system determines behaviors. You may not like how Nations, Corporations and individuals are able to amass so much wealth and power. You can effectively not play the game optimally for selfish gain, for greed, for power; you can cooperate and share instead. You won't become rich and if more people behaved in that way, some things would change for those people and their community, but not the system. Many of my colleagues in various enlightened circles believe we can usher in change by first changing ourselves, and our personal beliefs and behaviors.

If individuals refuse to choose cooperation or sharing, we can even politically neuter wealth and power through redistribution, but if we don't change the rules of the game of the system, what happens? Competition will once again lead to inequality and create Billionaires and Monopolies. While everyone is too busy engaging in us vs them debates, very few are learning how the system actually functions, leading us to conflict and demise.

How are we to ever make this a fair game again? Well, that's exactly what we haven't yet done and why I don't believe we have ever had civilization yet. The rules of behavior produce social interactions between humans leading to a wide variety of values, norms and customs. And because we are capable of believing in fictions and stories, how we organize ourselves (Governance) and allocate Property (Economics), offer myriad opportunities for different kinds of *Society*. Curiosity and human desire drive us to understand and influence the environment as knowledge develops continuously. Thus, society evolves.

Governance	+	**Economics**	=	**Society**
(rules of behavior)		(rules of Property)		

Language, art and trade have become the defining characteristics of humans. Along with the advent of the written alphabet, mathematics led to systems of measures, weights, accounting and ultimately currency. All of these fictions of our imagination are also technologies of coordination and organization, enabling ever more complex social structures composed of many cooperating and competing groups. From families to work places to villages to towns to cities and ultimately to nations.

The primary point I wish to impress upon you in regards to this simple formula is this: on the playing field of Earth, regardless of what the rules of behavior are within tribes— for the most part— it is economics which ultimately determines the relationship to power of the individuals within tribes and between tribes. It is the points which determine rank and not the substance or style of play— perhaps that should be reversed? Likewise, it is the rules of Property— especially the currency points— that we haven't yet codified for fairness which leads to peace and prosperity. Fighting each other over rules of behavior has been a massive distraction from the more important task of giving sufficient thought into the rules of Property and the coordination problems therein. First, let's explore these rules of behavior.

The Realm of Governance

Think for a moment about the US Government, what is it our *elected representatives* do? Is it Governance, making rules of behavior? Certainly that is part of their function, but the more important and contentious job they do is to make economic decisions and rules about Property; in many cases determining who wins and loses Property. What do you think taxes are? Do you actually think your sovereign Nation *needs* your money? The same Nation that constantly creates more money? The same Nation that lets private corporations called banks create most of the money out of fictional credit? Money is fictional Property.

States today control both Governance and Economics which mean they alone— top down— dictate what type of Society their subjects have. These decisions are forced upon us. Elon Musk tweeted that "government is just a monopolist corporation in the limit." That's because Nations were formed to control and protect Property. Not just private personal property, that's peanuts, but rather to enforce the private ownership of the common resources. So, when rich morons say they don't want to 'get political', that's bullshit. All politics today **is** Property which **is** life. Anyone who doesn't want to 'get political' simply doesn't want things to change because they are either in power or winning. Bertolt Brecht wrote: "The worst illiterate is the political illiterate. He hears nothing, sees nothing, takes no part in political life. He doesn't seem to know that the cost of living, the price of beans, of flour, of rent, of medicines all depend on political decisions. He even prides himself on his political ignorance, sticks out his chest and says he hates politics. He doesn't know the imbecile, that from his political non-participation comes the prostitute, the abandoned child, the robber and, worst of all, corrupt officials, the lackeys of exploitative multinational corporations."

The realm of Governance alone— just the rules of behavior— is more straightforward, even though it's been a tumultuous journey to get right. This was one of the roles played by religion, to codify human rules of behavior for peace and prosperity. But I don't believe these rules are that complicated.

It starts, and practically ends, with the golden rule and the non-aggression principle: Treat others how you wish to be treated and don't be a dick are maxims found in practically every religion. Like Jesus Christ taught "Do to others whatever you would like them to do to you."[19]

What is religion? Dr. Asatar Bair describes it as a "unique experience of the divine." Religion and law have much to do with codifying human behavior, ie. our freedoms. By nature we have individual agency and the freedom to do what we want, but unfortunately, in order to have working communities and society, no one should be allowed to have and exercise their full freedoms. Surely no one should be allowed to assault, rape or kill another? And this is where religion came in with their commandments and rules of behavior which help to produce order.

Still today we have Dictators, Rulers, Presidents, Government agents and agencies who have almost unlimited freedoms, even to torture, imprison and kill people. Some under the cover of complete secrecy. Everyone knows this is a bad idea. We had the Age of Enlightenment already, yet somehow we still have rulers not because we lack understanding of morality but because it's something deeper and hard coded in another domain of this world: the economic system that codifies our relationship to the physical world of Property. Almost always, those who control Property also happen to control the rules of behavior.

Religion is part of Governance, but fails to address the power of Property. Religion has always depended completely on donations of Property from its members and it has always had a dirty relationship with Property, throughout history causing wars and whatnot for power over Property. Religions taught

---

[19] Old Testament, Mathew 7:12

morality, tolerance, sharing and caring among their faith, but sometimes also called for converting, enslaving or murdering the *others*.

Everyone is well versed in morality by now, but our amoral economic system literally has us controlling each other, at war with each other over control and access to the Property in the game. That's the main problem. When we change the economics to win/win we'll find all else we need are just some simple basic rules of behavior.

Kwame Ture (Stockely Carmichael) expressed this distinction clearly when he said: "If a white man wants to lynch me, that's his problem. If he's got the power to lynch me, that's my problem. Racism is not a question of attitude; it's a question of power. Racism gets its power from capitalism. Thus, if you're anti-racist, whether you know it or not, you must be anti-capitalist. The power for racism, the power for sexism, comes from capitalism not attitude." Actions speak louder than words.

Everybody is free to lynch, rape or assault anybody they want, but not everybody is at liberty to do so, and that makes all the difference in the world. The rich in Game A have money to buy liberties and to deny others of theirs. Like George Orwell wrote in *Animal Farm*: "All animals are equal, but some animals are more equal than others."

We don't all need to become *one* in the sense of all believing in the same gods, the same religion, or of having the same customs or even the same language. As long as everyone is playing the same game of Property we can get along just fine. To each his own. Similar to having standard rules of driving, drive in the right lane (or left), red means stop, green means go; as long as we all agree on these and a few other standard protocols, driving becomes possible without crashing into each other. Access to the roads are not centrally planned. It doesn't matter the color, the type, or the speed of your vehicle. Out of the chaos of everyone driving what, when and where they want, these fictional protocols produce order. Driving is anarchy (without rulers), but by having simple standard rules, what looks like chaos actually produces order. Likewise with your beliefs: you have no rulers, there is nobody in central command of your mind, not even yourself, try as you might, haha. Nobody should tell you what to believe. If you want to live, then you better pay attention to your health, because your life is bound by the rules of biology and that's 100% connected to our ecology.

> Is the universe ruled by chance or choice?
> If the universe is really ruled by chance, then everything is ultimately random and any theories we make are meaningless (by definition). If it is ruled by

> choice the universe is unpredictable, but not random. At the heart of the scientific understanding of the choice-universe is a domain that cannot be rationally fathomed, but if choice is what rules the universe, this place is not empty, but FULL. It is the well of all things – the fountain of life. And the barrier to reaching this domain is... the MIND itself. Recognizing chance or choice as the ruling dynamic is truly a binary choice. One rules out the other, and so a culture that firmly believes in one will be totally different from a culture that firmly believes in the other.[20]

This is a very important distinction. In Albanian culture we have a saying that translates into 'it was written.' This notion that things happen by 'chance', or fate, as if it were always predetermined by God, as if 'it was written' in a book and was of course inevitable, thereby removing all choice from possibility. I find that absurd. There would be no point to life. More often than not, I hope, the idea that most are really implying is actually that of *choice*, that is, 'it was written' as in: of course it was destined to happen because of all the choices that led to the event. "Destiny is no matter of chance. It is a matter of choice. It is not a thing to be waited for, it is a thing to be achieved," expressed William Jennings Bryan.

In this September 17, 2018 Twitter thread Michelle Allison asks and answers what is the point of society:

> If the point of having a society *isn't* to care for each other, to ease suffering and realize each life's potential, literally what is the point? To hoard wealth? To build empires on other people's throats? Life is brief, nothing lasts. Wealth and empires are pointless violence. It will all be consumed by the sun. The question is not how can we make our mark, because it can't last and a mark alone is pointless, but how can we make meaning, ease suffering, be of service, express care, and sweeten our collective existence? Even temporarily, that matters. I live in a society that prioritizes violently subjugating and/or neglecting whole groups of people over taking care of all our basic needs, collectively, because violent subjugation and neglect makes a handful of folks feel superior and of historic consequence. Fuck all of that. History will go into the hopper, too, someday. Elevating a bunch of people with viciously antisocial values has been the most flagrant waste of human lives and limited time and scarce resources imaginable, but at least it also set us on a path to premature self-destruction. Wait. We have to start tearing this shit down, right now. We need societies that spend their money on caring for the precious, mortal people who comprise and cultivate those societies, not

---

[20] Rolf Jackson, Facebook Gameb Group, post, July 6, 2020

> on malignant growth and hoarding and immortalizing the violence that calls itself victory.[21]

Are we in a simulation? I don't know, and nobody does. It's like asking what happens after we die. It's in a different time and space and there are no links which connect from here to there. All the actions of all players and everything determine what comes about, so, even if we are in a simulation, that's still the process in which it unfolds. Even simulations aren't *written* until after they are run. You can set, *write* and control all the inputs— presumably like God did— but the purpose of running the simulation is to see what unfolds given the choices and actions of the agents. Even if God made all the physical and biological rules, how the players interact in the game is up to them individually and collectively, and what emerges is most certainly not pre-determined or *written*. It can be predictable, just like Game A predictably produces inequality, but it's not already *written* like some movie playing out.

I was born into the Muslim community of Albanians and then grew up in the USA which is mostly Catholic but there are also peoples from all over the world. They call this a 'melting pot' and maybe this is what led me to question God and religion, which angered believers. Everyone I knew growing up was a believer. My brother and cousins would constantly get mad at me, pleading with me to not share my questions or opinions with others and to just pretend I believe. My parents reacted the same way. They all wanted me to just shut up and not talk about it.

But I love to talk about it. Why do we exist and what does it mean to be human? As Martin Heidegger asked, why is there something rather than nothing? I'm fully fascinated with the mystique, the unknowability of these inquiries. The experience of life itself in this miraculous world is religious.

> We do not choose to exist. We do not choose the environment we will grow up in. We do not choose to be born Hindu, Christian or Muslim, into a war-zone or peaceful middle-class suburb, into starvation or luxury. We do not choose our parents, nor whether they'll be happy or miserable, knowledgeable or ignorant, healthy or sickly, attentive or neglectful. The knowledge we possess, the beliefs we hold, the tastes we develop, the traditions we adopt, the opportunities we enjoy, the work we do – the very lives we lead – depend entirely on our biological inheritance and the environment to which we are exposed. This is the lottery of birth.
>
> As newborns, we're not responsible for our own nature. We're endowed with genes we didn't ask for, and exposed to a world we played no part in

[21] Michelle Allison, https://twitter.com/fatnutritionist/status/1041674576558804993

> creating. So when do we become responsible for who we are? We don't! The fact is, by the time we're old enough to contemplate our own identity, we've already got one. By then, the way each one of us sees the world is framed by our prior conditioning. And that conditioning will inform any choices we make, even the choice to rebel against that conditioning. Long before we can shape the world, the world has firmly shaped us.
>
> if we judge a person or group to be ultimately responsible for an action, we blind ourselves to the deeper causes of the action: the confluence of economic, political, and cultural forces that allowed it to occur.
>
> The responsibility myth makes it seem that people get what they deserve. It helps to justify inequality and the economic system that produces it. When you realise that had you lived someone else's life, you'd be doing exactly what they're doing, a profound equality emerges – one that prevents us from putting ourselves, in any deep sense, above or below anyone else. This kind of empathy can be a revolutionary force for good. That kind of empathy, when multiplied across society, is a powerful liberating force, which in this time of turmoil and crisis, is our best chance of turning conflict into peace, division into unity, and hate into compassion.[22]

"Is God willing to prevent evil, but not able? Then he is not omnipotent. Is he able, but not willing? Then he is malevolent. Is he both able, and willing? Then whence cometh evil? Is he neither able nor willing? Then why call him God?" questioned Epicurus.

Not everyone believes in Gods but everyone is religious or *spiritual.* Everyone believes in *something*; we just use different terms. "What one man calls God, another calls the laws of physics," said Nikola Tesla. Like Astrophysicist Hubert Reeves said, "Man is the most insane species. He worships an invisible God and destroys a visible Nature. Unaware that this Nature he's destroying is this God he's worshiping."

Tesla believed that "If you want to find the secrets of the universe, think in terms of energy, frequency and vibration." In the split between spirituality and science, he thought that we don't have to choose between being rational believers in science or spiritual believers in the divine, they are the same.

King Haile Selassie saw it similarly. "We must stop confusing religion and spirituality. Religion is a set of rules, regulations and rituals created by humans, which was supposed to help people grow spiritually. Due to human imperfection religion has become corrupt, political, divisive and a tool for power struggle. Spirituality is not theology or ideology. It is simply a way of

---

[22] Raoul Martinez, *Creating Freedom*, Pantheon Books, New York, 2016

life, pure and original as was given by the Most High of Creation. Spirituality is a network linking us to the Most High, the universe, and each other…"

Indigenous elder Black Elk said, "The first peace, which is the most important, is that which comes within the souls of people when they realize their relationship, their oneness with the universe and all its powers, and when they realize at the center of the universe dwells the Great Spirit, and that its center is really everywhere, it is within each of us."

So go explore your mind, spirituality, and the cosmos, because that's where the real future is at. Nowadays more people are considering themselves atheist, but what do they believe when it comes to the rules to live by? As part of the 2014 book *Atheist Mind, Humanist Heart: Rewriting the Ten Commandments for the Twenty-first Century*, authors Lex Bayer and John Figdor held a contest in which atheists were asked to offer modern alternatives to the Ten Commandments.

Here are the winners of the "Ten Non-Commandments":

1. Be open-minded and be willing to alter your beliefs with new evidence.
2. Strive to understand what is most likely to be true, not to believe what you wish to be true.
3. The scientific method is the most reliable way of understanding the natural world.
4. Every person has the right to control of their body.
5. God is not necessary to be a good person or to live a full and meaningful life.
6. Be mindful of the consequences of all your actions and recognize that you must take responsibility for them.
7. Treat others as you would want them to treat you, and can reasonably expect them to want to be treated. Think about their perspective.
8. We have the responsibility to consider others, including future generations.
9. There is no one right way to live.
10. Leave the world a better place than you found it.

I love this except for #5; it needs altering. This list is about *how* we should live so it lacks any meaning or purpose of life. *Why* should we live? If God is not necessary for meaning, then what is? Carl Jung believed, "Meaning makes a great many things endurable. Perhaps everything." What is the point of doing, acting and behaving by these 10 commandments? "If I am not for myself, who will be for me? If I am only for myself, what am I?" expressed

Rabbi Hillel in "The Mishnah: Ethics of the Fathers." Where do we find purpose? In a word: Community.

What are you without your community? Nothing. Your purpose is your community and that's exactly where you will find your meaning. Ubuntu: "I am because we are." Perhaps community is God? So, #5: God (Community) is necessary to be a good person or to live a full and meaningful life.

Governance + Economics = Society = God(s)

Where are humans headed as a species? From Harari's book *Homo Deus*:

Hunter-Gatherers → Agricultural Revolution → Scientific Revolution

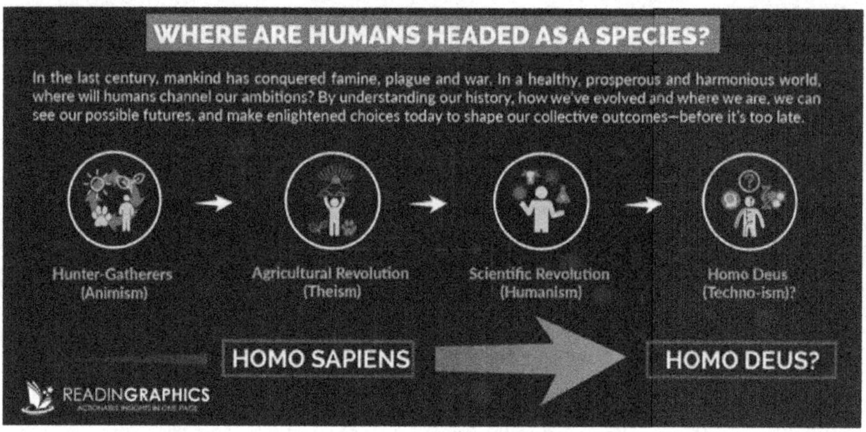

> The task is not to unify with a pre-existing consciousness – a "God". It is to become God, to create God consciousness from the universal unconscious. There is no conscious super-being (a Master, A Creator, an Other) standing separate from us. God is coming to consciousness through us. Each of us is an indispensable cell of the becoming God.[23]

Game A separates us into individual, self maximizing agents in competition with all other agents, with no regard at all for the community of the greater good. Those that accept and follow these perverse incentives, win, and those that don't, lose. Despite these competitive imperatives, many people still sacrifice their lives for others and for their community. Why? Love, that's why.

---

[23] Thomas Stark, *The Sheldrake Shift: A Critical Evaluation of Morphic Resonance*, 2019

"It is essential to our struggle for self-determination that we speak of love," wrote bell hooks. "For love is the necessary foundation enabling us to survive the wars, the hardships, the sickness, and the dying with our spirits intact. It is love that allows us to survive whole… But love is really more of an interactive process. It's about what we do not just what we feel. It's a verb, not a noun."

"Love is what we are born with, fear is what we learn. The spiritual journey is the unloading of fear and prejudices and the acceptance of love back in our hearts. Love is the essential reality and our purpose on earth. To be consciously aware of it, to experience love in ourselves and others, is the meaning of life. Meaning does not lie in things. Meaning lies in us," believes Marianne Williamson and so do I.

> We were told that we would see America come and go. In a sense, America is dying, from within, because they forgot the instructions of how to live on earth. It's the Hopi belief, it's our belief, that if you are not spiritually connected to the earth, and understand the spiritual reality of how to live on earth, it's likely that you will not make it.
>
> Everything is spiritual, everything has a spirit, everything was brought here by the creator, the one creator. Some people call him God, some people call him Buddha, some people call him Allah, some people call him other names. We call him Tunkaschila... Grandfather.
>
> We are here on earth only a few winters, then we go to the spirit world. The spirit world is more real than most of us believe. The spirit world is everything. Over 95% of our body is water. In order to stay healthy, you've got to drink good water. ... Water is sacred, the air is sacred. Our DNA is made out of the same DNA as the tree, the tree breaths what we exhale, we need what the tree exhales. So we have a common destiny with the tree.
>
> We are all from the earth, and when the earth, the water, the atmosphere is corrupted, then it will create its own reaction. The mother is reacting.
>
> In the Hopi prophecy, they say the storms and floods will become greater. To me, it's not a negative thing to know that there will be great changes. It's not negative, it's evolution. When you look at it as evolution, it's time, nothing stays the same. You should learn how to plant something. That is the first connection.
>
> You should treat all things as spirit, realize that we are one family. It's never something like the end. It's like life, there is no end to life.[24]

[24] Floyd Red Crow Westerman

The Realm of Economics

Economics— the rules of Property— determine how we manage Earth.

Small familial bands of hunter-gatherers were the first players. These individuals in small groups were equal to other animals when the game of life was more fair among all people and animals alike. Similar to how Indigenous tribes lived, and others still in larger tribes and their own nations and confederations too. Very harmoniously with nature. Sustainably. At one. The Iroquois Confederacy, founded by the Great Peacemaker in 1142, is the oldest living participatory democracy on earth.

Murray Bookchin believed: "It is impossible to achieve a harmonization of man and nature without creating a human community that lives in a lasting balance with its natural environment."

David Suzuki tells us that "The way we see the world shapes the way we treat it. If your mountain is a deity, not a pile of ore. If a forest is a sacred grove, not timber; if other species are biological kin, not resource; or if the planet is our mother, not an opportunity - then we will treat each other with greater respect. Thus is the challenge, to look at the world from a different perspective."

> How we see the world determines how we act. The Western philosopher Hobbes saw humans as engaged in a war with each other over resources making our lives solitary, poor, nasty, brutish and short. This view of the individual, fearful, working alone, in competition with others now dominates Western philosophical tradition. In Indigenous philosophy we are all related as individuals as part of a kinship based community and as part of nature in balance with the whole. In most Western thought Society is seen as an aggregate of self-interested individuals connected by competition with each other over limited resources creating fear, insecurity, hopelessness, a scarcity of spirit. Indigenous societies see prosperity in nature; resources are abundant, shared, collaboration fosters environmental stewardship and balance with nature. In the western worldview nature is feared, its value based on hierarchy, everything on Earth ranked, mineral, plant, animal with humans at the top dominating everything below. In the Indigenous worldview humans are an equal part of a vibrant interconnected whole, two worldviews two very different economic systems. The dominant Western market economy, like its worldview, driven by an assumption of scarce resources, intensive centralized production, individuals with insatiable appetites accumulating. By this standard the market economy works. 40% of the Earth's resources owned by just 1% of the population [inequality has increased since]... The Indigenous economy, like its worldview, inter-

> dependent, decentralized production, extensive use of resources, promoting responsible resource management, abundance, kinship, a belief in enoughness, encourages sharing and cooperation. Prerequisites for sustainability, the health of the economy measured by the health of the whole. Health in the market economy measured by gross domestic product. The more we produce, consume, the better the economy. Construction of buildings, manufacturing, transportation, all considered positive production but so is production of weapons, cigarettes, while investments like healthcare, education are considered costs, negative economic productivity. And the impact on GDP of the physical and emotional costs of warfare or the pollution that threatens 1/3 of the world's animal species irrelevant externalities outside the system, not even making it onto the balance sheet, an unsustainable system where scarcity of resources is a self-fulfilling prophecy. There is an alternative, Indigenous people's territory spans 24% of the earth's land surface but is home to 80% of its total biodiversity. This is not a coincidence. In Indigenous cultures balance and harmony aren't romantic notions but millennia-old design fundamentals. Nature essential for survival production and protection together, economic success sustainable creating well-being for all.[25]

Indigenous Americans didn't have certain technology, especially advanced weapons, so competition for Property remained fair and stable... until Europeans came to shore with their technology and their fictional Game A rules and everything went to shit thereafter. Two different fictions, two different results. One sustainable, the other not.

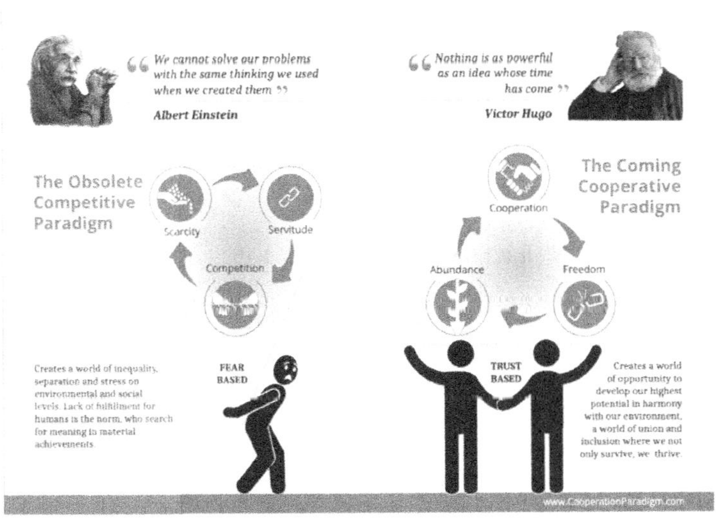

[25] First Peoples Worldwide, "ENOUGHNESS: Restoring Balance to the Economy", https://www.youtube.com/watch?v=RxPVrr44KHI

The Contract

We agreed, you know
before you were born,
back when the world was young,
that land would have owners,
which is to say,
that some shall serve,
and others rule
because of what they did,
not them, but an ageless Peer,
in some distant battle,
This is mine.

We agreed, also, that
if you bargain for your life
with a gun pointed at your head,
as long as the man with
the paper
and the man with
the gun
are two different men, say
your boss, and
your landlord,
why then it is not crime at all,
it's now called business.

The contract makes you responsible
for signing away your nature,
and one man with a gun,
and one man with a pen,
is all it takes for it all to be legal.

If there is no gun, they call it
anarchy.

If there is no pen, they call it
War.

poem by Vinay Gupta (@leashless)

Jean-Jacques Rousseau warned us, writing in 1754: "The first man who, having enclosed a piece of ground, bethought himself of saying 'This is mine', and found people simple enough to believe him, was the real founder of civil society. From how many crimes, wars, and murders, from how many horrors and misfortunes might not any one have saved mankind, by pulling up the stakes, or filling up the ditch, and crying to his fellows: Beware of listening to this impostor; you are undone if you once forget that the fruits of the earth belong to us all, and the earth itself to nobody."[26]

We have become undone. As soon as the first human players claimed common Property as private (and others agreed to the fiction), the game was afoot. The mad scramble to *own* as much of the commons as possible was completed centuries ago, when all the Earth was finally claimed by 'someone'. People were the original owners, but today most owners are fictional entities called Corporations or Nations. It has led to the ridiculous situation in the US whereby Corporations are considered legal persons. What lunacy.

Ownership is based on past events. When something becomes *owned*, it means others have no right to access or use without the owner's permission. Ownership of the commons is selfish and leads to disuse, abuse or waste.

Thomas Paine wrote one of the earliest proposals for real civilization, for a Common Planet, in 1796 called "Agrarian Justice":

> There is not, [among the Natives], any of those spectacles of human misery which poverty and want present to our eyes in all the towns and streets in Europe. Poverty, therefore, is a thing created by that which is called civilized life. It exists not in the natural state… Civilization, therefore, or that which is so called, has operated, two ways, to make one part of society more affluent, and the other more wretched, than would have been the lot of either in a natural state. The thing therefore now to be done is to remedy the evils and preserve the benefits that have arisen to society by passing from the natural to that which is called the civilized state. Taking then the matter up on this ground, the first principle of civilization ought to have been, and ought still to be, that the condition of every person born into the world, after a state of civilization commences, ought not to be worse than if he had been born before that period. It is a position not to be controverted, that the earth, in its natural uncultivated state, was, and ever would have continued to be, the COMMON PROPERTY OF THE HUMAN RACE. In that state every man would have been born to property. He would have been a joint life-proprietor with rest in the property of the soil, and in all its natural productions, vegetable and animal. Man did not make the earth, and, though he had a natural right to occupy it, he had no right to locate as his property

[26] Jean-Jacques Rousseau, *Discourse on Inequality*, 1754

> in perpetuity any part of it; neither did the creator of the earth open a land office, from whence the first title-deeds should issue.[27]

As brilliant as Paine's proposal was for that time period, it could not slow down or alter Game A so that today, all Property is *owned* by one of three different kinds of players: humans, Corporations and/or Nations. Humans are the only biological players and they control the levers of power of Corporations and Nations which both, in turn, control all the human players, the weakest players, the lowest in the hierarchy, except, of course, for those few humans who get to control the levers of power.

In today's economic game, the only two roles available to you are either a master or a slave. Most of us get to play as both, some more as master, and too many unfortunate souls stuck mostly as slaves. The entire *labor* sector and *service* industry exists to cater to our desires as we play the role of master.

These are the 3 classes of Game A human players today:

1. Masters: Property owners, rulers or bourgeois.
2. Slaves: Property managers, workers or proletariat.
3. Useless: underpaid, unemployed or Propertyless.

Property— the fountain of life from which all players must drink or perish — was captured a long time ago. Sadly, it's in the hands of the few who control the entire flow of life on Earth.

My heart breaks for all these people in the third class, the useless class. These are people who do not get sufficient access to the fountain of life. A fountain which is full, overflowing even, but, according to the old rules we still play by, since these people can not or do not serve the interests of the Property owners, well then, they do not deserve to live. They *cannot* play because either they are underemployed, underpaid, lost their job, got fired, or can't or don't want to play the game of master and slave anymore. Game A is a demoralizing amoral game. It's breaking so many people.

"Under capitalism," says Jason Hickel, "private property is not about the right to have your own home and belongings. It is about the right of elites to enclose and appropriate commons: forests, subsurface minerals, water, the atmosphere, public goods, even knowledge itself."

---

[27] Thomas Paine, "Agrarian Justice", https://www.thomaspaine.org/major-works/agrarian-justice.html

Here's George D. Herron, an American clergyman, lecturer, writer and Christian socialist activist, in Lecture Four of a series of eight Monday-noon lectures for the Christian Citizenship League (Chicago) given between October 24 and December 12, 1898:

> The common ownership of natural resources follows a clear line of Christian teaching from the beginning of that teaching with Jesus Christ. Nearly all His statements of religious principles are in terms of human relations; and His idea was altogether more communistic than we care to discover. Reduced to economic terms, the realization of His ideal of the kingdom of Heaven could mean nothing less than an all-inclusive, non-exclusive communism of opportunity, use, and service. It may be a debatable matter whether any form of communism is practicable; but it is not open to question that Jesus never contemplated anything else than an organization of human life in which all men should work together for the common good, and each have according to his needs or power to use.[28]

It all accelerated with surplus food which led to some larger societies turning into class based hierarchies. Property became fiercely sought and unequally distributed giving some significant material advantages (unfair) and these class divisions in turn became hereditary (more unfair). The means and tools with which this inequality was maintained changed over time but the structural existence of master/slave, employer/employee or rich/poor dynamics has always been rooted in the control and appropriation of Property. John Adams saw this in 1776: "Power always follows Property. This I believe to be as infallible a Maxim, in Politicsks, as, that Action and Re-action are equal, is in Mechanicks. Nay I believe We may advance one Step farther and affirm that the Ballance of Power in Society, accompanies the Ballance of Property in Land."[29]

Jim O'Reilly calls this the 'Adams Maxim' in his 2015 book *Capitalism as Oligarchy*. "There has always been a strong correlation between the two in complex societies and it's reasonable to assert that to a very large degree, power *is* wealth and wealth *is* power; they're really just different words expressing the same idea... Wealth is minority power over the majority and it's the antithesis of democracy. It's the essence, in fact, of domination and is thereby *tyranny*." He goes on to tell us:

---

[28] George D. Herron, *Between Caesar and Jesus*, New York, 1899, pp. 105-140.

[29] John Adams 1776 letter to James Sullivan. https://founders.archives.gov/documents/Adams/06-04-02-0091

> Throughout every age, a tiny elite has always wielded tyrannical power to subjugate 'its' population into producing goods and services for its aggrandizement. The ever changing historical means by which this has been accomplished are secondary to the unrelenting persistence of a deeply ingrained structural power. Wealth is the root of tyranny and its flip side is servitude. Slavery and serfdom were the icing on the servitude cake; but the cake itself is made of inequality and it's perfectly edible without the icing. First, wealth diverts production into serving its wealth defense and luxury motives that could otherwise have gone toward improving the living standards of the population. It thereby does hurt the majority. Second, the key fruit of wealth turns out to be the ownership of the economic plane itself. Wealth isn't just luxury; it's above all else power and ends up with everything. It becomes the owner of the system. The success of the minority thereby becomes the subjugation of the majority. History is clear on this point and it's the essential meaning of the Adams Maxim. Imagine an agrarian civilization in a remote desert oasis in which all arable land is owned by a tiny minority which has imposed slavery. Most of us today would find this objectionable; but what changes if the population is freed while ownership remains the same? Eliminating slavery is no doubt a significant human rights advance, but the population still owns nothing and must therefore continue working for the owners in a subservient position. The Adams Maxim tells us the balance of power hasn't budged.[30]

Individuals become trapped within the system. Upton Sinclair writes in *The Jungle:* "There is one kind of prison where the man is behind bars, and everything that he desires is outside; and there is another kind where the things are behind the bars, and the man is outside." In Marx's own words, "the worker, whose sole source of livelihood is the sale of his labour power, cannot leave *the whole class of purchasers, that is, the capitalist class,* without renouncing his existence. He belongs not to this or that capitalist, but to the *capitalist class.*"[31]

Master or slave, the only two options in Game A. Guess who doesn't want to change the game? Guess who wants to convince you there is no alternative? The same people who convinced you that you are not a slave, because you too get to play as master sometimes.

Pyotr Kropotkin observed the same phenomena, writing in 1887: "It has happened in the long run of ages that everything which permits men to increase their production, or even to continue it, has been appropriated by

---

[30] Jim O'Reilly, *Capitalism as Oligarchy*, 2015, pp. 40-41

[31] Karl Marx, "Wage Labour and Capital" in R. Tucker (ed.) *The Marx-Engels Reader*, second edition, New York: W.W. Norton, p. 205

the few. The land, which derives its value precisely from its being necessary for an ever-increasing population, belongs to the few, who may prevent the community from cultivating it. Who is the sophist who will dare to say that such an organization is just? But what is unjust cannot be beneficial to mankind; and *it is not.* In consequence of this monstrous organization, the son of a workman, when he is able to work, finds no acre to till, no machine to set in motion, unless he agrees to sell his labor for a sum inferior to its real value. And the workman is compelled to accept the feudal conditions which we call "free contract," because nowhere will he find better conditions. Everything has been appropriated by somebody; he *must* accept the bargain, or starve."[32]

In the language of game play: "There is no finite game unless the players freely choose to play it. No one can play who is forced to play. It is an invariable principle of all play, finite and infinite, that whoever plays, plays freely. Whoever must play, cannot play."[33] James Carse's book *Finite and Infinite Games* is practically a must read. Playing games is something we are all intimate with, but what this book is able to do, in such simple language, is break down all the nuances of game play that we already know intuitively but hardly think about.

The economic equation of having to work in order to live is very much a game. Unfortunately, it's very much like musical chairs: there are more people who need to work than jobs available, and it's only going to get worse as job-killing technology continues its exponential growth. Recently, Elon Musk said Tesla's Optimus Human Robot is the most important thing Tesla will be working on this year and has "the potential to be more significant" than its car business. The one thing about business is they sure are masters of efficiency, masters of cutting costs. Labor is one of the biggest costs to business, so to be the most efficient means paying labor as little as possible or cutting jobs, which means removing chairs. What if these people can't find another chair? What if there are no chairs even available to them? Even if chairs are available locally, that doesn't mean they are open to just anyone. And there are borders everywhere so you can't even look for a chair at the table next to yours.

Yuval Harari calls this growing tide of people the 'useless class.' He isn't making a value judgement on these people, rather he is using this derogatory

---

[32] Pyotr Kropotkin, "Anarchist Communism", 1887, https://www.fourmilab.ch/etexts/www/kropotkin/ancom/

[33] James Carse, *Finite and Infinite Games*, The Free Press, New York, 1986

word on purpose to expose how they are rendered useless by Game A. "In the twenty-first century we might witness the creation of a massive new unworking class: people devoid of any economic, political or even artistic value, who contribute nothing to the prosperity, power and glory of society. This 'useless class' will not merely be unemployed - it will be unemployable."[34]

All Property is *owned* and the only way to get Property from those that own it, is to exchange another Property of equal value. Manifesting currency (a measure of value) into money (Property) solved the issue of trust and the double coincidence of wants problem to facilitate trade. Those who own all the real Property became willing to accept money in exchange. Soon, everybody needed money in order to live, but if the only way for most people to get money is by working, and there are not enough jobs due to no fault of their own, then we must figure out another way to get money to these people.

Just before he died recently, Stephen Hawking wondered: "If machines produce everything we need, the outcome will depend on how things are distributed. Everyone can enjoy a life of luxurious leisure if the machine-produced wealth is shared, or most people can end up miserably poor if the machine-owners successfully lobby against wealth redistribution. So far, the trend seems to be toward the second option, with technology driving ever-increasing inequality."

Here's what Pope Francis has to say about that:

> No to an economy of exclusion
>
> 53. Just as the commandment "Thou shalt not kill" sets a clear limit in order to safeguard the value of human life, today we also have to say "thou shalt not" to an economy of exclusion and inequality. Such an economy kills. How can it be that it is not a news item when an elderly homeless person dies of exposure, but it is news when the stock market loses two points? This is a case of exclusion. Can we continue to stand by when food is thrown away while people are starving? This is a case of inequality. Today everything comes under the laws of competition and the survival of the fittest, where the powerful feed upon the powerless. As a consequence, masses of people find themselves excluded and marginalized: without work, without possibilities, without any means of escape.
>
> Human beings are themselves considered consumer goods to be used and then discarded. We have created a "throw away" culture which is now spreading. It is no longer simply about exploitation and oppression, but

[34] Yuval Harari, *Homo Deus*, 2017, p. 330

> something new. Exclusion ultimately has to do with what it means to be a part of the society in which we live; those excluded are no longer society's underside or its fringes or its disenfranchised – they are no longer even a part of it. The excluded are not the "exploited" but the outcast, the "leftovers."[35]

The simple but wrong solution is to give everyone a UBI, to continue Game A and ignore the structural inequality problem and the ecological problem. This is what almost all of today's top Game A winners like Musk, Gates, Zuck and their silicon valley brethren want, nay, think is inevitable. Economists Milton Friedman and Friedrich Hayek believed a UBI is the easiest way to end poverty. So did MLK. Even Pope Francis is calling for it. If it were truly a universal, global amount that all people on Earth got, then yeah, it could help alleviate some of the massive poverty, but at the cost of continuing or increasing ecological destruction, as well as inequality. After all, it's the same game. But with more money circulating, it could drive more production, which is at present inefficient and destructive ecologically. It would be like adding gas to a fire. Plus, all that new money would eventually end up in the hands of the oligarchs anyway, because *owners* collect all profit.

That said, a UBI might be a good first step toward Game B, since it exists in the economics of a Common Planet too. But by itself, a UBI is not enough, and many of today's proponents like it precisely because it continues their power and privilege since it doesn't change the equation or the game.

Game A is set up like a finite game, with clear winners and losers already, but the game of life for humanity is infinite. The winners won a long time ago, the spoils already claimed so the game is basically over. Political societies "multiplied and spread over the face of the earth," Rousseau wrote, "till hardly a corner of the world was left in which a man could escape the yoke."[36] Today, which individuals occupy the top of the Property owning table is a direct reflection of exactly how much they have won, and how much power they currently have. Those at the top of the Game A table altogether command, and fight over, 99% of the Property on Earth.

We are still in the era of the Game of Thrones. To be sure, which individuals occupy which position on the table changes relative to net worth, but that there is a table— a hierarchy of real wealth and real power— there is

---

[35] Pope Francis, Apostolic Exhortations, https://www.vatican.va/content/francesco/en/apost_exhortations/documents/papa-francesco_esortazione-ap_20131124_evangelii-gaudium.html

[36] Jean-Jacques Rousseau, *Discourse on the Origin and the Foundation of Inequality*, 1755

no doubt. You don't even have to be really good at Game A trading like Warren Buffett or Jeff Bezos. You can be *entitled* to wealth created or stolen by others, born into your position with inherited wealth like the Walmart heirs or Paris Hilton, or you can be a gifted artist (actor, athlete, musician), or a lucky lotto winner or a government leader, politician or a lucky *executive.*

Then there's the individuals most closely connected to the real source of all wealth and power: people in finance. The bankers who created the money have ancestors with hidden accounts who aren't listed in the rankings for good reason because secrecy is their key to continued power. According to mafia expert Roberto Saviano, the UK is the most corrupt country in the world. "It's not the bureaucracy, it's not the police, it's not the politics but what is corrupt is the financial capital. 90 per cent of the owners of capital in London have their headquarters offshore."[37]

Jamie Dimon is a billionaire investment Banking *executive* who's amassed almost $2 Billion as an employee in just 40 years time. That's $50 Million every year! Exactly what value has Dimon produced in the world deserving of such extraordinary wealth? Could his *profession* be any more parasitic? At least the inventors and entrepreneurs of real industry can point to tangible value creation but Dimon's entire wealth is skimming money from financial trades. Warren Buffet, the most successful and famous investor of all time, is a skilled Game A trader. He's often admitted that in a different system, his *skill* is useless. Indeed, he is skilled at trading Property, which means he is excellent at capturing more of society's pie for himself and his investors, but this skill doesn't produce anything that adds to the pie; he's just really good at *legally* valuing and taking more of what society produces.

Aristotle thought: "The most hated sort [of moneymaking], and with the greatest reason, is usury, which makes a gain out of money itself, and not from the natural use of it. For money was intended to be used in exchange, but not to increase at interest. And this term usury which means the birth of money from money, is applied to the breeding of money, because the offspring resembles the parent. Wherefore of all modes of making money this is the most unnatural."

"Those who make money with money deliberately keep it scarce. Money is not wealth. Wealth is the accomplished technological ability to protect, nurture, support, and accommodate all growful needs of life. Money is only

---

[37] Peter Yeung, Independent, online, https://www.independent.co.uk/news/uk/home-news/roberto-saviano-britain-corrupt-mafia-hay-festival-a7054851.html

an expediency-adopted means of interexchanging disparately sized, nonequatable items of real wealth."[38]

Evidently the table of Game A is not based on merit or any other semblance of fairness. It is truly not justifiable as much as economists would have us believe. The worst is Dimon's heirs will inherit his ill gotten Property. Timothy Mellon, the billionaire grandson of the previous US Treasury Secretary and banking tycoon Andrew Mellon, just donated $53.1 Million worth of stock to help privately fund the Texas border wall. No doubt as a tax write-off. Also no doubt he didn't *earn* that money. Not to mention this isn't even his native country. If you are an American, your heritage is either Native American, refugee, slave, or immigrant, that's it.

Check out how and how much this lady just got and tell me this game ain't dog-shit. Bloomberg placed this ad on my Twitter timeline:

Elon Musk, the current *richest* player, has a net worth now higher than the market capitalization of all but 25 *public* companies. "If a monkey hoarded more bananas than it could eat, while most of the other monkeys starved, scientists would study that monkey to figure out what the heck was wrong with it. When humans do it, we put them on the cover of Forbes," observed Nathalie Robin Justice.

The Forbes ranking celebrates the top Property owning humans, making it appear that Game A has only human players. Looking at the list, you'll notice that every single human is a *citizen* of some Nation. Every person on the planet is a subject of the real players: Corporations and Nations. Is there an

[38] Fuller, p. xxvi

equivalent table that measures the ranking of all Game A players? Nope. They are separate. The stock market measures Corporate future value and Nations measure themselves on GDP (the past).

In all cases, rankings based on money, used as proxy for wealth (surplus), conveniently allows Nations and Corporations to completely ignore what is actually happening to the ecology of the Earth.[39] It's easy to project prosperity by measuring numbers because numbers are unlimited, but what about the numbers that represent the real quantities of real resources? This graphic shows the divergence of what these two ways of measuring look like. Global GDP number going up, up and away along with income for the 0.01% amidst the reality of devastating ecological destruction.[40]

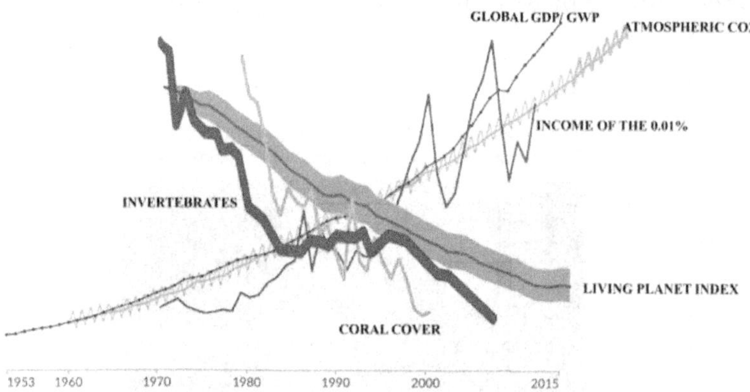

Most of the fictional numbers of value are controlled and *owned* by just a few players. For example, only two financial companies, Vanguard and BlackRock, just happen to *own* the most shares of *public* companies all over the world. Basically, they hold a monopoly in all industries in the world. Bloomberg calls BlackRock "The fourth branch of government", because it's the only private agency that closely works with the Federal Reserve (FED). BlackRock develops the software used by the central bank, it advises them and it lends money to them. BlackRock itself is also owned by shareholders. Who are those shareholders? Funny enough, the biggest shareholder is Vanguard. Guess what? Vanguard is a private company and we cannot see

39 Nate Hagens, "The Human Predicament", https://www.youtube.com/watch?v=MNzLkdr7UIU

40 Sune Nightingale, https://www.linkedin.com/posts/sune-nightingale-a94ba724_its-just-a-coincidence-theyre-not-connected-activity-6858736133040340992-sXFq/

who the shareholders are. The combined assets of the FED and BlackRock alone equate to 82% the size of the entire US economy. Add Vanguard with another $7 trillion and you're looking at 115% of GDP. Fidelity adds another $4 trillion+ for a 134% of GDP total. BlackRock is the world's largest asset manager, despite its size and global power, it isn't even regulated as a "Systemically Important Financial Institution" under the Dodd-Frank Act, thanks to pressure from its CEO Larry Fink, who has long had cozy relationships with government officials. From BlackRock's website: "Our purpose is to help more and more people experience financial well-being. Together with our clients, we're contributing to a more equitable and resilient world – today and for generations to come." How does helping clients capture as much profit as possible for themselves— at the expense of everyone else— produce an 'equitable world'? It's oxymoronic. These bastards are also said to be buying up residential real estate in the US right now, at much lower rates of interest than is available to human players.[41]

Do you want to continue fighting over resources in constant chaos or gallivant in opulence and order?

Imagine if a million people left Earth to settle a new planet, do you think they would organize themselves by separating themselves into hundreds of different tribes, each of various membership and geography, starting with a totally unequal distribution of wealth and power? Do you think any reasonable person, family or tribe would choose that over fair distribution and harmonious union?

According to MLK, "If we are to have peace on earth… our loyalties must transcend our race, our tribe, our class, and our nation; and this means we must develop a world perspective."

Activist Peter Schurman, in his quest for global unity, has written this sweet and short history of nations and about our need to become *one*:

> Humans took over the Earth by cooperating based on shared stories and ideas, and by using technology, beginning with fire. We invented farming and banded together in villages, using force to defend our food from raids. Our ideas led to social systems, such as laws, money, and religion, that transcended villages, enabling the growth of city-states, kingdoms, and empires. Wars were common for thousands of years as states and empires clashed. The idea of national "sovereignty" was established in 1648, when rival monarchies agreed to treat each other as the ultimate holders of power.

[41] Bloomberg, https://www.bloomberg.com/news/articles/2022-01-28/rental-home-demand-from-wall-street-has-land-prices-soaring

> Soon after, the Enlightenment introduced concepts such as liberty and constitutional government. New industrial technologies took hold. In a wave of political revolution that followed, the United States and France became the first countries built on a story of national identity, less than 250 years ago. Since then, society has transformed rapidly, with complex ideas like corporate capitalism and new communication technologies connecting the world as never before. European empires have dissolved. Many countries have split apart through civil wars, while others have joined in multinational systems such as trade agreements, the EU, and the UN. Since the end of World War II, violence has declined to the lowest level in human history, as our stories, ideas, and systems increasingly connect us. Yet, tragically, war continues. Today our main challenges are global, and it's increasingly clear that the concept of separate countries is outdated, and no longer enough to handle the threats we face.[42]

Never in the history of mankind has there existed a global coordinating system with standard rules because never has there existed a human society based on the notion of a global identity, of a global tribe.

Yale Professor of Psychology Paul Bloom tells that, "Responses to others: fear, hatred, disgust. Any category of humans is something you either belong to or you don't. In group, out group… We extend our compassion to strangers when we think of them as real people. In particular, we think of them as if they're our friends and family."[43]

We have never been we. It's always been us vs them. Are you a citizen of the United Nations or of a *United* Nation? What is it your Nation is united to do exactly? It exists to compete to control Property and people, that's what. It exists to survive to further its own interests. Why do you think the US allocates such an enormous amount of *our* money on *self defense*? What is it defending? Its own power.

What is a Nation? A Nation is a fictional ruler whose instruments of power are controlled by class 1 human players. Harari tells us "The very notion of a nation is itself a fictional story. It's not an objective truth. Nations are not biological or physical entities. They are imagined realities. They are stories that exist only in our own minds. A mountain or a river is an objective physical entity. You can see it. You can bathe in the river. You can listen to the murmur of the waves in the Mississippi. United States is not a physical reality. You cannot see the United States. You can see the Mississippi

---

42 Peter Schurman, et al, One Global Democracy, https://oneglobaldemocracy.com/

43 Paul Bloom, Big Think, "The Psychology of Everything", online, https://www.youtube.com/watch?v=328wX2x_s5g

River, but that's not the United States. The Mississippi River was there two million years ago, the United States wasn't. The United States might disappear in 200 years or 500 years, the Mississippi River will probably still be there. So it's not a physical entity. It's a story."

"Nations are concerned about themselves, not about the planet, and this kind of problem will keep coming at us as we discover more and more such potential catastrophic consequences," warned Carl Sagan.

History shows humans forming various size tribes in competition with one another for Property; where winners take all and make the rules, often with help from some new technology.[44] This is where we have hit an evolutionary dead end. It's Game A, a free for all to own and control as private property what is really the commons. It's pure chaos, a constant global war for control over Earth's bounty. There is practically zero global coordination despite the creation and existence of the so-called United Nations (UN); there is no such unity. We are not united. If we were, we would be seeking sustainability.

Finally, on October 8, 2021 the UN Human Rights Council recognized, for the first time, that having a clean, healthy and sustainable environment is a human right. Was that not obvious before? It doesn't matter though. Their recognition doesn't change the actions of Nations or of multinational Corporations. It's just words, literally. Winners are above the rules. They make and remake rules to suit themselves. The World Trade Organization (WTO) determines bargaining power based on GDP so countries that got rich from the theft of the past now get to make the rules of international trade to maintain and further their interests. Is that fair?

On June 21, 2021 a total of 184 countries of the UN General Assembly voted in favor of a resolution to demand the end of the US economic blockade on Cuba, for the 29th year in a row, with only the United States and Israel voting against. A resolution supported by a 184-2 vote did not pass. 184 Nations don't have a real voice and can't stop the biggest Nation from bullying and cheating smaller Nations. How is that possible? Isn't the UN a democratic institution? No. It was created by the winners to maintain their power and this is how:

> The creators of the United Nations Charter conceived that five countries — China, France, the Union of Soviet Socialist Republics (USSR) [which was succeeded in 1990 by the Russian Federation], the United Kingdom and the

---

[44] Ollie Bye, YouTube, "The History of the World: Every Year", https://www.youtube.com/watch?v=-6Wu0Q7x5D0

> United States —, because of their key roles in the establishment of the United Nations, would continue to play important roles in the maintenance of international peace and security.
>
> They were granted the special status of Permanent Member States at the Security Council, along with a special voting power known as the "right to veto." It was agreed by the drafters that if any one of the five permanent members cast a negative vote in the 15-member Security Council, the resolution or decision would not be approved.[45]

Political Coordinator for the US Mission, Rodney Hunter, said during the vote that sanctions are "one set of tools in Washington's broader effort toward Cuba to advance democracy, promote respect for human rights, and help the Cuban people exercise fundamental freedoms." This level of projection is disgusting. Apparently, democracy is only important for the people of Cuba, but not for the people of the *Kingdom* of Saudi Arabia, or for the people in the US or for the Nations in the UN. Is it fair the US gets to bully the world and dictate not only who can trade with whom, but at what cost? Denying Cuba and others the right to trade freely in the so-called free market makes a mockery of even Game A. There isn't even a pretense for fairness or democracy. It's all lip service and projection.

For thousands of years now, all the major religions have preached sharing and caring; at least among their respective tribes because we know they don't always extend those courtesies to *them*, to those *others*. There wouldn't be any *others* if we were united by a global game. We would be us. The secret to ameliorating, to reducing, poverty is by sharing and caring, however, it should be clear to you now that the secret to eliminating poverty has more to do with the fundamental rules of Property in the game, not just our morals. Redistribution schemes like taxes and donations wouldn't be necessary if Property were accessible or distributed more fairly in the first place.

"In order to have the continued opportunity to express their 'generosity,'" wrote Paulo Freire in *Pedagogy of the Oppressed*, "the oppressors must perpetuate injustice as well. An unjust social order is the permanent fount of this 'generosity,' which is nourished by death, despair, and poverty." Former *New York Times* columnist Anand Giridharadas wrote a book about the moral virtue signaling of the rich *giving* to the poor. In *Winners Take All: The Elite Charade of Changing the World*, he introduces us to the new gilded age, same as the old, where the rich and powerful act to fight for equality and justice any way they can, except ways that actually threaten their wealth and power. They

[45] UN Security Council, https://www.un.org/securitycouncil/content/voting-system

hire PR agents to brand themselves as saviors of the poor; and they constantly seek to do more good, but never less harm.

> For a long time now our species has been building something bigger than ourselves. We haven't designed it. We didn't plan it. We're not sure what it does to us, or what it might do to us in future. It's a nest, a nest made of all the things that we've surrounded ourselves with over millennia. For a long time our nest grew only slowly. Recently, though, it started changing a lot, and thus so have we. The first big change came about 5,000 years ago, with writing. Then about 800 years ago we started codifying much of the world's written knowledge. About 500 years ago we began a printing revolution. About 300 years ago we started a scientific revolution. Then about 200 years ago came an industrial revolution. About 50 years ago we entered an information revolution. Today, we're in an intelligence revolution. We've now made our nest so powerful and interlinked that, within decades, it may be about to wake up.[46]

Indeed, we do have God-like technologies. Imagine all people working together on a network of open information resource management. Imagine the possibilities.

Believe it or not, trees may have beat us to this information revolution. An ecology professor, Suzanne Simard, recently discovered that vast webs of mycelium (mushroom roots) act as an information superhighway which trees use to communicate and behave like a single organism.[47] We assumed trees were competing with each other for nutrients (Property), but Simard showed us trees were also cooperators, sending the elements back and forth to each other until the entire forest is balanced. "An old-growth forest is neither an assemblage of stoic organisms tolerating one another's presence nor a merciless battle royale: It's a vast, ancient and intricate society. There is conflict in a forest, but there is also negotiation, reciprocity and perhaps even selflessness. The trees, understory plants, fungi and microbes in a forest are so thoroughly connected, communicative and codependent that some scientists have described them as superorganisms."[48]

---

[46] Rawlins, *Shoulders of Giants*

[47] Suzanne Simard, Noeme, "The Intelligent Forest", https://www.noemamag.com/the-intelligent-forest/

[48] New York Times, "The Social Life of Forests", https://www.nytimes.com/interactive/2020/12/02/magazine/tree-communication-mycorrhiza.html

A superorganism can be defined as "a collection of agents which can act in concert to produce phenomena governed by the collective"[49] What about the human superorganism, what does it look like today?

Unfortunately, Game A is not a superorganism made up of humans only. It is presently dominated by fictional enterprises we call States and Corporations. All humans are the subjects of these institutions. We are not equal players at all. One can make the argument that humans are not even players in Game A today. Definitely not at the macro global level. The States are sovereign and the Corporations are limited liability, and together, they totally command all global Property.

The accounting records of these fictional entities reveals the evidence showing just a tiny percentage of humans (oligarchs) own the majority. They get to control all Property and all the other human players as their subjects. They use these entities like Iron Man suits, or drone operators vs the rest of us. They surveil and manipulate us as much as possible, much more than most of us realize. These guys so pervade our lives it's rage inducing. It's not a fair playing field, more like a killing field. It is the reason we feel so helpless and powerless, because we are; we totally are. But don't worry, the source of all their power in Game A is just a story and we can re-distribute this power with a new story.

Now if we zoom in to the micro level of the individual, the family and the local community, we can finally see individual agency and power. It is on this local playing field where most people focus their life's attention as it is the primary arena in which they are allowed to play. This is where we make most of our transactions, obviously, as it is where we live, play and work. At this level, Game A competition is mostly composed of smaller players like sole proprietors, small business owners and even small local banks, giving an appearance of fairness. In America, we used to have a lot more smaller players but things have gotten outrageously concentrated, homogenized and monopolized. Local players do still have an outsized impact locally, as they should, where even voting is consequential. However, local players have practically zero impact nationally or globally. Presumably we get to vote on the big boy playing field in our state or nation, but it doesn't mean jack shit. We don't actually have a *voice.* Everybody knows this. We are frequently reminded that America is a republic, not a democracy meaning we only get to

---

[49] Kevin Kelly, *Out of control: the new biology of machines, social systems, and the economic world.* Reading, MA, Perseus Books (1994), p98

vote for representatives. So they give us a *choice* of representatives, but they're approved, paid-for, or hand-picked by the oligarchs. Apparently this is freedom, but freedom for what and for whom? It is the libertarian notion of freedom to compete to *own* Property, no holds barred, a never-ending winner takes all battle royale.

More Property is continuously extracted or produced for profit from production or from trade whenever and wherever possible on Earth. There's plenty of Property that is created and circulated even locally, but most is *owned* by the oligarchs. Most of us trade our time for a wage to some corporation and in turn we spend most of it locally, so that our wage (our Property), circulates to our neighbors. But tragically, what used to be just a trickle out of our pockets into the pockets of the oligarchs is now gushing out of ours into theirs. More and more local transactions are conducted with large multinational corporations. Industry intentionally concentrates through acquisitions, resulting in monopoly power increasing prices and decreasing wages all made possible with political corruption. Inequality is what the game *always* produces; it concentrates more and more Property to fewer and fewer hands. A real life game of Monopoly:

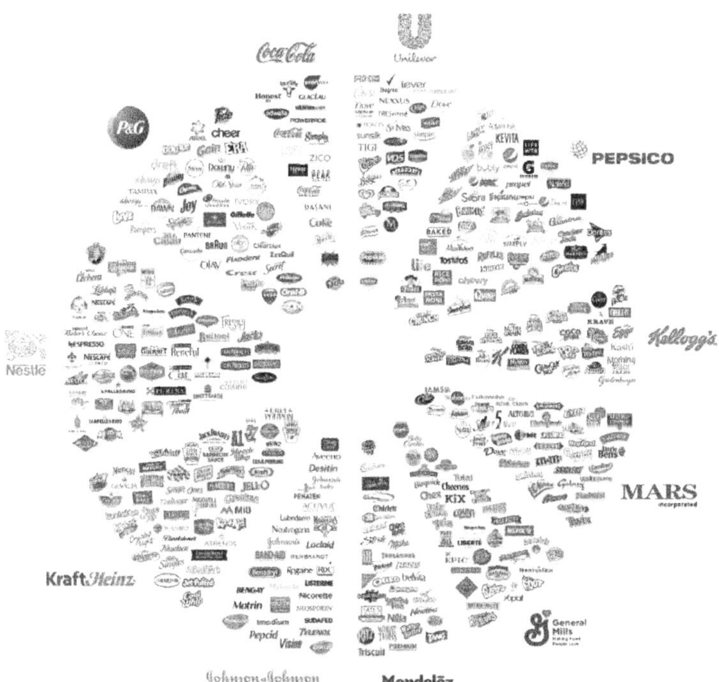

The complete picture of the superorganism today contains Nations, Corporations and people all at war for the Property in the game, to trade, because without Property they perish as players. Wendell Berry wrote this about the dangers of corporate power in his 2003 book *Citizenship Papers:*

> The folly at the root of this foolish economy began with the idea that a corporation should be regarded, legally, as "a person." But the limitless destructiveness of the economy comes about precisely because a corporation is not a person. A corporation, essentially, is a pile of money to which a number of persons have sold their moral allegiance. Unlike a person, a corporation does not age. It does not arrive, as most persons finally do, at a realization of the shortness and smallness of human lives; it does not come to see the future as the lifetime of the children and grandchildren of anybody in particular. It can experience no personal hope or remorse, no change of heart. It cannot humble itself. It goes about its business as if it were immortal, with the single purpose of becoming a bigger pile of money. The stockholders essentially are usurers, people who "let their money work for them," expecting high pay in return for causing others to work for low pay. The World Trade Organization enlarges the old idea of the corporation-as-person by giving the global corporate economy the status of a super government with the power to overrule nations.[50]

These fictions called Nations and Corporations are not bound by the laws of biology like humans are. When these fictional entities can't play the game anymore they simply cease to be or are gobbled up by other fictional entities. But when a human player loses all of their Property and ability to play the game, they become part of the useless class because they are still alive biologically. People still require Property to live. The game may not offer them access to Property any longer but that just means the rest of us must figure out other means of giving them some of our Property. Unfortunately, helping others is a losing strategy but 'greed is good' in Game A.

Here's what Pope Francis wrote about the useless class: "Human beings are themselves considered consumer goods to be used and then discarded. We have created a 'throw away' culture which is now spreading. It is no longer simply about exploitation and oppression, but something new. Exclusion ultimately has to do with what it means to be a part of the society in which we live; those excluded are no longer society's underside or its fringes or its disenfranchised – they are no longer even a part of it. The excluded are not the 'exploited' but the outcast, the 'leftovers.'" That's #53 in

---

[50] Wendell Berry, *Citizenship Papers*, 2003

the 2013 *Apostolic Exhortations*, which is defined as an address or communication emphatically urging someone to do something.[51]

That someone is us folks. Hence the need for this book. We must evolve. Otherwise Game A will forever remain fundamentally unfair and rivalrous.

Maybe it's just human nature to war? Author Robert Ardrey posited, in his 1961 book *African Genesis,* that man is driven by inherited instincts to acquire land and defend territory, and that the development of weapons was a fundamental turning point in his evolution. In his 1966 follow up, *The Territorial Imperative*, he further explored these ideas to elucidate the role that inherited evolutionary instinct, particularly what he calls the 'territorial imperative', plays in modern human society in phenomena such as property ownership and nation building.

> A bird does not fly because it has wings; it has wings because it flies... Just what is the relationship of body to behavior? Do we think because we have brains, or do we have brains because we think?... ecology is the relationship of an animal to his environment. But you will find no mention of behavior at all. And yet biology is in general agreement today that it is behavior—such behavior as territory, or the manner in which animal evades predators—that determines whether bodily characters have a selective advantage or not. It is behavior, in other words, that evolves and is central to the evolutionary process.[52]

Ardrey's book was not without controversy but it does make you wonder how much control of our mind and body do we actually have? Humans are adaptable but our behaviors are very much responses to our environment. According to behavioral economist Dan Ariely, "One of the big lessons from behavioral economics is that we make decisions as a function of the environment that we're in."

Today's anthropological evidence is more complete and it shows humans are not inherently violent & competitive. Nor are we inherently peaceful & collaborative. If you are required to be violent and compete to survive, that is what your biology compels you to do. If peace and collaboration is a better survival strategy, then that is what your biology compels you to do. Are either of those strategies inherently *human nature* and built into our biology? No. Humans are adaptive with a vast range of predispositions in response to short and long term stimulus. We are wired to survive. We are what the social

[51] Pope Francis, "Apostolic Exhortation", 2013

[52] Robert Ardrey, *The Territorial Imperative*, 1966

system requires us to be to survive. People will continue to fight and kill for personal reasons, but homicide is not war. War is social, with tribes organized to kill people from other tribes.

> Humans, they argue, have an obvious capacity to engage in warfare, but their brains are not hardwired to identify and kill outsiders involved in collective conflicts. Lethal group attacks, according to these arguments, emerged only when hunter-gatherer societies grew in size and complexity and later with the birth of agriculture. War appeared at different times in different places. The preconditions that make war more likely include a shift to a more sedentary existence, a growing regional population, a concentration of valuable resources such as livestock, increasing social complexity and hierarchy, trade in high-value goods, and the establishment of group boundaries and collective identities.[53]

Forming tribes leads inevitability to group identities, of in-group and out-group, of us vs them. This is what Nations are, large formal tribes. When America was *discovered* over 500 years ago there were already tens of millions of Indigenous peoples with "approximately five hundred different nations inhabiting the continent, each with their own customs and traditions."[54] What happened to them? Remember when I said Game A is 'finders keepers, losers weepers', well, I wasn't kidding, that's exactly how many Nations were formed. The first order of business for any Nation is to claim sovereignty over a specific geography and all Property within *its* borders. That is how the USA was created.

A mob playing by the fictions of Game A infiltrated the Indigenous way of life, killed them and stole their land. That's what happened. Good old fashioned genocide. In Raoul Peck's recent HBO documentary "Exterminate All The Brutes", toward the end of the 2nd episode of the 4 episode series, he says: "Contrary to what has been asserted about the birth of the United States and its domination of the continent, it was neither superior weapons, nor technology, nor a superior number of settlers, nor disease, that is to say, 'not guns, steel, and germs,' that can account for it. The determining factor of this domination was the willingness to eliminate whole civilizations of people in order to possess their land."

---

[53] R. Brian Fergusan, Scientific American, "War Is *Not* Part Of Human Nature", https://www.scientificamerican.com/article/war-is-not-part-of-human-nature/

[54] World Atlas, https://www.worldatlas.com/articles/tribes-that-populated-north-america-prior-to-the-arrival-of-europeans.html

According to Max Weber, a Nation is a political institution or entity that has the monopoly over the use of force in a certain territory over a certain population. A Nation can be identified by these four combined elements: sovereignty (independence), government (ruling body), territory (geography), and population (citizens).

But wait, there's more. Humans are considered Property in Game A. Millions of people were stolen from their lands in Africa and transported on ships to the Americas and used as slaves to work the newly acquired lands to profit from trade.[55] Today, the USA is the self-proclaimed richest Nation on Earth. A fictional entity is the current *winner* of Game A. Well done guys.

"'The slave trade did not end the world's hunt for cheap labor. To satisfy that hunger, colonial governments devised various strategies to compel native Africans to work. These included oppressive taxes and laws restricting the independence of indigenous peoples. In some cases, such measures were accompanied by missions intended to "civilize" native Africans. The continued economic exploitation of native peoples could therefore be justified by colonial administrators as an educational exercise."[56]

Here's Kwame Ture speaking in 1966: "Now when the missionaries came to civilize us because we were uncivilized, educate us because we were uneducated, and give us some–some literate studies because we were illiterate– they charged a price. The missionaries came with the Bible, and we had the land. When they left, they had the land, and we still have the Bible. (applause) And that has been the rationalization for Western civilization as it moves across the world and stealing and plundering and raping everybody in its path. Their one rationalization is that the rest of the world is uncivilized and they are in fact civilized. And they are uncivilized."[57]

Because labor is an expense for sellers, Enterprises have been known to do whatever it takes to keep their costs down as much as possible. Every penny cut from costs equals a penny in profit. Sellers raise profit margins when cutting production or acquisition costs. The world may have ended chattel slavery in the 1800s, but slaves of Game A production and trade we remain.

---

[55] Guardian, Built on the bodies of slaves: how Africa was erased from history, https://www.theguardian.com/news/2021/oct/12/africa-slaves-erased-from-history-modern-world

[56] John J. McCusker, *History of World Trade Since 1450*, p3 quote by Justin Crawford

[57] Kwame Ture (Stokely Carmichael), "Black Power", Speech, Oct 29, 1966

> Colonial officials used racist stereotypes to justify their tax and labor policies. They claimed that Africans were lazy and that whites had to teach Africans the "dignity of hard labor." Officials argued that taxes and forced labor were simply tools for turning Africans into good workers. The fact was that colonial employers needed cheap labor to survive. Settlers, mine owners, and company plantations lacked the capital and expertise they needed to compete on the world market. African wages were the only expense they could control, and they used every available method to force Africans to work more for less pay. Critics denounced forced labor policies, but their protests had little effect. In the early 1900s the Congo Reform Campaign raised a public outcry over the violent measures used to force Africans to collect rubber. The Belgian government promised to abolish forced labor in the colony, but company plantations continued to impose labor rents on tenants. The International Labour Organization's Forced Labour Convention of 1930 called on governments to outlaw all forms of forced labor. However, the document permitted the use of forced labor on public projects. This loophole allowed colonial labor practices to continue essentially unchanged until the 1950s.[58]

Colonial refers mostly to European governments. Nations and Corporations work together to control the people in pursuit of perpetual Property.

> Government was instituted to guarantee that property would remain stolen. The chief function of every cop, every judge, every bureaucrat is to see that property remains stolen. The first kings were conquerors. They stole the land by shot and shell, period. Then, they settled down to rob the survivors at a certain rate per year, called taxation. Next, they divided up the land among their relatives or officers in the army, who all became lords-of-the-land, landlords, and were empowered to rob the citizens at a certain other rate per year, called rent. When science and industry appeared, other satraps and sycophants of the royal families received charters to monopolize the resources and means of production, and to rob at a certain rate per year, called capital interest or profit. When banks were formed to circulate the medium of exchange (money), other charters were handed out to others in the bandit-gang, who became bank directors with a license to rob at another rate per year, called money interest or economic interest.[59]

The USA was formed by decree, claiming all the land where they had already displaced Indigenous peoples. The rest of the land, they stole by continued

---

[58] McCusker, *History of World Trade Since 1450*, p5

[59] Robert Anton Wilson & Robert Shay, "Anarchism and Crime", Green Egg, Vol. VII, No. 62, Beltane, May, 1974, http://www.rawillumination.net/2013/08/anarchism-and-crime-by-wilson-and-shea.html

genocide or by trickery of trade and *legal* contracts. The Homestead Act of 1862 in the United States accelerated the land theft. Giving individuals from the US and around the world the opportunity to claim free government land allowed nearly any man or woman a chance to live the American Dream while helping to continue the Indigenous nightmare. During the homesteading era over 1.6 million people claimed and settled (found and kept) more than 270 million acres of the Indigenous peoples' land.

Over 17% of land in my state of Oregon was *homesteaded* (stolen); that's more than 8 million acres. The State and Federal government claimed the rest pushing Natives onto reservations. Thanks Lewis and Clark.

Here's a link to a Game A "infographic, created all the way back in 1931 by a man named John B. Sparks, which maps the ebb and flow of global power going all the way back to 2,000 B.C. on one coherent timeline."[60] It's quite impressive.

"If I were asked to answer the following question: What is slavery? and I should answer in one word, It is murder!, my meaning would be understood at once. No extended argument would be required to show that the power to remove a man's mind, will, and personality, is the power of life and death, and that it makes a man a slave. It is murder. Why, then, to this other question: What is property? may I not likewise answer, It is robbery!, without the certainty of being misunderstood; the second proposition being no other than a transformation of the first?"[61]

Nobody wants to believe their position in life is built on genocide, but it is because all property is stolen land.[62] This 1764 English folk poem captures this essence:

> They hang the man and flog the woman
> Who steals the goose from off the common,
> Yet let the greater villain loose
> That steals the common from the goose.
>
> The law demands that we atone
> When we take things we do not own,
> But leaves the lords and ladies fine
> Who take things that are yours and mine.

---

[60] Visual Capitalist, online, https://www.visualcapitalist.com/histomap/

[61] Pierre-Joseph Proudhon, *What is Property?*, 1840

[62] The Guardian, https://www.theguardian.com/commentisfree/2021/nov/15/new-england-once-hunted-and-humans-for-money-were-descendents-of-the-survivors

What is the structural significance of all land already being owned? What is this economic coordination problem which makes Game A fundamentally unfair, *over*, and self terminating?

This reminds me of an experience in sixth grade at Schaghticoke Middle School in New Milford, CT, USA. A school named after the Schaghticoke Indigenous peoples whose land we now called ours.

Everyone was seated as the school bell rang to signal the beginning of class. Our math teacher, Mr. Paul Bourdeau[63], had drawn a tic-tac-toe board on the chalkboard. Towards the end of class he starts telling us about his favorite restaurant, Chuck's Steak House, and how they have the best steak in the area and then he says, "whoever can beat me in tic-tac-toe wins a free dinner at Chuck's Steak House." All the kids immediately raise their hand to challenge him. The teacher chooses his opponents, then goes first. He ties the first two games and wins the third. More hands go up as he explains that's it for the day, however the offer will be open until someone beats him, and that also, he had never yet been beaten. Challenge accepted.

Tic-tac-toe was a game familiar to kids that age. It's a simple game really. There are only 2 players and a board with 9 squares. To win you have to place 3 of your objects in a row diagonally, vertically or horizontally. After choosing an object of X or O, each player takes turns placing their object on the board which leads quickly to either one player winning or nobody winning, which is usually called a tie.

I played against my friends during lunch and the bus ride home because I wanted to win a dinner at Chuck's Steak House. Then I played against my brother at home and finally by myself over and over until I realized something: the game is rigged mathematically to favor the player going first. There are not many moves possible, so with very little practice you should be able to win or tie every time you go first. And, even if you go second, with a little practice, you can tie and not ever lose. Therefore, our math teacher was playing a game he knew he could never lose. His bet was a lie.

The entire setup seems so perfectly fair, but it isn't a fair game at all. But how could that be? Well, the facts are both players are equal in taking turns, number of objects played per turn, and both start on an empty board; all of which gives the appearance of fairness, except, as soon as play begins, the first player to fill a square gains immediate advantage. Imagine running a

---

[63] The Zone, obituary, https://thezone.rep-am.com/goal-zone/2018/01/08/legendary-soccer-official-paul-bourdeau-dies-at-age-87/

track race where you can't begin until your opponent has already finished the first lap. Is that fair? Of course not. It's the same with Property *ownership*.

The next day, every kid raised their hands in the air to play. A load chorus of 'ooh-oohs' filled the room. The teacher went first again and won. I grumbled out loud that the teacher ought to let the kids go first and so he did, thus ending in the inevitable tie. I wondered why they bothered but I didn't dare say anything. I don't know what your school was like, but 1980s American youth culture meant that anyone who stood out was open to ridicule, including being smart as a 'teacher's pet.' So I kept quiet.

This went on for days, maybe weeks. Kids kept on playing thinking they had a real chance at winning a dinner at Chuck's Steak House. Surely they must know this game is a farce? Eventually, I could stand it no more, raised my hand and blurted, "you're cheating."

He replied with a coy, "Oh, how so?"

"It's impossible to lose if you know how to play. I'll bet you dinner at Chuck's Steak House you can't beat me either," I said.

Without pause he continued, "Ok then, who wants to play next?" And again hands in the air. Just unbelievable. He can't be beat! Or did they think it was just my opinion that he couldn't be beat, because, after all, it was possible to win in the game. So maybe they could be the lucky one to finally beat him?

Any kid who actually thought they could win, clearly did not understand the math of the game. Imagine it was a real game with real consequences and the loser had to pay the winner. Mr. Bourdeau would've eaten steak dinners every night.

Economics has really to do with only one thing: allocation of Property. That's it. Game A is very much like tic-tac-toe because whoever gets the Property first has immediate advantage.

There is a presumption that because humans must consume resources to survive they must also compete for these resources, especially if they are scarce. Thus, the primary struggle in our evolution has always been over access to and control of resources. Whoever controls Property, rules. The history of the world is an ongoing series of battles for control over Property. Competition is presumed to be the only option. There is no doubt we must *compete* for goods that are sourced from the Earth, but is it possible for us to make this a fair competition, a win/win game? Especially considering food grows perennially. At any given moment there is a finite amount of food, but food is not scarce because more is continually growing. Many other resources are also regenerative, while some are truly scarce.

Now let's go back and examine the game of tic-tac-toe for a moment. Imagine the X and O to be the resources and the Earth is the playing field, or the game board. These are the 3 possible outcomes.

#1 Competition		
X	X	X
X	O	O
O	O	X

#2 Competition		
O	X	O
O	X	X
X	O	X

#3 Cooperation		
X	X	X
X	X	X
O	O	O

If teams compete, the game ends when there's a winner (#1) or when both lose (#2). If the teams cooperate (#3), they maximize prosperity for all.

There are 2 competing interests: Tribe X takes resources for their side, and Tribe O takes for theirs. Team X goes out and collects their first X, meanwhile team O is also competing to collect resources and so they get their first O. As the game proceeds, the tribes continue to collect resources until suddenly, they realize the resources are getting scarce.

This ultimately leads to the class conflict the *Communist Manifesto* focuses on and is expressed right from the start of the book:

> The history of all hitherto existing society is the history of class struggles. Freeman and slave, patrician and plebeian, lord and serf, guild-master and journeyman, in a word, oppressor and oppressed, stood in constant opposition to one another, carried on an uninterrupted, now hidden, now open fight, a fight that each time ended, either in a revolutionary reconstitution of society-at-large or in the common ruin of the contending classes.[64]

Marx and Engels are saying that we have always been playing the same game, X vs O, and its results look just like options #1 and #2 of tic-tac-toe above, and then it repeats over and over again. Presumably, what Marx called communism would be a lasting and stable #3. Why haven't we been able to achieve a lasting peace? Let's continue examining the game for the answer.

Round after round of competition was found to not produce the best results so they decide to try cooperation since there are enough resources for all. Because X starts first they will collect more resources than O does at first, but if they continue cooperating and take turns, both tribes can win and

---

[64] Karl Marx and Friedrich Engels, *The Communist Manifesto* (London: Verso, 2012), 34-35.

produce everything they need and desire in perpetuity. A true win/win organizing system. However, in order for that to happen, they need to trust each other to play by the rules or have standard incorruptible rules. Trust has been, so far, the evolutionary hurdle we haven't overcome and there has never been standard incorruptible rules either.

When one of the teams lies or cheats, cooperation as a strategy breaks down. The aggressor wins at the other's expense. Cooperating suddenly becomes a losing strategy. In the previous example both teams trusted each other to cooperate. What happens if one decides to cheat?

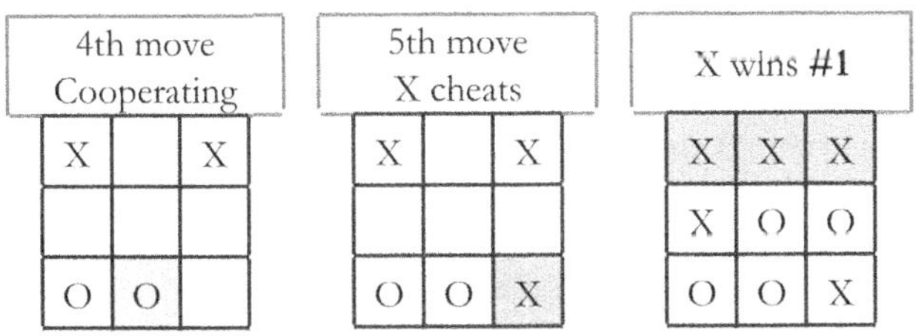

Team O makes the 4th move and continues to cooperate. Then, on the 5th move, Team X changes its strategy from cooperate to compete instead, choosing to cheat, thereby gaining advantage and assuring itself victory as outcome shown in #1. Thus, the struggle continues and society goes from #3 cooperating back to competing again resulting in #1 and #2 outcomes until future generations discover the mutual benefits of #3 which lasts until the newer players realize they can win and dominate by competing against their cooperative counter-party and they end up back to #1, then #2, repeating the cycle forever. But why?

> Justly or unjustly, society has made wealth a measure of worth. It is easy on general principles to prove that it is not such a measure. All will admit that, taken in the abstract, the principle is unsound, and yet all act upon it. Not rationally, not perhaps consciously, but they still do it. It is "human nature" to respect those who have and to care little for those who have not. There is a sort of feeling that if one is destitute there must be a reason for it. It is inevitably ascribed to some personal deficit. In a word, absence of means is, in one form or another, made to stand for absence of merit. Its cause is looked for in character. This is most clearly seen in the marked contrast between the indisposition to help the unsuccessful and the willingness to help the successful. Aside from the prospect of a *quid pro quo*, no one wants to waste time, energy, or money on what is worthless - and possession is a primary test of worth... Thus it comes about that wealth, in the existing state of society, is a tremendous power. It gives not only ease, plenty, luxury, but,

> what is infinitely more, the respect of all and the envy of the less favored. It gives, in a word, superiority; and the strongest craving of man's nature is, in one way or another, to be set over his fellows. When all this is considered, the futility of the proposal of certain reformers to eradicate the passion for proprietary acquisition becomes apparent.[65]

Ok then, it seems humans strive to always be *better* than their peers. The primary measure of better is more material possession, of more Property, of higher net worth. Is that 'human nature', Game A incentives or both?

Let's examine another decision making and game theory paradox called the prisoner's dilemma, as presented by mathematician Albert Tucker in 1950.

> Two men, charged with a joint violation of law, are held separately by the police. Each is told that (1) if one confesses and the other does not, the former will be given a reward ... and the latter will be given a large fine ... (2) if both confess, each will be given a small fine ... At the same time each has good reason to believe that (3) if neither confesses, both will go clear. Each argues that, whatever the other does, he has a better deal by confessing.[66]

Predictably, individuals typically choose what's best for themselves at the expense of the other person. If they could coordinate with each other they would deny and both walk free, but coordination is difficult. So they both confess and receive a small fine. The decision to cooperate from an individual standpoint is irrational because they don't know how the other person is going to choose. It's too risky. There is no trust. Even if they could talk, there is no assurance they will do what they say they will do. It's easy for us to see from the outside that cooperate-cooperate is a better outcome than confess-confess, but neither prisoner inside the system can make it happen. What is needed is a system where their decisions are openly chosen before execution, assuring cooperation and thereby producing better results than confession.

Our current economic system suffers from these same multipolar traps, arms races and malthusian traps. You can join in the race to the bottom or be outcompeted and destroyed. Not much of a choice really. If you want some value, then you must go after the only thing of value in the game. Like gladiators thrust into the arena, there is no choice but to battle over Property.

---

[65] Lester F. Ward, "Plutocracy or Paternalism", Forum, November 1895

[66] Albert Tucker bio, online, https://mathshistory.st-andrews.ac.uk/Biographies/Tucker_Albert/

What can we learn from game theory about how to solve and avoid these coordination failures? Game theory can help us to understand not only why it can be difficult for players to work together in the best possible way but also how we can reach more optimal outcomes by coordinating using better information sharing. With a sufficient push towards a new equilibrium, we can substantially improve our collective circumstances in a short time.

The Open Source and Maker movements are examples of decentralized information systems unlike the siloed, centralized information and decision making which most Nations and Corporations practice today. It is not just us humans caught up in these multipolar traps, it is also our Nations and Corporations too, and they are the biggest perpetrators, and we the victims, of our economic system and the biggest cause of our decline. They literally can't help themselves. Just like individual humans must obey the *law* of self preservation so too must these fictional entities seek self preservation via profit. Humans can't combine themselves into a physically larger biological human. We would've if we could've. Instead, we found that we could combine ourselves into fictional entities like Corporations and Nations to better compete for more Property in Game A.

Just because information is open or transparent to all doesn't guarantee best use of resources either. Aristotle observed the phenomena that "What is common to many is taken least care of, for all men have greater regard for what is their own than for what they possess in common with others." More recently in 1968 ecologist Garrett Hardin observed, land without a single owner often becomes overgrazed, eroded and polluted in what he labeled "The Tragedy of the Commons"[67] in an article with that title in *Science* magazine, about a parable arguing that if everyone had free access to common property, the resource would be lost to all. "The 'tragedy of the commons' refers to the situation when individuals, acting rationally in their own self-interest, nonetheless act irrationally as a collective group by irreparably depleting a resource that is owned in common. The current climate change crisis is an example of 'the tragedy' on a global scale… "Ruin is the destination toward which all men rush, each pursuing his own best interest," [lamented Hardin]. 'The tragedy' is therefore a puzzle to many

[67] Garrett Hardin, "The Tragedy of the Commons", Vol. 162 *Science p.1243* (December 13, 1968), https://www.science.org/doi/10.1126/science.162.3859.1243

observers, in particular rational choice economists, as, what appear to be rational actions are in fact irrational when viewed in the long term."[68]

If owning things in common leads to ruinous resource usage, then it seems that the only solution is private ownership, right? Like that of Game A. According to Ian Angus, "The tragedy of the commons is a useful political myth -- a scientific-sounding way of saying that there is no alternative to the dominant world order."[69]

The original author, Hardin, did reassess his views 30 years after his infamous essay, saying it's not that the resource is a commons, but that it is an 'unmanaged' commons, an open-access regime:

> The weightiest mistake in my synthesizing paper was the omission of the modifying adjective "unmanaged." In correcting this omission, one can generalize the practical conclusion in this way: "A 'managed commons' describes either socialism or the privatism of free enterprise. Either one may work; either one may fail: 'The devil is in the details.' But with an unmanaged commons, you can forget about the devil: As overuse of resources reduces carrying capacity, ruin is inevitable.[70]

To make sure this point is crystal clear: Game A is a global battle royale over unmanaged commons, thus: 'ruin is inevitable.' There is no global commons management. It's just humans wielding the powers of fictional entities battling each other for control over our global commons.

Here's Daniel Schmachtenberger talking about this in a recent interview:

> This is a key piece of the game theoretic challenge in global coordination and the two primary way ways it expresses itself is arms races and tragedy of the commons. And the tragedy of the commons scenario is if we don't overfish that area of virgin ocean, but we can't control that someone else doesn't, because how do we do enforcement if they're also a nuclear country? That's a tricky thing, right? How do you do enforcement on nuclear equipped countries, so us not doing it doesn't mean that the fish don't all get taken, it just means that they grow their populations and their GDP faster which they will use rivalrously, so we might as well do it, in fact, we might as well race to

[68] Maebh O'Gorma, "Global Warming: A Tragedy of the Commons", https://core.ac.uk/download/pdf/232618203.pdf

[69] Ian Angus, "Refutation of the Tragedy of the Commons", https://wiki.p2pfoundation.net/Refutation_of_the_Tragedy_of_the_Commons

[70] Garrett Hardin, https://www.garretthardinsociety.org/articles/art_extension_tragedy_commons.html

> do it faster than they do. That's the tragedy of the commons type issues. The arms race version is, if we can't ensure that they don't build AI weapons or they don't build surveillance tech and they get increased near-term power from doing so, we just have to race to get there before them. That's the arms race type thing. It just happens to be that while that makes sense for each agent on their own in the short term, it creates global dynamics for the whole in the long term that self-terminate, because you can't run exponential externality on a finite planet. That's the tragedy of the commons one and you can't run exponential arms races and exponential conflict on a finite planet. So the thing that has always made sense which is just keep winning at the arms races has had a world where we've had lots of wars increasing in their scale and lots of environmental damage. We started desertification thousands of years ago, it's just it has been a long slow exponential curve that really started to pick up with the industrial revolution and is now really verticalizing the digital revolution and the cumulative harm of that kind of thing becomes impossible now. So basically, with the environmental destruction, with the wars and, with the kind of class subjugation things that civilizations have in the past, pretty much anyone would say we have not been the best stewards of power. And technology is increasing our power. Exponential tech means tech that makes better versions of itself, so you get an exponent on the curve… We could say the central question of our time is if we've been poor stewards of power for a long time and that's always caused problems but the problems now become existential, they become catastrophic. We can't keep doing that.[71]

In 2009, Elinor Ostrom became the first woman to receive the Nobel Prize in Economics. The reward was for her "analysis of economic governance, especially the commons" which showed while the tragedy of the commons is one possible result, it's not inevitable. Ostrom demonstrated how common property could be successfully managed by groups using it. Common resources thrive when people manage them in an open environment of self-determination and group decision-making. She and countless others have since used these principles to effectively mobilize local management of common pool resources around the world, offering an alternative that lets people thrive towards a common pursuit. The good news is, the economic protocols introduced in this book enable Ostrom's commons management methods throughout the world.

All this talk about coordination problems and critiques about fair and unfair, "so what?" you might ask. Well, let me ask you, how many games, of

---

[71] Center for Humane Technology interviewing Daniel Schmachtenberger, "What's Really Driving Global Problems in the World Today?" https://www.youtube.com/watch?v=wO1WVguNQAM&t

some consequence, do you voluntarily play that are not fair? Can you think of any games for fun or sports or any competition where the primary rules are not known upfront, not applied equally or don't demand fairness? I bet you can't. Why would we not demand fairness from the most consequential game of all: the game of life?

Not only are games initially set up as fair, but they are constantly changed and upgraded to increase fairness. They are divided further along size or skill to make them even more fair. Modern technology (VAR, goal line tech) is now used to correct decisions of imperfect humans so the game can be still more fair. Reciprocity or fairness is one of the twin pillars of morality along with empathy or compassion. It's a primal instinct and demand.

Dr. Sarah Brosnan and Frans de Waal wrote an article in 2003, "Monkeys reject unequal pay"[72] where they report on an experiment with Capuchin monkeys who didn't react too kindly to being treated unequally. A pair of monkeys in separate cages did some defined task, after which, they each got a piece of cucumber. All was good when they got the same reward, a bland cucumber, they still repeated the task and ate their cucumber just fine. But guess what happened when one monkey got a piece of cucumber, while the other got a delicious grape instead? The one that got the cucumber got pissed off, immediately threw the cucumber out of the cage and rattled the cage in rage.[73] They sensed the unfairness. The video is hilarious until you realize the monkey in rage is what Game A is doing to the majority of humans.

Abraham Lincoln believed "The land, the earth god gave to man for his home ... Should never be the possession of any man, corporation, (or) society ... Any more than the air or water." He's right about that. It's access to and decision making of Property that is the real key and design challenge.

There are only 3 possible ways to organize society:

1. Hierarchy = Leaders + Subjects = Rulers + **Rules = Order**
2. Freedom = No Rulers + **No Rules = Chaos**
3. Liberty = Anarchism + Democracy = Self Rule + **Rules = Order**

What is the thing that a society <u>must</u> have if we are to have order? **Rules.** It would be chaos if all people were free to do whatever they want. Chaos is

---

72 Sarah Brosnan and Frans de Waal, "Monkeys reject unequal pay", Nature, September 18, 2003, https://www.nature.com/articles/nature01963

73 Frans de Waal, TedTalk excerpt, https://www.youtube.com/watch?v=meiU6TxysCg

the default state until rules are either agreed upon or imposed, and then an order is produced. It doesn't matter if there are rulers or no rulers as long as there are rules, an order results. Who makes the rules makes all the difference in the game and determines if the game is even legitimate.

Carse says: "The rules must be published prior to play, and the players must agree to them before play begins... *The agreement of the players to the applicable rules constitutes the ultimate validation of those rules...* Rules are not valid because the Senate passed them, or because heroes once played by them, or because God pronounced them through Moses or Muhammad. They are valid only if and when players freely play by them."[74]

By the way, this is the key for the transition, for how we can change the game. Using a sports analogy: we may be forced to play American football, but once the soccer ball and the new rules are agreed upon, we can finally stop playing football and take the field to start playing soccer, if and whenever we want.

"Somebody once declared that the only two political theories that are completely consistent are anarchy and totalitarianism. Anarchy fully embraces the concept of self, totalitarianism fully rejects that concept," according to Darrell Anderson. So far, having rulers is the primary method of achieving order. Many incorrectly believe hierarchy is the *only* way, even if they don't admit it directly. Having rulers is certainly one way to achieve order, except, by definition, this is the opposite of democracy and by extension it leads eventually to an unfair order, then breakdown into chaos, then new leaders then re-ordering all over again. History repeating itself.

Rulers make rules thus order is produced. As long as there are rulers there will always be rules, hence order. Problem with this is that rules usually apply only to the subjects and not the rulers which means it's not fair or just. If things become chaotic, a ruler can make commands of new rules to create an order. Police and courts enforce the rules of the rulers. Obviously there will be an order of one kind or another if someone or government is in charge, but if the ruler is removed then often rules are either dismissed or ignored and chaos ensues. Nobody wants chaos. A power vacuum occurs until either a new ruler or new rules are imposed to once again restore order.

All Nations are #1 hierarchy societies. Yes, you are a subject of your Nation. That's why there are borders for humans but not for Corporations. Ken MacLeod reminds us that, "From space you can see no borders." How much say did you have in forming or agreeing to the rules of your

[74] Carse, *Infinite and Finite Games*, The Free Press (NY 1986).

community, your state, your Nation, or the world? Zero! Hierarchy means top-down. Rules come down from above. Do you really believe the people of the US wish to allocate $768 Billion this year on military expenditures? Why is it happening then? Because we have rulers, not a democracy. Amazingly, we Americans somehow never see this for what it is: economic 'central planning.' Because we vote to choose our rulers somehow that equals democracy? Amazing. "The United States is also a one-party state but, with typical American extravagance, they have two of them," remarked Julius Nyerere, the first President of Tanzania.

Why do Nations even go to war? Hubert H. Harrison tells us "Wars are not fought for ideals but for lands whose populations can be put to work, for resources that can be minted into millions, for trade that can be made to enrich the privileged few. When King Leopold of Belgium and Thomas Fortune Ryan of New York joined hands to exploit the wealth of the Congo they did it with oiled phrases on their lips. They called that land of horrors and of shame 'The Congo FREE State!' And, so, when Nations go to war, they never openly declare what they want. They must camouflage their sordid greed behind some sounding phrase like 'freedom of the seas,' 'self-determination,' 'liberty' or 'democracy.'"

Democracy throughout antiquity meant serfdom for most of the population. Aristotle was very clear on this, saying, "Many cities have constitutions that appear to be democracies, but they're really oligarchies." And in fact, every democracy, Aristotle wrote, tends to turn into an oligarchy, as wealthy people get rich, and then the oligarchy makes itself into a hereditary aristocracy, and lords it over the rest of society.

The US is a republic, a representative democracy, and it too is run by an oligarchy. *Representatives* make decisions on our behalf, but in whose interests? We don't have a seat at the table, nevermind a voice. As Liz Fosslien and Molly West Duffy tell in their book, *No Hard Feelings*, "Diversity is having a seat at the table, inclusion is having a voice, and belonging is having that voice be heard." People seem to forget, it was impossible before to include everyone in the decision making for obvious logistical reasons, but not today, not in a world of computers with instant communication.

What is the reason we are not allowed to have a full, functioning direct democracy yet? Now, like then, those above us don't believe we are wise or worthy enough to have a say. Rulers want to continue ruling and that's why we don't have a democracy. Like Voltaire laid bare, "The comfort of the rich depends upon an abundant supply of the poor."

We've tried authoritarianism, totalitarianism, feudalism, imperialism, colonialism, democracy, capitalism, fascism, socialism and communism in various combinations and degrees. None have been able to evolve beyond the Game A construct. None. Not ever. A Nation can organize and distribute Property among its citizens around the ideals and fictions of any system they want. They are the rule makers. But when coordinating with other Nations they must play by the same rules of Property or they can't play. Instead they will end up competing. One will inevitably annihilate the other and then resume play according to their own rules.

This is what happened in the *new* worlds of North and South Americas hundreds of years ago. Back then, nobody could say, "hey, you Europeans, you can't just invade others' territory, kill its inhabitants and claim their land. Stop it. We won't recognize it and there will be consequences." Nobody could stop it and everybody agreed to just recognize the new *owners*. Was it legitimate? According to Game A rules of winners take all… yeah. Finders keepers, losers weepers. Is it legitimate for the US to dominate all the other Nations? What are you gonna do about it? Nothing will change as long as we agree to play by their rules. Our acquiescence gives them legitimacy, gives them the power to rule us.

There is one economic ideology centered on fairness, democracy and freedom. For much of the last 200 years, various lovers of mankind have been inspired by the same vision: an idea called socialism, where Property is the common heritage of all, eliminating the source of greed, envy, poverty and strife. It is perhaps the most popular economic idea in history, and the most elusive.

I really want to copy and reproduce all four pages of the 1908 Eugene Debs article "Socialist Ideals" because it is as clear a description of socialism as you'll find anywhere, but a brief selection shall suffice here:

> Socialism is not so much a cut-and-dried program as it is a method by which industry is to be operated. It does not say what it will do or what you shall do, but only that the people, the workers and producers, shall be master

> of themselves and do with industry and the proceeds of their toil what they may think best. It is a continuation of the old fight against monarchy and in favor of democracy, which was begun in 1776, and which has since been growing into an enlarged world-demand. Then the ideal was for the overthrow of the political autocracy that prevailed and the establishment of political democracy in its stead. After our forefathers won in that revolution of blood, the ideal inspired France to a glorious but unintelligent struggle for popular rule, and it has been growing and spreading ever since…
>
> Democracy has been so successful that it is safe to say that the people will never permit a return to absolute kingly rule. **Socialism is merely an extension of the ideal of democracy into the economic field.** At present, industry is ruled by the owners of machines of production and distribution, who have literally the power of life and death over the subjects… In many lines the prices of necessary articles of consumption are fixed arbitrarily, and in all cases a tribute of profit is exacted on all things bought and all things sold. Through these means the entire people are constrained and made helpless before the system… Socialism proposes to put industry in control of the people so that they may no longer be dependents on others for a job, so that they may be freed from the tribute of profit, and so that they may manage industry in their own way, as seems best to them.[75]

There are some so-called *socialist* and *communist* Nations today whose state capitalist regimes are playing Game A using variable degrees of power and decision making over Property but pretending to be playing a different game.

100 years ago, many communists, like Vladimir Lenin, thought the path forward was to concentrate all political and economic power in the hands of the State. In Lenin's own words:

> For socialism is merely the next step forward from state-capitalist monopoly. Or, in other words, socialism is merely state-capitalist monopoly *which is made to serve the interests of the whole people* and has to that extent *ceased* to be capitalist monopoly.
>
> There is no middle course here. The objective process of development is such that it is *impossible* to advance from *monopolies* (and the war has magnified their number, role and importance tenfold) without advancing towards socialism.
>
> Either we have to be revolutionary democrats in fact, in which case we must not fear to take steps towards socialism…
>
> There is no middle course.
>
> And therein lies the fundamental contradiction of our revolution.

---

[75] Eugene V. Debs, "Socialist Ideals", The Arena, vol. 40, whole no. 227 (Nov. 1908), pp. 432-434, https://www.marxists.org/archive/debs/works/1908/1100-debs-socialistideals.pdf

> It is impossible to stand still in history in general, and in war-time in particular. We must either advance or retreat.[76]

The Soviets advanced from a #1 hierarchy Nation into what had elements of a #3 type society among themselves. However, the Nation itself remained a #1 type competitor within the global Game A construct, requiring a small group of men to lead. Lenin argued that once collective production advanced far enough beyond scarcity into abundance, into socialism, then the State would just wither away. But how? Only if all the other Nations agreed to change the global game. We were and remain in a Game of Nations world. Our population represents a 'trading block' in the market battlefield of Game A. We can't not play as a Nation. The Game A economic equation still determines distribution of property and wealth between Nations. That has never changed yet. For this reason, many say real socialism has never existed.

Some, like Kropotkin, even warned in 1919 that state capitalism was doomed to failure. "Unhappily, this effort has been made in Russia under a strongly centralized party dictatorship… I owe it to you to say frankly that, according to my view, this effort to build a communist republic on the basis of a strongly centralized state communism under the iron law of party dictatorship is bound to end in failure. We are learning to know in Russia how not to introduce communism, even with a people tired of the old regime and opposing no active resistance to the experiments of the new rulers."[77]

Because what was implemented was called *socialism* or *communism*, many people in the world associate both ideologies as being synonymous with state capitalism, dictatorial central planning, totalitarian or as a police-state. All of those things are the complete opposite of freedom or self-rule. Nobody wants those things. The aim or direction of the theory of socialism and communism were fine and commendable but choosing the economic path of state capitalism (or Game A socialism or whatever label we put on it) proved to be a dead end. Almost like an obvious forced error even.

The dream of global liberty, of democracy, of communism or a classless society has never been achieved, obviously. This failure was seized upon by our rulers, who have twisted, maligned and poisoned the meanings of both words: socialism and communism. It is common in America to hear people

---

[76] Marxists Internet Archive, Vladimir Lenin, "The Impending Catastrophe and How to Combat It", 1917, https://www.marxists.org/archive/lenin/works/1917/ichtci/11.htm

[77] Pëtr Kropotkin, "The Russian Revolution and the Soviet Government: Letter to the Workers of Western Europe" (PDF), 1919

casually complain of authoritarian impulses and erroneously label them as socialist or communist.

Humans have always been combining their population and their Property into tribes called Nations so as to be more powerful in Game A, in competition for Property against all the other humans and their tribes. Where might makes right, size and strength become important. After all, "History is written by the winners" as they say. Game A is a hierarchical game of power over Property. All Nations are authoritarian. This graphic illustrates what has been tried, so far, in practice.

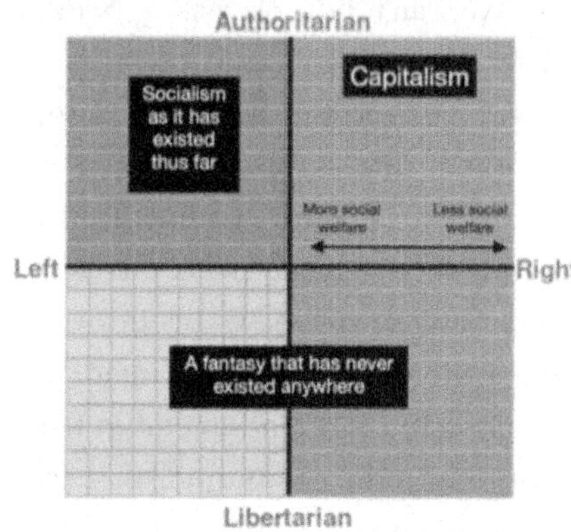

The problem with the "libertarian" to "authoritarian" axis is that all states use authority, and the term "authoritarian" spectacularly fails to recognize this, ending up as an ad hoc device to separate the US and its allies, who are never seen as authoritarian, to those countries that stand outside US hegemony, who are, unless they serve a useful political function to the US empire, in which case they are never labeled authoritarian even if they fit the criteria quite well (think Israel, Saudi Arabia, Suharto's Indonesia, etc.).

These axes, are of course, class-blind, and hence they ignore the central division in the world economy, that between workers and the tiny group of bourgeoisie who rule the US empire, and through that, shape the policies that regulate the global economy.

What we have are many examples of countries in the blue (northeast) quadrant, for capitalism is the globally dominant mode of production in the world. Some have more of a social safety net, others have less, but the main division among the capitalist nations is whether they are rich or poor, and that has an awful lot to do with two related factors: (1) was the country an early adopter of capitalism and (2) did it benefit from the modern imperialism that occurred under capitalism (about the last 300 years), or was it the victim of it? In the red quadrant, we have socialism, which the libertarians would like us to believe is "authoritarian." But I wonder, whose interests are served by having us focus on whether or not there was more than one political party, was there state media, what was the voting like, etc. Why is there so little focus on how people are actually living?[78]

---

[78] Dr. Asatar Bair, Twitter, https://twitter.com/asatarbair/status/1399175226903072768

In this Twitter thread, the organization Black Socialists in America clarify this point further.

> Anyone who accepts or supports top-down, hierarchical social relations is authoritarian. Both Liberals and Conservatives are authoritarian by this metric, since they support Capitalism. Forces Libs and Conservatives typically label "authoritarian" are usually authoritarian too. What most Liberals, Conservatives, and authoritarian "Leftists" don't grasp is that anything truly "Left" is where direct democracy begins, and exploitation + domination ends. Hierarchy and extraction, whether upheld by private corporations or a state, can only be authoritarian. Look past surface aesthetics and rhetoric and ask yourself these questions when evaluating whether or not political orgs and/or tendencies are authoritarian: Are they okay with hierarchy and individual leaders giving orders from the top? Are these "leaders" instantly recallable? Worth noting that there are both formal and informal hierarchies, and different forms of authority. The key question is whether or not these hierarchies or authorities have been consented to and are recallable, or if they have been imposed. Hierarchies, however, beget problems. The paradigm we are currently suffering under is a paradigm of authoritarianism. Whether you're in the U.S. or China, you most likely have someone ordering you around and monitoring your every move each day. What happens to most if they refuse these orders? They starve or die.[79]

Out of the ashes of the global great depression in 1937, George Orwell wrote his book *The Road to Wigan Pier*, about the terrible lives of workers and the poor in northern UK, along with his views on socialism:

> Meanwhile what about Socialism? We are living in a world in which nobody is free, in which hardly anybody is secure, in which it is almost impossible to be honest and to remain alive… Socialism, as a world-system and wholeheartedly applied, is a way out. It would at least ensure our getting enough to eat even if it deprived us of everything else. Indeed, from one point of view, Socialism is such elementary common sense that I am sometimes amazed that it has not established itself already. The world is a raft sailing through space with, potentially, plenty of provisions for everybody; the idea that we must all cooperate and see to it that every-one does his fair share of the work and gets his fair share of the provisions seems so blatantly obvious that one would say that no one could possibly fail to accept it unless he had some corrupt motive for clinging to the present system. Yet the fact that we have got to face is that Socialism is not establishing itself. Instead of going forward, the cause of Socialism is visibly

[79] Black Socialists in America, https://twitter.com/BlackSocialists/status/1385579244441546758

> going back. At this moment Socialists almost everywhere are in retreat before the onslaught of Fascism, and events are moving at terrible speed... the idea of Socialism is less widely accepted than it was ten years ago. The average thinking person nowadays is not merely not a Socialist, he is actively hostile to Socialism. This must be due chiefly to mistaken methods of propaganda. It means that Socialism, in the form of which it is now presented to us, has about it something inherently distasteful--something that drives away the very people who ought to be nocking to its support.[80]

In the last sentence of a 1949 article by Albert Einstein titled "Why Socialism" he talked about this situation too: "Clarity about the aims and problems of socialism is of greatest significance in our age of transition. Since, under present circumstances, free and unhindered discussion of these problems has come under a powerful taboo."[81]

A few years later, then US President Harry S. Truman made similar remarks in a 1952 speech: "Socialism is a scare word they have hurled at every advance the people have made in the last 20 years. Socialism is what they called public power. Socialism is what they called social security. Socialism is what they called farm price supports. Socialism is what they called bank deposit insurance. Socialism is what they called the growth of free and independent labor organizations. Socialism is their name for almost anything that helps all the people."[82]

Today's political climate is exactly the same. Full of fear mongering over socialism and communism. They are tossed around as smear words. It's a tried and true method of dividing the people, of creating an us vs them. Socialists vs Capitalists or whatever group or ideology you happen to think you belong to, nevermind that we are all just human on the same planet. As you can see, this taboo over exploring economic systems has never stopped.

School fed us limited information on history and told us what to believe. All versions of history taught in school are heavily revised to favor one's own nation's agenda while hiding its crimes. They do this to further an unrealistic sense of false patriotism used to manufacture allegiance to a corporate entity masquerading as government.

---

[80] George Orwell, *The Road to Wigan Pier*, 1937, chapter 11, https://george-orwell.org/The_Road_to_Wigan_Pier/10.html

[81] Albert Einstein, "Why Socialism?", Monthly Review, 1949, online, https://archive.org/details/AlbertEinsteinWhySocialism/mode/2up

[82] Harry S. Truman, Oct 10, 1952, https://www.trumanlibrary.gov/library/public-papers/289/rear-platform-and-other-informal-remarks-new-york

They taught us to follow rules, to be obedient, or else. They told us we are a free peoples whose form of representative democracy begun in 1776 is the greatest and most perfect system ever. It is so good in fact that our wars are said to be our way of spreading freedom and democracy to others, and not the Game A theft and murder that it really is. Even in war we must paint ourselves as the good guys.

Einstein's "Why Socialism" describes the history of Game A and why we need system change using better thinking and language than I'll ever do in this chapter. Go ahead and click away and read it first if you want but if you can't then here is his conclusion:

> I am convinced there is only one way to eliminate these grave evils, namely through the establishment of a socialist economy, accompanied by an educational system which would be oriented toward social goals. In such an economy, the means of production are owned by society itself and are utilized in a planned fashion. A planned economy, which adjusts production to the needs of the community, would distribute the work to be done among all those able to work and would guarantee a livelihood to every man, woman, and child. The education of the individual, in addition to promoting his own innate abilities, would attempt to develop in him a sense of responsibility for his fellow men in place of the glorification of power and success in our present society.
>
> Nevertheless, it is necessary to remember that a planned economy is not yet socialism. A planned economy as such may be accompanied by the complete enslavement of the individual. The achievement of socialism requires the solution of some extremely difficult socio-political problems: how is it possible, in view of the far-reaching centralization of political and economic power, to prevent bureaucracy from becoming all-powerful and overweening? How can the rights of the individual be protected and therewith a democratic counterweight to the power of bureaucracy be assured?[83]

In the next chapters you will learn how sovereignty, opportunity and liberty in Common Planet is the answer to Einstein's question at the end, on 'How can the rights of the individual be protected.' It's by design. It's simple math.

Much of the focus in mainstream media (msm)— oligarch run Corporations— is on the failures of socialism or communism in Game A. Unless you're a curious reader you might not even know of the many

---

[83] Einstein, "Why Socialism?"

different kinds of socialist experiments (praxis) and their massive achievements. For example: Chile's Project Cybersyn in the early 1970s.[84]

The economic problems of central planning are kinda obvious. Many economists like Ludwig von Mises, Friedrich Hayek and Carl Menger each pointed out the flaw in central planning: those who try, lack the information and ability to analyze in determining how to best allocate resources. Because people's transactions are information about values, the genius of a pricing system is its capacity for converting that pricing information into resource allocation. Central planning can result in overproducing goods consumers don't want and not producing goods they do want. Pointing to all the negatives of central planning, Western liberals (rich Property owners) concluded that capitalism, despite its limitations, is therefore by default, the superior system of economic organization.

"It is not intelligent, it is not beautiful, it is not just, it is not virtuous — and it doesn't deliver the goods," declared Keynes. "In short, we dislike it, and we are beginning to despise it. But when we wonder what to put in its place, we are extremely perplexed."[85]

There is little serious attempt in the academic or professional field of economics to search for an alternative. Anyone who does is mocked. Watch what happens to me. TINA and don't even try because it will always lead to failure. We've heard it so many times they must be right? "I leave aside the deeper concern that the primary role of mainstream economics in our society is to provide an apologetics for a criminally oppressive, unsustainable, and unjust social order," wrote Jeremy B. Rudd, Federal Reserve Board, in 2021.

Here is how Bucky Fuller described the situation in his 1969 *Operating Manual For Spaceship Earth:* "Then we have the great pragmatic ideologist Marx running into that entropic-Malthusian-Darwinian information and saying, "Well, the workers who produce things are the fittest because they are the only ones who know how to physically produce and therefore they ought to be the ones to survive." That was the beginning of the great "class warfare." All of the ideologies range somewhere between the Great Pirates and the Marxists. But all of them assume that there is not enough to go around. And that's been the rationalized working hypothesis of all the great sovereign claims to great areas of the Earth. Because of their respective

---

[84] https://en.wikipedia.org/wiki/Project_Cybersyn

[85] John Maynard Keynes (1933). National self-sufficiency. *Studies: An Irish Quarterly Review, 22*(86), 177–193.

exclusivities, all the class warfare ideologies have become extinct. Capitalism and socialism are mutually extinct. Why? Because science now finds there can be ample for all, but only if the sovereign fences are completely removed. The basic you-or-me-not-enough-for-both ergo, someone-must-die- tenets of the class warfaring are extinct."[86]

Just as States concentrate power in Game A socialist economics, likewise monopoly power created by capitalist private property itself becomes concentrated and centralized too. Political economists ceaselessly debate and pretend to know the present while never searching for future alternatives. Since someone must *own* Property, then there are only two options: distributed private ownership or concentrated state ownership.

William Stanley Jevons and Léon Walras are two economic thought leaders of the early twentieth century who both understood Property as the source of the problem and solution. Theirs was called the 'marginal revolution.'[87] Jevons wrote, "Property is only another name for monopoly." Walras stated, "Declaring individual land ownership ... means ... thwarting the beneficial effects of free competition by preventing the land from being used as is most advantageous for society." Along that thinking, one of the more interesting ideas of the time was called competitive common ownership. Those who wanted to use the land productively could rent out the land from the government, who could then terminate the lease if it finds someone better able or more willing than the current tenant. In this way, people rent land but do not own it, thus, private property in land is abolished.

Don't confuse this as central planning, which Walras hated, fearing that planners would themselves become monopolistic overlords. Walras described his approach as 'synthetic socialism', where land is owned by the state and the rents it generated returned to the public as a 'social dividend.' He wanted landed property to be controlled by society through a process of competition and wanted returns on that property to be enjoyed by society.

This reminds me of the 'Just Third Way' proposed by Norman Kurland at the Center for Economic & Social Justice. His is one of the better Game A proposals we found during research. He calls it 'capital homesteading', 'own or be owned', as outlined in Economic Democracy Act.[88] By making every citizen essentially a beneficial owner of 'public' company shares, the

[86] Buckminster Fuller, *Operating Manual For Earth*, 1969, p.11

[87] https://en.wikipedia.org/wiki/Marginal_utility#Marginal_Revolution

[88] CESJ.org, https://www.cesj.org/learn/capital-homesteading/

dividends can then flow to all individuals in the community rather than to just a few as they do now. If this proposal were combined with Henry George's 'land value tax' (LVT), Game A economics would rid itself of massive inequality, making what I believe to be the best possible version of Game A. It's no wonder Kurland has dedicated his life to this pursuit. Unfortunately, even when combining these two radical ideas it doesn't produce an alternative because value distribution is still rooted in the exchange of Property. The people of your Nation would become more egalitarian with each other while remaining in trading competition with other Nations.

As these widely divergent ideas of socialism indicate, a society can manage resources it controls in many ways. In the late nineteenth century, socialism was a rather amorphous term and was not always associated with central planning. Socialists agreed on only one point: that traditional private property and the inequality of its ownership posed significant challenges to prosperity, well-being and social order.

The idea of tribes having kings or rulers was coming to an end as democracy became the new clarion call. The newest cool idea was to have Nations and leaders instead. What's the difference between a ruler and a leader? In theory, everything; in practice, nothing. The Nation of Russia had a long monarchy who ruled for centuries. All power and decision making was concentrated to just a few, and then there was a bloody revolution, and they went from being a Monarchy to Socialism, which they believed to be the first step toward communism, that elusive #3 or third way.

A new leader rose up, once again concentrated all power and decision making to just a few. What changed? The Adams maxim tells us the balance of power didn't change even though the words to describe their system did. In reality, Lenin and Stalin painted a picture that they would be good rulers, not bad like those other guys before them. It doesn't matter if they were good rulers or not, people don't want to be ruled!

It was worse in fascist Germany under Hitler and his *National Socialist German Workers' Party*. Masterful branding really. It's not like they could've just admitted to being fascist fuckers. Oh wait, they did, but people either liked it or didn't believe them. What is that saying about history repeating itself? But seriously, who could be against any of those party principles? Who doesn't like their country (National), wants to be like Jesus (Socialist), is proud of their heritage (German) and recognizes the value of work? Aside from the blatant vulgar hatred of Jews, the Nazis practically guilted everyone into belonging; classic us vs them. It's like Ronald Reagan's 'Make America Great

Again' (MAGA) slogan— copied by Trump— who doesn't want greatness for their country? Especially when your economic fortune and freedoms depend on it. Except there's just one problem, party's have leaders but Nations have rulers and as John Dalberg-Acton said: "Absolute power corrupts absolutely."

Franklin D. Roosevelt said in 1941: "They [who] seek to establish systems of government based on the regimentation of all human beings by a handful of individual rulers...call this a new order. It is not new and it is not order."

Is there a just way to organize society and what would such a system look like? Many thinkers, old and new, have similar foundational design criteria for a Game B, but almost all of them lack any real specific economic details which would actually deliver the results they seek. Here's what Pyotr Kropotkin suggested in 1887: "The means of production and of satisfaction of all needs of society, having been created by the common efforts of all, must be at the disposal of all. The private appropriation of requisites for production is neither just nor beneficial. All must be placed on the same footing as producers and consumers of wealth. That will be the only way for society to step out of the bad conditions which have been created by centuries of wars and oppression. That will be the only guarantee for further progress in a direction of equality and freedom, which have always been the real, although unspoken goal of humanity."[89]

Equality and freedom, the real unspoken goal of humanity. Let's speak on it. There is one ideology with these twin pillars: Anarchism. I know, it's a totally taboo word, but, nevertheless, it is an ideal. The goal of anarchism is a society which enables the full and free development of every individual. Not Nation, not Corporation, but **every individual**. Like Malatesta said, "By definition an anarchist is he who does not wish to be oppressed nor wishes to be himself an oppressor; who wants the greatest well-being, freedom and development for all human beings." An anarchist society would be #3 above, it would have rules but no fixed rulers. This would be self-rule, bottom up decision making in an open, fair playing field like Ostrom's work proves is also most advantageous to the whole.

An absence of government, no rulers, is the original definition of anarchy, derived from the ancient Greek *anarkhia* (without a ruler), composed of *an-* 'without' + *arkhos* 'chief, ruler.' What happens to a community when the ruler dies? There's chaos and so the word anarchy (no rulers) came to also be

[89] Kropotkin, *Anarchist Communism*

synonymous with chaos and so this then became the modern dictionary definition of anarchy:

- #2. Chaos. A state of disorder due to absence or nonrecognition of authority or rules.
- #3. Society freely constituted without authorities, regarded as a political ideal. Self-rule.

As you can see, #3 is a political ideal, however, rulers do not like that because they want to rule and so they convinced us that if there are no rulers there is automatically chaos. Thus anarchy is chaos and nobody wants chaos. Thus anarchists are smeared as dangerous fools just like socialists today are smeared for being dangerous central planning fools. The radical change most anarchists seek is a form of direct democracy where people learn to collectively rule themselves so we may prevent societal breakdown.

> Today, there must be a place on the political spectrum where a body of anti-authoritarian thought that advances humanity's bitter struggle to arrive at the realization of its authentic social life -- the famous "Commune of communes" -- can be clearly articulated institutionally as well as ideologically. There must be a means by which socially concerned anti-authoritarians can develop a program and a practice for attempting to change the world, not merely their psyches. There must be an arena of struggle that can mobilize people, help them to educate themselves and develop an anti-authoritarian politics, to use this word in its classical meaning, indeed that pits a new public sphere against the State and capitalism.[90]

That place is where anarchists converge. "Are You An Anarchist? The Answer May Surprise You!" wrote David Graeber in 2009:

> Chances are you have already heard something about who anarchists are and what they are supposed to believe. Chances are almost everything you have heard is nonsense. Many people seem to think that anarchists are proponents of violence, chaos, and destruction, that they are against all forms of order and organization, or that they are crazed nihilists who just want to blow everything up. In reality, nothing could be further from the truth. Anarchists are simply people who believe human beings are capable of behaving in a reasonable fashion without having to be forced to. It is really a

[90] Murray Bookchin, "What is Communalism"

> very simple notion. But it's one that the rich and powerful have always found extremely dangerous.
>
> At their very simplest, anarchist beliefs turn on to two elementary assumptions. The first is that human beings are, under ordinary circumstances, about as reasonable and decent as they are allowed to be, and can organize themselves and their communities without needing to be told how. The second is that power corrupts. Most of all, anarchism is just a matter of having the courage to take the simple principles of common decency that we all live by, and to follow them through to their logical conclusions. Odd though this may seem, in most important ways you are probably already an anarchist — you just don't realize it.[91]

Anarchy means without rulers and my use throughout this book uses that definition and not chaos. If I want to say something is chaos I will write chaos or disorder but never anarchy, because anarchy means no rulers. By this definition, I am an anarchist because I don't want rulers, and not because I don't like rules or because I want chaos. No. The whole reason I wrote this book is to help avert the upcoming chaos that will ensue if we let the existing economic order continue its path toward self termination.

If you ask the average person they'd likely say they are against anarchy, yet as I've already said: today's economics is anarchy. There are no rulers in charge of what, where or how much resources we can extract in game play. This anarchy of chasing our self interest, masquerading as economics, was recognized by Samuel M. Jones is this glorious 1899 article (the link below to twitter shows the complete article): "The people are beginning to understand that we have been pursuing a policy of plundering ourselves, that in the foolish scramble to make individuals rich we have been making all poor. "For a hundred years or so," says Henry D Lloyd, "our economic theory has been one of industrial government by the self-interest of the individual; political government by the self-interest of the individual we call anarchy." It is one of the paradoxes of public opinion that the people of America, least tolerant of this theory of anarchy in political government, lead in practicing it in industry. We are coming to see that the true philosophy of government is to let the individual do what the individual can do best."[92]

---

[91] David Graeber, "Are You An Anarchist? The Answer May Surprise You!", https://theanarchistlibrary.org/library/david-graeber-are-you-an-anarchist-the-answer-may-surprise-you

[92] Municipal Affairs, Sept 1899: "The New Patriotism: A Golden-Rule Government for Cities." https://twitter.com/RemziBaj/status/1494356516417069069

Simon Springer said it best: "When I say 'Anarchism' you hear 'Chaos, Violence, Mayhem.' When I say 'Anarchism' I mean 'Cooperation, Voluntary Association, Mutual Aid.'" Eric Fleischmann writes that "Anarchism is not an ideology of violence but one which opposes violence at a systemic level and seeks liberation and voluntary interaction in all spheres of life."[93] The rulers are too busy fighting each other for domination, inexorably leading us to eco-suicide. That is the 'tragedy of the commons' right there. "Anarchism is not a romantic fable but the hardheaded realization, based on five thousand years of experience, that we cannot entrust the management of our lives to kings, priests, politicians, generals, and county commissioners," explained Edward Abbey. When we the people make the rules, from bottom to top, then there will be an order of *our* choosing, real Civilization.

Karl Hess wrote in his autobiography: "Some years ago I was asked what great ambition drove me. I answered only that I wanted to be the perfect anarchist. Queried further on what I meant by the perfect anarchist, I added good friend, good lover, and good neighbor."[94]

Anarchism stands for a social order based on the free grouping of individuals, with rules and with liberty. "The basic premise guiding anarchist political philosophy is simple: Humans are fundamentally cooperative by nature and, when given the chance, flourish in situations of collective self-governance. By self-governance, anarchists typically mean an arrangement in which every person has an unalienable right to participate fully in any political decision made on their behalf—and to leave any association that makes a decision they find unconscionable."[95]

Anarchists recognize the human capacity for cooperation, kindness and love but also oppression, domination and exploitation. It's well understood humans can behave good or bad, and for this reason, we should abolish relations of power which give people the opportunity or motivation to oppress or subject others to their will. We must be realistic, society will not become better if we replace evil rulers with good rulers. Any person or group who is placed in a position of authority will be corrupted by it and so we must abolish the principle of rulership itself. The only thing required for a functioning society is clear, standard and fair global rules.

---

[93] Eric Fleischmann, "No Really, What is Anarchism?", https://c4ss.org/content/53720

[94] Karl Hess, *Mostly on the Edge: An Autobiography*, 1999

[95] David Flood, "Anarchism in Practice Is Often Radically Boring Democracy", https://www.sapiens.org/culture/anarchism-democracy/

"Anarchism, to me, means not only the denial of authority, not only a new economy, but a revision of the principles of morality. It means the development of the individual as well as the assertion of the individual; self-responsibility, not leader worship… I die, as I have lived, a free spirit, an Anarchist, owing no allegiance to rulers, heavenly or earthly," declared Voltairine de Cleyre.

According to Georges Lechartier, "The true founder of anarchy was Jesus Christ and … the first anarchist society was that of the apostles." Ivan Illich said similar, "Jesus was an anarchist savior. That's what the Gospels tell us." Ernest Renan saw it similar too, "Jesus, in some respects, was an anarchist … A great social revolution, in which rank will be overturned, in which all authority in this world will be humiliated, was his dream."

Anarchism is a political philosophy that advocates self-governed societies with voluntary institutions. These are often described as stateless societies, but several authors have defined them more specifically as institutions based on non-hierarchical free associations. Anarchism holds the state to be undesirable, unnecessary or harmful. While anti-statism is central, anarchism entails opposing authority or hierarchical organization in the conduct of human relations, including, but not limited to, the State system. As an anti-dogmatic philosophy, anarchism draws on many currents of thought and strategy. Anarchism does not offer a fixed body of doctrine from a single particular world view, instead fluxing and flowing as a philosophy.

There are many types and traditions of anarchism, not all of which are mutually exclusive. Anarchist schools of thought can differ fundamentally, supporting anything from extreme individualism to complete collectivism. Anarchism is usually considered a radical left-wing ideology, and much of anarchist economics and anarchist legal philosophy reflect anti-authoritarian interpretations of communism, collectivism, syndicalism, mutualism, or participatory economics.

If you want to get a taste of what order out of chaos (#3 above) could look like, in the 2013 book *Binding Chaos*, author Heather Marsh facilitates the process of examining past efforts and imagining alternative futures by exploring "what ideas have not worked and why, and what ideas seem to be working." She examines ideas of consensus, anonymity, peer-to-peer (P2P) networking, and the hive mind that have largely arisen through collaboration made possible by the internet. Marsh writes that "old authoritarian systems can no longer bind the natural chaos of a free society, but we can show the power of chaotic order and the beauty and creativity of collaborative freedom."[96] Marsh engages the reader with questions about representative democracy vs direct democracy, personality vs idea, individual vs group affiliation, trade economy vs 'approval economy.' By having old and new ideas dialogue with one another, she builds a bridge and takes the first steps over them. Marsh's thoughts are threads that 'bind chaos' and help us trust our tentative steps in this period of uncertainty and transition as the old world-order crumbles. She's a wonderful thinker with wonderful words.

Kropotkin was a proponent of a decentralized communist society free from central government and based on voluntary associations of self-governing communities and worker-run enterprises:

> ANARCHISM, the no-government system of socialism, has a double origin. It is an outgrowth of the two great movements of thought in the economic and the political fields which characterize the nineteenth century, and especially its second part. In common with all socialists, the anarchists hold that the private ownership of land, capital, and machinery has had it's time; that it is condemned to disappear; and that all requisites for production must, and will, become the common property of society, and be managed in common by the producers of wealth. And in common with the most advanced representatives of political radicalism, they maintain that the ideal of the political organization of society is a condition of things where the functions of government are reduced to a minimum, and the individual recovers his full liberty of initiative and action for satisfying, by means of free groups and federations-freely constituted--all the infinitely varied needs of the human being.
>
> Anarchists recognize the justice of both the just-mentioned tendencies towards economic and political freedom, and see in them two different manifestations of the very same need of equality which constitutes the very essence of all struggles mentioned by history. Therefore, in common with all socialists, the anarchist says to the political reformer: "No substantial reform in the sense of political equality and no limitation of the powers of government can be made as long as society is divided into two hostile camps, and the laborer remains, economically speaking, a slave to his employer." But to the state socialist we say also: "You cannot modify the existing conditions

---

[96] Heather Marsh, *Binding Chaos: Mass collaboration on a global scale*, 2013

> of property without deeply modifying at the same time the political organization. You must limit the powers of government and renounce parliamentary rule. To each new economic phase of life corresponds a new political phase. Absolute monarchy corresponded to the system of serfdom. Representative government corresponds to capital rule. Both, however, are class-rule. But in a society where the distinction between capitalist and laborer has disappeared, there is no need of such a government; it would be an anachronism, a nuisance. Free workers would require a free organization, and this cannot have any other basis than free agreement and free cooperation, without sacrificing the autonomy of the individual to the all-pervading interference of the State. The no-capitalist system implies the no-government system."
>
> Meaning thus the emancipation of man from the oppressive powers of capitalism and government as well, the system of anarchism becomes a synthesis of the two powerful Currents of thought which characterize our century.[97]

Kropotkin also wrote one of the best definitions of anarchism in the 1910 edition of *The Encyclopedia Britannica*:

> Anarchism, the name given to a principle or theory of life and conduct under which society is conceived without government – harmony in such a society being obtained, not by submission to law, or by obedience to any authority, but by free agreements concluded between the various groups, territorial and professional, freely constituted for the sake of production and consumption, as also for the satisfaction of the infinite variety of needs and aspirations of a civilized being. In a society developed on these lines, the voluntary associations which already now begin to cover all the fields of human activity would take a still greater extension so as to substitute themselves for the state in all its functions. They would represent an interwoven network, composed of an infinite variety of groups and federations of all sizes and degrees, local, regional, national and international temporary or more or less permanent - for all possible purposes: production, consumption and exchange, communications, sanitary arrangements, education, mutual protection, defence of the territory, and so on; and, on the other side, for the satisfaction of an ever-increasing number of scientific, artistic, literary and sociable needs. Moreover, such a society would represent nothing immutable. On the contrary - as is seen in organic life at large - harmony would (it is contended) result from an ever-changing adjustment and readjustment of equilibrium between the multitudes of forces and influences, and this adjustment would be the easier to obtain as none of the forces would enjoy a special protection from the state.

[97] Kropotkin, *Anarchist Communism*

> As to their economical conceptions, the anarchists, in common with all socialists, of whom they constitute the left wing, maintain that the now prevailing system of private ownership in land, and our capitalist production for the sake of profits, represent a monopoly which runs against both the principles of justice and the dictates of utility. They are the main obstacle which prevents the successes of modern technics from being brought into the service of all, so as to produce general well-being. The anarchists consider the wage-system and capitalist production altogether as an obstacle to progress. But they point out also that the state was, and continues to be, the chief instrument for permitting the few to monopolize the land, and the capitalists to appropriate for themselves a quite disproportionate share of the yearly accumulated surplus of production. Consequently, while combating the present monopolization of land, and capitalism altogether, the anarchists combat with the same energy the state, as the main support of that system. Not this or that special form, but the state altogether, whether it be a monarchy or even a republic governed by means of the *referendum*.
>
> The state organization, having always been, both in ancient and modern history (Macedonian Empire, Roman Empire, modern European states grown up on the ruins of the autonomous cities), the instrument for establishing monopolies in favour of the ruling minorities, cannot be made to work for the destruction of these monopolies. The anarchists consider, therefore, that to hand over to the state all the main sources of economical life - the land, the mines, the railways, banking, insurance, and so on - as also the management of all the main branches of industry, in addition to all the functions already accumulated in its hands (education, state-supported religions, defence of the territory, etc.), would mean to create a new instrument of tyranny. State capitalism would only increase the powers of bureaucracy and capitalism. True progress lies in the direction of decentralization, both *territorial* and *functional*, in the development of the spirit of local and personal initiative, and of free federation from the simple to the compound, in lieu of the present hierarchy from the centre to the periphery.[98]

One of my favorite modern thinkers, Daniel Schmachtenberger, has a website and a blog post titled "New Economics Series: Design Constraints for a Viable Economic System"[99] written on October 12, 2017, which is a masterful outline of where we are as a society, where we need to go and what we must do to get there. "This document is intended mostly for people working on developing new macroeconomic systems – to make clear and

---

[98] Pyotr Kropotkin, *The Encyclopedia Britannica*, 1910, http://dwardmac.pitzer.edu/Anarchist_Archives/kropotkin/britanniaanarchy.html

[99] Daniel Schmachtenberger, "New Economics Series", https://civilizationemerging.com/new-economics-series-1/

explicit the necessary macro scale behavioral dynamics – so they can be taken as design constraints."

This outline was used to examine if the Common Planet economic protocol is compatible with these design criteria, and it is. The next chapters will make that clear. We had already understood, considered and incorporated most of these during numerous conversations about the design of and implications of our new protocol. Drawing from a deep well of knowledge, Schmachtenberger has thought long and hard about what is and what should be, given the vast diversity of all the disciplines.

All I did was to focus specifically on the economics and re-imagine and rearrange them to see what results. I had three young children; there was no time before to indulge learning biology, psychology, sociology, anthropology or history— though I've been catching up for the past 7 years now.

Walter Burke, my senior high school math teacher, used to call us 'surface learners.' He was so right. I was the ultimate surface learner, except in one field: finance. I dug deep by reading or listening to many, many books— including newspapers, magazines, blogs and podcasts— about finance, investing, real estate, insurance, sales and self-help. All of which for the purpose of succeeding in Game A, trying to make as much money as possible. Only when I suffered a catastrophic defeat in Game A did I care to actually look at the underlying structure of our system and realized, right away, that it's leading us either to another economic collapse, or worse, civilizational collapse and ultimately extinction.

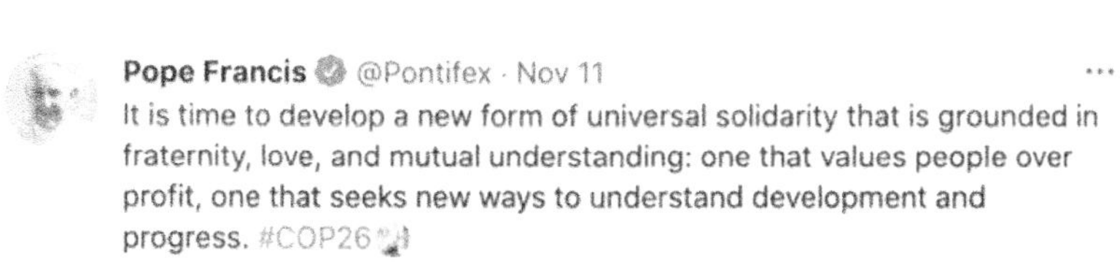
Pope Francis @Pontifex · Nov 11

It is time to develop a new form of universal solidarity that is grounded in fraternity, love, and mutual understanding: one that values people over profit, one that seeks new ways to understand development and progress. #COP26

It saddens me now when I think about how much of my time I spent learning information which will be useless to me in Common Planet life. If we are to get there, then it will have been worth the sacrifice.

Here's Schmachtenberger's outline:

- Economics has to do with two primary areas of concern:

  1) allocation of resources to meeting needs and creating value, and
  2) a system of coordination of human activity.

- Our current global economic system is not only sub-optimal with regard to both goals, but is fundamentally unstable and ultimately self-terminating. The problems originate at the level of foundational axioms so all proposed retrofits (eg, gold-back the dollar or replace it with a crypto equivalent, reinstate Glass-Steagall, etc) to the current system still fail.

- The level of technological advances that have contributed to modern economics' instability also change many of the foundational axioms upon which it was built.

- Economics is a facet of social architecture, inseparable from infrastructure, culture, governance, law, defense, information systems, education and human development, etc. These systems co-evolve and co-influence each other. They are currently all fundamentally inadequate to the scope, urgency, and nature of the issues and dynamics civilization now faces and must undergo a discrete phase shift to axiomatically restructured, higher order systems.

- The emergence of a new adequate system of economics (and attendant systems) requires three interrelated categories of work: 1) developing and implementing transitional systems that are intelligible to and can interface with the current system, while vectoring towards post-transitional systems, 2) the development of post-transitional systems that are adequate to the long term needs of a civilization with the degree of anthrocomplexity and distributed exponential technology we are facing, and 3) protective work to ensure that none of the catastrophic scenarios made possible by and incentivized by the current system come to pass. These three taken together (following the criteria outlined below), constitute a necessary and sufficient set of activities to ensure humanity's survival and increased thriving into the foreseeable future

- This economic system will be inextricably interconnected with new systems of:

  - Governance (collective choice making)
  - Law (collective choice enforcing)
  - Intelligence (collective sense-making)
  - Infrastructure (collective need-meeting)
  - Worldview (collective coherence and values)

Essential Design Constraint: At all points, the system must vector towards omni-win-win dynamics. (At no points can the system incent win-lose dynamics.)

Schmachtenberger says that "Our current global economic system is… "fundamentally unstable and ultimately self-terminating." That's a serious situation. The Indigenous peoples have long understood this self-terminating feature of Game A. Many of them have interesting prophecies. Tȟašúŋke Witk (Crazy Horse) predicted: "Upon suffering beyond suffering: the Red Nation shall rise again and it shall be a blessing for a sick world. A world filled with broken promises, selfishness and separations. A world longing for light again. I see a time of Seven Generations when all the colors of mankind will gather under the Sacred Tree of Life and the whole Earth will become one circle again."

The Anishinaabe (Good People) have "The Prophecy of the 8th Fire" and final fire, an eternal fire of peace, love, brotherhood and sisterhood: "They will come to a fork in the road. One road will lead to Materialism and Destruction... for almost all living creatures... The other road will lead to a Spiritual Way upon which the Native People will be standing... This path will lead to the lighting of the 8th fire, a period of eternal peace, harmony and a "New Earth" where the destruction of the past will be healed."

The Hopi prophecy is nice: "When the Earth is ravaged and the animals are dying, a new tribe of people shall come onto the Earth of many colors, creeds and classes, and by their actions and deeds shall make the Earth green again. They shall be known as the warriors of the rainbow."

Chapter 3

Common Planet

=>÷ Equals is greater than division

With tremendous joy and optimism, we present you with a Common Planet: a restoration of **Sovereignty, Opportunity and Liberty** for every person on Earth. It's a new game of life, but this time without debt, without taxes and without masters. It's time for self-rule. Do you want to play?

Common Planet is an alternative global economic system that ends poverty, homelessness, nuclear weapons and war by rearranging the flow of currency and the control, use and access to all the land, resources, buildings and houses on the planet.

The foundational design of the socio-economic system dictates and determines behavior and thus the outcomes that we see. The problems caused by our current for-profit, growth dependent economic system are a direct result of the private ownership of natural resources, production and information along with the amorality and power of circulatory currency. Based on winner-take-all competition for money, it produces scarcity, poverty and constant warfare. Most concerning is ecological overshoot. And with 8 billion people on a finite planet, change is now absolutely necessary. Regulations and reforms can reduce some of these negative externalities but can not stop the inevitable dangers that loom: the potential social, economic and/or ecological collapse. The only solution that can really change everything is to share the resources and decisions again, but this time as a global unit.

Buckminster Fuller envisioned "The World Game"[1] in the 1960s. A place where individuals or teams of people came and competed, or cooperated, to: "Make the world work, for 100% of humanity, in the shortest possible time, through spontaneous cooperation, without ecological offense or the disadvantage of anyone."

This is the task we must commence at once. Nothing less than a total redesign out of extractive, exclusionary, hierarchical Game A to regenerative, inclusive, contributory Game B will do.

These are the 2 major areas of structural reform proposed hereto:

1. **Currency:** Transition from Circulatory to Flow currency system. Where the currency flows in as Credit (to enable or incentivize) rather than as circulatory debt money (to limit or control). Credit currency is created constantly. It flows into existence to each and every person. Then flows out in exchange for goods or activities. Everyone gets some regularly. And, it can't be lost, stolen or used to control others.

2. **Property:** Manage the Commons democratically and account for everything in shared, open radical transparency. Most housing, cars and other personal possessions remain private, but all non personal resources such as corporations, land, buildings and equipment become the Commons. Current owners can 'cash out' their equity or maintain a role as beneficial caretaker as they choose.

Game A: Trade. All value comes from trading.
To extract value by trading Property. It is a rivalrous, win/lose game using money that is created by banks who tap into free credit and issue it as interest-bearing debt to Nations, Corporations and people. Money is used to value and exchange all the Property on Earth. Only Property is valuable.

[1] The Buckminster Fuller Institute, https://www.bfi.org/about-fuller/big-ideas/world-game

Common Planet: Contribute. All value comes from contributions.
To create value by managing Property as stewards, not owners. Credit currency flows to all people and all use it to satisfy their needs and desires in the open market of goods produced from the Commons. People are valuable.

Let's begin with an examination of how value (currency) works in Game A. Before continuing it's important to point out that some of this may be complicated. How money works is convoluted, so I'll probably be repeating things using different words to make it as clear as possible. Circulatory currency is confusing— Marx's *Capital* is a testament to that— especially when contrasted against the simplicity of Flow currency. You'll recognize and appreciate the differences right away. I'll be using some terminology and definitions from Marx since many readers are already familiar with those and also because they are quite clear and precise.

First, we've already met the 3 kinds of players: People, Corporations and Nations. People are really the only players but they organize themselves by combining into larger more powerful players called Corporations and Nations. All the people are competing to own as much Property as possible for its value.

Every person must play Game A to trade as themselves (for their own account), but they can also play as legal entities called Corporations and own Property there too. Since most corporations consist of more than one human owner, think of them as a family or a gang. These owners receive all corporate value and profits. Nations, as already discussed, are different. Their members consist of both people and corporations. Nations are run by people (rulers, representatives, bureaucrats) empowered to regulate the flow of a Nation's Property to its members. Inevitably, many Nations distribute value (spend $) or take it away (tax $) unfairly and unevenly between its members. People in politics get to act very much like the head of a family or a mob boss, controlling the actions of its members by controlling the flow of value.

Game A is a failed system of competition over value based only on profit from trade. Profit is a kind of information which reveals just the difference between the purchase price and the sale price. Buy low, sell high. Using price signals to determine allocation of resources— a requirement of markets— is proven to mostly work, however, this one crude measure of value via trade also determines the allocation of the real value to all of the various players. If there is one thing that should be obvious to you about this game is that it most definitely does not result in anything closely resembling a fair distribution of value. Obviously, the rising inequality is the direct result of this value equation.

Game A does not offer or recognize any value at all in people, except via trade. In this game, it is only Property which has value, so, for any player to get value they must capture Property and trade it for its value in order to realize value for themselves. Those who don't acquire Property become valueless (useless). Anyone who does not trade, does not get value because all value is found only upon some trade of Property. It is only through transactions that all value (currency) today circulates.

While all of the players compete to own Property— called 'investing'— what they're typically after is not really the Property itself (its use-value), but rather its exchange-value as represented by numerical prices. I'll be using Marx's symbols of C-M-C (commodity to money and money to commodity), and M-C-M (money to commodity and commodity to money), or what Marx called "the general formula for capital" in the sphere of circulation. This will help us to analyze the circuit of how goods and money circulate within the Game A equation. Here's the three roles available to players:

- **Owner**: C-C: Barter (exchange commodity for commodity), or C-M: commodity (C) for money (M).

- **Trader**: M-C then C'-M' which completes the circuit M-C-M': use money M to exchange for commons C then combine Cs to create a more valuable commodity (C') for sale in the market for more money M' ('surplus value' or profit).

- **Consumer**: M-C(MS): use money M to exchange for commodity (means of subsistence) C(MS).

Because trade is the only way to collect value in Game A, players must either already own something to exchange for its value or engage in trade (buying then selling things for M' profit). Nobody trades their money for a commodity M-C in the market simply to sell it again for the same price C-M. So the formula M-C-M' illustrates Game A market exchange. Traders buy commodities C, including labor power (LP), and the means of production (MP) with money M in order to combine them into production (P) and sell the resulting commodity C' for more money M' than they began with. That looks like this: M-C…P…C'-M or shortened: M-C-M' (Buy-Transform-Sell). Not until C is thrown into P does it come out as a more valuable commodity C' which is exchanged for its equal counterpart of M'.

Ok, if you didn't understand that last paragraph you will need to reread it 10 times… just kidding. I apologize to some of you here for the use of these symbols and some math, but I promise I'm going somewhere with this. Don't waste too much time making sure to understand every circuit of Game A if you're having too much trouble. The point here isn't to make you an expert on Game A finance, but to give you the overall happenings and movements so when we get to describing the Flow currency system, you will understand the logic between the two.

Most call these actors Capitalists but I'm using the term Traders instead. Traders don't buy Cs for its use-value, that is they aren't buying to consume, but buying for exchange-value, to sell it for more money. For our purposes M=C, since they are both Property. M-C, therefore, represents a kind of barter, an equal exchange of value. It just so happens that M is an easier and safer Property to accumulate than most Cs. In the final analysis of value flows, these forms of exchange-value (C and M) are merely numbers, thus the same. I call any thing of value that is exchanged: Property. Whereas Marx called it Capital. I prefer Property because I suspect many people think of only money or currency when they see the word 'capital', especially non-economists.

Money may be the central, dominant Property in Game A, however it's transformed into just a unit of measure as a Flow currency in Game B. The real Property then takes center stage, as it should.

Common Property— the source of all value— is extracted, combined, distributed, traded, and ultimately transformed or consumed but in every case, it's value originates from what Marx called 'primitive accumulation.' Take common resource C and trade it for M. Accounting of value is what Game A is all about.

Since everything on Earth is already owned, it might help us to understand things easier if we imagine owners taking their common resources C and placing them inside the 'refrigerator' where things go to be sold. The fridge is a restricted market. Anything owners want to sell is put in the fridge: the trees, minerals, oil, rice, fish, etc. When players take pieces of our commons and put them in the fridge whenever they want without our permission or knowledge is the multipolar trap which leads to the 'tragedy of the commons.' This is the basis of all Game A foundational value extraction accounting and money. All things in the fridge have a price or value, and those who 'own' them have the sole right to extract and distribute these things on their terms. These things, though, are the commons which all life on Earth depends upon.

Owners sell. Traders and consumers buy. Owners decide what Cs go into the fridge, then sell them for M. Traders buy things C from the fridge, mix them in production P turning them into finished goods C' and place them back into the fridge for sale for more money M'. In all cases, everything is priced in M.

All people are consumers, first and foremost. You depend on access to the means of subsistence C(MS) in the market, otherwise you die. If you don't have any M then you can't go into the fridge. For evidence, take a walk in any American city today and you'll see poor homeless people wandering around, locked out of the fridge and completely dependent on charity for C(MS).

Here's an incredible passage written by Robert Tressell in 1914:

> Poverty is not caused by men and women getting married; it's not caused by machinery; it's not caused by "over-production"; it's not caused by drink or laziness; and it's not caused by "over-population". It's caused by Private Monopoly. That is the present system. They have monopolized everything that it is possible to monopolize; they have got the whole earth, the minerals in the earth and the streams that water the earth. The only reason they have not monopolized the daylight and the air is that it is not possible to do it. If it were possible to construct huge gasometers and to draw together and compress within them the whole of the atmosphere, it would have been done long ago, and we should have been compelled to work for them in order to get money to buy air to breathe. And if that seemingly impossible thing were accomplished tomorrow, you would see thousands of people dying for want of air – or of the money to buy it – even as now thousands are dying for want of the other necessities of life. You would see people going about gasping for breath, and telling each other that the likes of them could not expect to have air to breathe unless they had the money to pay for it. Most of you here, for instance, would think and say so. Even as you think at present that it's right for so few people to own the Earth, the Minerals and the Water, which are all just as necessary as is the air. In exactly the same spirit as you now say: "It's Their Land," "It's Their Water," "It's Their Coal," "It's Their Iron," so you would say "It's Their Air," "These are their gasometers, and what right have the likes of us to expect them to allow us to breathe for nothing?" And even while he is doing this the air monopolist will be preaching sermons on the Brotherhood of Man; he will be dispensing advice on "Christian Duty" in the Sunday magazines; he will give utterance to numerous more or less moral maxims for the guidance of the young. And

> meantime, all around, people will be dying for want of some of the air that he will have bottled up in his gasometers. And when you are all dragging out a miserable existence, gasping for breath or dying for want of air, if one of your number suggests smashing a hole in the side of one of the gasometers, you will all fall upon him in the name of law and order, and after doing your best to tear him limb from limb, you'll drag him, covered with blood, in triumph to the nearest Police Station and deliver him up to "justice" in the hope of being given a few half-pounds of air for your trouble.[2]

Imagine yourself with no money and no ability to buy anything for consumption or trade. How do you get money? You must find some thing to sell for M. It's the only way. What can you put in the fridge for sale? What do you own? Yourself. You own yourself. People, as owners of themselves, sell themselves to a Trader or consumer for M, otherwise they remain valueless and starve.

And this is how you and your labor power itself too becomes just another commodity in the market; LP = C. Your value is determined in the same way as other commodities, and it is used by traders just as any other commodity in the production process (or by consumers typically for sex). Traders combine all the different kinds of inputs: the C, LP, and MP together which represent the total cost of production. The resulting commodity C' is then sold for maximum price, yielding maximum M' profit. With your share of the value for your LP varying depending on the dynamics of power.

Marx said this capitalist economic system was an alienated form of human life because workers are forced to sell their labor – regarded as the essence of human existence – to the capitalists, who use this labor to accumulate more capital, which further increases the power of the capitalists over the workers. Capitalists become rich, while wages are driven down to the bare minimum needed to keep the workers alive.

Each in competition over these variable values causes a constant struggle between what's good for owners vs what's good for the workers, consumers and the planet. Profit from trade may be one good metric for resource allocation, but it is most certainly a terrible way to distribute value to people. It's true that all world resources have value: water, food, animals, minerals, trees, oil, etc. But still, why begin an economic game giving *ownership* of these commons— of all the valuable resources— to private persons, corporations and nations? Combined, all their individual economic interests of chasing

---

[2] Robert Tressell, *The Ragged Trousered Philanthropists*, 1914, ch 15, https://www.marxists.org/archive/tressell/works/1914/index.html

profit do not result in what's best for our collective wellbeing. It never has and never will.

In a recent message, here's what Pope Francis said about profit and value:

> This system, with its relentless logic of profit, is escaping all human control. It is time to slow the locomotive down, an out-of-control locomotive hurtling towards the abyss. There is still time… But what is one of the greatest dangers we face today? We will not come out of this pandemic crisis the same. Come out better or come out worse but: the same as we were before? No. We will never emerge the same. And today together, always together, we have to face this question: "How will we emerge from this crisis? Better or worse?" Of course, we want to come out better, but to do so we have to break the bonds of what is easy and the docile acceptance that "there is no other way", that "this is the only possible system." Such resignation destroys "us" and substitutes the isolation of "every man for himself." And so, we must dream. It worries me that, while we are still paralysed, "there are already projects underway to restore the same socio-economic structure we had before" because it is easier. Let us choose the difficult path. Let us come out better.[3]

A person must have possession of their labor power (not be a slave) in order to be able to sell it. A trader must have possession of the means of production (having taken them from the Earth or fridge). This pattern of possession shows two parties who are 'free' to act. Here, this 'freedom' to trade appears as an act of 'free will' as well as an act between two freely consenting property owners. If you trap yourself into thinking this property relationship is somehow natural, necessary and an inalterable method of exchange, then you end up with the Libertarian logic of 'freedom.' When I was younger and a Libertarian, this was my thought process: "If trade is both necessary and good, and the goal is maximum personal freedom for people, and people are traders, then any actors interfering with trade of private property is a distortion of and abuse of the functioning of the free market." I was merely following the logic of Game A value flow. I never considered that it could be any other way. Why would I? Did you? I was intensively engaged in trying to 'see' how it all worked. Not because I thought there was a better way, but so that I could win in Game A. I was a capitalist. We all are. We still live in Game A. We must follow the logic of its value flows, or starve.

---

[3] Pope Francis, Oct 16, 2021, https://www.vatican.va/content/francesco/en/messages/pont-messages/2021/documents/20211016-videomessaggio-movimentipopolari.html

Yes, many capitalists seek profit aggressively, and in doing so, money organizes society by shaping the lives of most people around jobs and markets. When money or profits are invested, it creates jobs, and jobs make it possible for people to live and improve their lives, thus business profit-seeking 'contributes' to society. From this, capitalists develop a sense of responsibility for the general social welfare. If anything hinders production or trade for profit it also reduces jobs. Since businesses are 'job creators', this process of exploitation appears a kind of benevolence of necessity.

If you've ever been a boss and hired employees, you'll know that feeling of responsibility for your employees livelihood and that of their families, along with the overall community too. How could you not. You're a major part of the value flow. Production produces valuable Cs. That's indisputable. The fridge gets filled up. But what produces the money necessary to purchase things from the fridge? Where does the money come from? Sounds like a chicken and egg situation. To answer this question, we must go back to the beginning of Game A.

Let's start with a brief history of trade and money. The traditional story is that humans started with barter, then invented money, and last came credit. This is backwards actually. Credit came first. People assume, like Adam Smith did in his Wealth of Nations, that it must've all started when someone had something someone else wanted and so they simply swapped stuff. A man with lots of chickens wanted a cow so he went to a man with cows and they negotiated a trade. They made a deal and swapped 20 chickens for 1 cow = barter. Eventually it happened that the man with cows didn't need or want any chickens or anything else the man with chickens had, so no deal could be made. So they had to invent something to use as a medium of exchange. Voila, enter money. Then eventually came banking and credit. This was— probably still is— the story told in modern economics, but anthropologists could find no record of this magical society of barter. It doesn't exist.

"Prehistoric society and many pre-modern societies did not use barter to allocate resources," writes Darren Allen in his book *33 Myths Of The System*, "but informal, non-usurious, credit, centralized distribution and the so-called 'gift economy'— just as friends and families do today. Both money and barter were used only for ritual and for trade with enemies — which is what they are still used for. The difference is that now everyone must be considered an enemy (the official term is COMPETITOR) or as a tool (official term; EMPLOYEES) in the insane activity known as BUSINESS."[4]

In the 2012 masterpiece, *Debt: The First 5,000 Years*, anthropologist David Graeber investigated the origins of money, providing much needed clarity. There were records of barter that came later between strangers but trade between neighbors was the original scenario; if there's somebody you're never going to meet again, you had to swap things, but if it's people that are your neighbors, people with whom you have regular contact with, trading was different. There were no barter systems within societies. Economists just assumed neighbors deal with each other in spot trades: I give you something, you give me something, we walk away but if we can't settle the deal right now, that's it. But that's not how people who know each other deal. If I have cows but I don't want your chickens, I know you're gonna have something I want at some point and so I just give you the cow now until you have something I want. That's credit and debt. That's how it all started. That's how we relate to one another with *our* property.

Here's Graeber in his own words from a 2012 interview:

> Graeber: if you just praise an object that belongs to someone else, they kind of have to give it to you, so what would really happen is you go up and you say, "wow that's a beautiful cow", and there's really no appropriate response. There's nothing you can say other than "it's not much, but take it please, you know, you're my neighbor, I love you, and don't even think about giving me something back", but of course we all know now I owe him one. So what you get is a sort of credit and debt situation, but it's not a specific one where you can quantify exactly how many of one thing equals another... It's not necessarily an object. It could be a favor; I need help with something. It's good to have people in your debt. So, what they're making up, these economists, is a story which imagines that essentially social relations don't exist, that people are only thinking about the stuff. Which is fine if you're inventing economics which is the study of people who are only thinking about the stuff but that's not how actual people normally behave.
>
> Kolhatkar. So is there evidence that societies, whole societies, behaved on credit and lending and borrowing items, and keeping tabs if you will, before currency existed?
>
> Graeber: Absolutely. That is what all evidence comes to indicate.[5]

---

[4] Darren Allen, *33 Myths Of The System*, 2018, 1st edition version, p. 35

[5] David Graeber Interview with Sonali Kolhatkar, 2012, https://www.youtube.com/watch?v=zSnReXI4gKk

So it all started when one person got a thing of value C and gave it to someone else. In other words, an IOU is created with one person extending a credit to another who is now in debt. Game A trading started so innocently.

Clay is valuable in making pottery, among other uses. If Tom takes clay from the Earth and shapes it into pottery for cooking, it suddenly has more value. Where did this value come from? It's obvious that without Tom spending his time working the clay it would not become pottery. Therefore, the clay and labor are both valuable, for without them no pottery can be had. Production produces value. It is a positive sum game and we are all better off for it.

Most production consists of two main parts: raw materials (common property) from the earth C (in this case the clay) + Tom's labor LP creates pottery, a commodity C' = a more useful/valuable Property. The value or price of C' in the market minus its total costs (clay + labor, C+LP) = profit. Profit (or loss) is what you're left with after trading a commodity C'.

How much of the value of C' is the clay itself vs how much is from Tom's labor? And how much should the price, thus profit be? There are no standard rules which regulate these value determinations in Game A. This 'class conflict' is settled entirely by the actors themselves. Economists have been pondering this question of value ever since because in Game A all value flows via exchange. That there are no standard, universal or fair rules determining values and who gets the value is a major problem. This produces a constant struggle where each participant tries to ascertain then claim as much of the value for themselves. This is where the terms 'class struggle' and 'free market' emanate from. In this Twitter thread, economist Arash Kolahi explores these owner/worker power dynamics:

> Like most prices in capitalism, wages (price of labor) are determined by markets. Markets are an allocation system whereby prices are reflective of the relative bargaining power between buyers & sellers of goods and services… Since wages in capitalism are bought & sold on the labor market, wages too are set by the relative bargaining power between the employer (buyer) & worker (seller)… With markets, bargaining power is EVERYTHING. Employers know it, executives know it, MBA's know it. Economists know it. Yet the propaganda is the opposite. Work hard & you'll earn more. Be more productive & you'll earn more. Produce more value for your employer & you'll earn more. ALL LIES for the masses…. Lie #1: Wages are based on productivity: Between the 1950s & today worker productivity has increased multiple times over, yet wages remained stagnant. Zero historical correlation between productivity & wages. Per worker productivity has skyrocketed, yet

> virtually none of those gains have benefited workers because worker bargaining power has remained flat. The one-sided war against unions over the past 50 years has contributed greatly to keeping workers' bargaining power low. Lie 1 debunked: No correlation between productivity & wages. Lie #2: Wages are based on the value of your labor: If by 'value' we mean 'valued by society,' this is obviously not the case as workers in some of the highest societally valued products & services (i.e. teachers) receive the lowest wages. If by value we mean value that can translate into profits for employers, this is obviously also not true since workers in some of the most profitable industries (i.e., iPhone factory workers) also receive some of the lowest wages. Regardless of profit levels (so long as there is no loss), the STRONGEST correlation is between workers' wages & worker's level of bargaining power in that industry, NOT profit levels and NOT the value of labor. Lie 2 debunked. And finally, the favorite lie of all. Lie #3: Wages are based on hard work, effort, sacrifice or duration of work. No one works 100x or 1,000x or 10,000 times longer or harder than anyone else – but some earn 100x or 1,000x or 10,000 times more income than others. As I've shown in a separate thread, if wages were remotely equitable, the average worker, working the average duration at an average effort, would receive the average income of roughly $130,000 a year! Obviously this is not the case. But what about the duration of work? For many workers there is SOME correlation between duration of work & income. But that correlation is only because of the minimum wage, not because of market forces. And much of the fight for a minimum wage was based on the understanding that if left up to normal market forces, i.e. relative bargaining power between workers & employers, wages would be driven so far down that most workers would earn dire poverty wages. Thus, as we have shown, market capitalism rewards bargaining power, NOT productivity, NOT value & certainly NOT hard work, effort, sacrifice, or duration of work. And because market capitalism rewards only bargaining power, it is inherently inequitable. The only fair & equitable criteria for wages is rewarding hard work, effort, sacrifice & duration of work. Capitalists lie about it because it resonates as fair, but capitalism is inherently NOT fair."[6]

In Marx's analysis in *Capital*, he too says the capitalists are the stronger class, defining what workers will be paid. The very essence of a capitalist is the desire to gain surplus-value. The capitalist system requires exploitation. Their primary method is to exploit workers by not paying workers for the full value of their labor power. In order to survive, the capitalist must exploit.

However, this power doesn't come from capitalists themselves, but rather from individuals within social institutions who make the property laws. Thus,

---

[6] Arash Kolahi, Twitter thread, https://twitter.com/ArashKolahi/status/1210332075787608065

the tension between workers and capitalists is structural (systemic). Measures to ease workers' hardships, such as a minimum wage, unions or welfare are simply band-aids (ancillary value flows); they do not change the equation of capitalism, serving instead to continue and perpetuate it. The values flowing from the mode of production reflects the economic system of capitalism. It will continue to do so, and continue to favor the capitalists, until it self-destructs, according to Marx.

A trader must trade his C' in order to collect its value as priced in money M, but at what price? This 'labor theory of value' is the question considered by Smith, Ricardo, Marx and Menger. Wherein each posits their theory on why and how certain agents receive the value they do. Lucky for you, we don't have to go into those. As I will show, they've been analyzing the wrong value equation altogether. The way trade works now is war over values and prices as Kolahi just explained.

If Tom trades *his* pottery (C') to Sam for a fish (C' of equal value), a barter transaction occurs C'-C', Property ownership changes, but there is no new creation of value. Sam spent equal time catching fish as Tom did making pottery. They both produced and then exchanged C' of equal value. Their initial production added C's to the fridge of the market, but the trade did not. One person may gain or lose value upon trade, but no new value is created or destroyed, it's just exchanged is all. There's still just one pottery and one fish available to the players in the game; either of which can be consumed by their new respective owners or be placed back into the fridge for sale.

In Game A, all C's (real and fictional) either keep their value, gain value or lose value as represented by prices affected by supply and demand. Prices are often variable and change constantly as people are want to haggle. If Tom sells the pottery for more than it's worth, he collects more value (profit) and Sam loses an equal amount. But that's still zero sum because no new C' or value was added to society's balance sheet, or the fridge.

Since the market is a collection made up of C's, we can say production is positive sum, trading is zero sum and consumption is negative. This is where the analogy of the fridge becomes useful. Production adds things into the fridge, trade swaps things, and consumption deletes things. Once the pottery is used and the fish eaten, they are gone, transformed. All exchange value is lost. Value is negated by consumption. You can add C's to the market, you can trade C's in the market or you can consume C's from the market. Paying attention to the real C's is what economics should be all about, but that's not the case today. Money and other financial C's distort the real C's.

But suppose Sam doesn't have anything of value to trade for the pottery, what then? There are only two kinds of trade possible: a spot trade (barter) or an IOU (credit/debt) situation. Since Sam has no money and no C' to trade with, he can take the pottery now and be in debt (owe one) to Tom. The circuit of trade value must be completed— as it is with barter— otherwise it would be a gift or theft, and not trade. In this example, the trade is executed by the creation of value (money) as credit/debt but the circuit of value flow continues and remains unfinished as Sam pays Tom with an IOU. **This IOU is money.** It's easy to see now why most economists assumed people had to barter before money was *invented.*

Tom can give the pottery to Sam as a credit in return for an IOU (a promise to pay equal value in the future). If we represent the transaction on an accounting ledger, it would show Tom extending credit to Sam, who is now in debt. Tom gave Sam value or money equal to the pottery. Let's say the market price of the pottery C' = $3 = C+LP+M' (the price of the clay + Tom's labor + profit). We know Tom took the clay C from the Earth at no cost beyond his own time and labor, but where did Tom get the credit ($3, the price of the pottery) to lend to Sam? It's just a human fiction, a make believe value. All values are subjective. It's just accounting, but for all intents and purposes it is now real value that Tom can use in future transactions. The IOU is now money for Tom and debt for Sam. It's a recognition of the value attributed to the positive sum contribution made by Tom. He added something to the fridge. Of course, only the two individuals recognize the exchange of this specific contribution, but still it's real. Anything the mind of man can imagine and believe becomes real so long as others believe it too. It's a shared fictional accounting. A game of points. Marx said this value or money, "crystallizes out of exchange."

Tom produced the C' (+$3) and Sam consumed it (-$3). How long can Sam continue consuming without producing before others no longer extend credit? This is called the free rider problem in economics, where some people consume without helping to produce anything. You can't just keep taking from the fridge without also putting stuff in. It's fundamentally unfair and as we've already discussed, fairness is deeply embedded in our psychology of social relations. These notions of fairness are what push people like Sam to reciprocate by creating value and continuing to play the game. I repeat: accounting of value is what life is all about. It's precisely because we demand things be equal and fair that we're even playing this game of measuring values of production and consumption of the real Property to begin with.

So Sam goes out and catches six fish (+$18), pays Tom back with a fish, thereby closing out the debt and completing the value circuit. He then trades two fish to other tribe members for equal exchange in barter or IOUs. Those exchanges look like this: C'-C' (barter) or C'-M (commodity for money). If barter for consumption, value is exchanged then consumed. If the exchange was for money, the circulation merely pauses until the money circulates in future exchange.

Sam still has 3 fish left, so he gives them to Tito who transports and trades them to other tribes. Tito has some physical defects making him a terrible hunter, fisherman and pottery maker, so instead he handles trade with other tribes to prove his value. Sam tells Tito to keep one fish for himself if he can trade the rest at full price. All benefit from the division of labor of specialized production and trade, as made famous by Adam Smith.

Tribe X doesn't have nearby access to rivers or lakes but they are masterful craftspeople who trade baskets for fish. With access to information only a trader has, Tito learns that tribe X values fish twice as high as the others. So he trades 2 fish for 4 baskets, gives Sam his share of the trade, the 2 pottery, and ends up with a profit of 1 fish and 2 baskets for his efforts (+$9). Sam produced the value by fishing (+$18) and received equal value in return, minus the one fish (-$3) he paid for Tito's services. After all transactions Sam ends up with value = +$15. Tribe X produced a value of 4 baskets (+$12) but only received a value of 2 fish ($6). They lost half their value (-$6) in the trade, which is exactly the amount of value (+$6) Tito got to keep for his efforts from that trade.

We could run that scenario dozens of times with the same or different agents using the same exact resources and end up with different value allocations for each of the three agents. That's because price is a reflection of value, of desire in the market, whether of a need or a want, and is always subjective in time. It's whatever the individual agents believe it to be at that moment, ie. who has the most 'power.' It's not scientific or fair. The values are completely variable in Game A. None of the actors know upfront how much value they will end up with for their roles until after all trade is complete. This example illustrates how trading creates winners and losers. This is what produces the constant struggle for value, and ultimately fighting and war over value.

Tito the trader produced no new C's of value for the fridge, yet ended up with value for his services. How and why? It was the others who labored to produce C's into the fridge, but they can't receive their share of value until it's sold. The producing players would not have been able to convert their labor into value if no trade was made. That's Tito's job. If you've ever wondered why companies spend so much on marketing and why 'salespeople' are among the highest paid 'workers', now you know why.

However, exchanging physical goods requires real labor too, in the form of pickup, safe-keeping and delivery. Therefore, the value of Tito's real labor of delivery/sale can be embedded or reflected in the final price of the finished goods too. In this way, Tito's labor does add value to the C' even though he didn't have a direct hand in producing the C'. His labor was a part of and necessary to move goods from producers to users and all benefit from it.

But what about trading that doesn't require any real labor, like modern speculators trading currencies, stocks, bonds, RE, crypto, NFTs, etc? What actual value do they add in the market? Zero. None. Trading is zero sum. Financial traders use asymmetric access to information (power) to collect value that is produced by society but they don't produce any actual value themselves. That's how Michael Bloomberg got so filthy rich. Yet somehow they have convinced themselves that theirs are the most important transactions in the market for the good of all.

I traded stocks for over a decade. Trading was said to be good and necessary for the market because we were providing liquidity for investors. Is that all? Yup. Investors, governments and banks all provide M to producers, thus determining what goes into the market. Without M to prime the pump of production there would be no market, based on this logic. So of course they are important in this equation. They have all the M, hence all the power.

It was Smith in 1776 who recognized the three main sources of income: profits, rents and wages. As discussed, owners make profits by selling but nowadays they mostly sell access to their Property instead. This is called rent. Much of today's economy is rentierism defined as income derived from interest, dividends, rent and capital gains. Rentier income is unearned income.

Never did I question the equation of Game A and how it came to be that this group of people and fictional entities had all the money and power to begin with. Where did all this money swirling around come from?

We have to realize something straight away: where did the clay C that Tom molded into pottery C' originally come from? The Earth right? Whose is it? Every single thing on Earth is God's property first and foremost. That a person or fictional entity can take OUR property and sell it as their own is theft from the commons, plain and simple.

"Perhaps the most interesting thing about libertarian thought is that it has no way of coherently justifying the initial acquisition of property," writes Matt Bruenig. "How does something that was once unowned become owned without nonconsensually destroying others' liberty? It is impossible. This means that libertarian systems of thought literally cannot get off the ground. They are stuck at time zero of hypothetical history with no way forward."[7] He goes on to quote Robert Nozick, whom he calls a 'serious libertarian': "It will be implausible to view improving an object as giving full ownership to it, if the stock of unowned objects that might be improved is limited. For an object's coming under one person's ownership changes the situation of all others. **Whereas previous they were at liberty (in Hohfeld's sense) to use the object, they now no longer are."**

Suppose the tribal leader claims he now owns all the clay in the territory. Suddenly he becomes the sole commander of who and how much clay can be taken and for what purposes it might be used. As you can see, this new *owner* has some serious power of something valuable in the game. And so begins the battle to claim all the things from our collective commons as private in order to extract and control its value.

No formal record keeping is necessary when you know people, but eventually even these relations and transactions came to have more formal arrangements with different tribes valuing things differently among themselves using both spot and IOU trades. However, when it came to trade between tribes, values and accounting became serious. There was lots of experimentation with all kinds of different inventions of tools of record keeping making accounting easy between individuals and tribes who had ongoing relationships. But how do you trade with people or tribes you're not likely to deal with soon or ever again?

You can't do an IOU with someone you don't trust or won't deal with again so the only option you have is a spot trade. If some far away tribe came for your stuff without an equal value of stuff you wanted, what can you do? This is called the double coincidence of wants problem, where both parties must coincidentally have what each wants in order to make a trade. Enter money as a medium of exchange. You may not have what I want in goods, but if you have money of equal value to my goods then we can trade. Money

---

[7] Matt Bruenig, Jacobin, "How Did Private Property Start?", 2018, https://jacobinmag.com/2018/03/libertarian-property-ownership-capitalism

is an alternative piece of property, itself also a C— physical like shells, coins, etc— with some specific generally agreed upon exchange value. Basically, money became a physical representation of value which you could trust and which both parties will accept, and therefore can always solve the double coincidence problem to facilitate any trade. When M=C then M-C mimics C-C, a spot trade or barter. It closes the circuit. The deal is done. The trade is complete. It's important to point out that a C with a use-value also has an exchange value, but in the M form there is only an exchange-value. You can't eat money. By itself it's useless. Also, money doesn't have an exchange value in itself, but only in its relationship with other objects. You can only use it to exchange for something else, and so it circulates. This is a very important distinction because in C-C after the value circuit completes, if both Cs are consumed then so too is all value and no more circulation is possible, whereas the value of M is never consumed. Its value continues to circulate, forever, especially in its physical form of precious metals.

As far as accounting using numerical value is concerned, there is no difference even though the two things are most definitely different. One is real, the other imaginative. "The true goal of economic theory, then, is to look "through" money, as one looks through a window, at what is really going on "behind" it, and not be deceived by monetary illusions. The nominal is a veil over the real."[8] What is happening to the common resources of the world (those extracted and sold in the fridge) are really the only material values that matter. The currency in Game A has become an abstraction and a distraction from what we are doing to our ecology, or the balance sheet of life. What started innocently enough through desirable and necessary trade was changed forever with the introduction of this new super valuable property called money.

Since all money comes into existence when the commons are extracted, more value was created as production and trade increased. Tribes grew into cities, food and goods became plentiful but needed to be stored. That's not easy. Food doesn't last very long but money does. It should be easy to see from this perspective how, eventually, money became the most desired Property in Game A. The race to own Property for value extraction enters high gear, and is near supersonic today. Have you seen the enormous size of our excavators that dig the earth and super-trawlers dragging nets in the oceans? Not to mention the many oil and gas drilling right now sucking up

---

[8] Colin Drumm, *The Difference That Money Makes*, 2021, https://drive.google.com/file/d/1IZy2o238Ef3zOIfI724dt95UqookVe0b

resources out of the ground. Why? Because owners claimed pieces of the commons in order to trade them for money. Extract C from the commons to trade for M; use M buy C; sell C for M'. So on and so forth, forever.

Claiming things from the commons as private property, then all geography too, became just the way things work. Then trade unleashed a forever battle over the values of all this Property in the game. Eventually, silver and gold became the main forms of money for thousands of years. They are easy metals to mold, to store, and they do not degrade. They proved to be the most trusted physical representations of value to facilitate trade. Money is a social agreement. As long as everyone agrees something has value, then it does. We believe in money because it is the unit of exchange for **everything**. Currency is great at measuring prices to determine allocation of resources, but trade is terrible at distributing 'value.'

Consider the word 'value.' When economists talk about value they are really talking about money, or, more precisely, about whatever it is that money is measuring; also, whatever it is that economic actors are assumed to be pursuing. When we are working a job, or buying and selling things, we are rewarded with money. But whenever we are not working or buying or selling, when we are motivated by pretty much anything other than the desire to get money, we suddenly talk about 'values.'

What people really want is not money, but the conditions that they believe only money can provide. Most want a carefree life that is full of opportunities. They want autonomy (liberty), they want growth (mastery), and they want contribution (purpose, meaningful work); even if they are not aware of it. Notice that all of these things are intrinsic motivators, not extrinsic. Chasing money isn't the key to happiness. Graeber said, "For me this is what's so pernicious about the morality of debt: the way that financial imperatives constantly try to reduce us all, despite ourselves, to the equivalent of pillagers, eyeing the world simply for what can be turned into money."

In his wonderful book *Team Human*, Douglas Rushkoff says about money:

> Central currency turned simple transactional tokens - a utility for exchange into a scarce commodity. The Renaissance's chartered monopolies transformed craftspeople and cooperative commons users into expendable employees, competing for a day's work.
>
> We must learn to distinguish between the natural world and the many constructions we now mistake for preexisting conditions of the universe. Money, debt, jobs, slavery, countries, race, corporatism, stock markets, brands, religions, government, and taxes are all human inventions. We made

> them up, but we now act as if they're unchangeable laws. Playing for Team Human means being capable of distinguishing between what we can't change and what we can.[9]

But there's a major problem with currency as a commodity. Quantity. Each of the various physical forms of money have changing quantities in the Earth and that in turn affects the relative values between them.[10] Supply and demand. That's the first lesson of economics. That makes determining the values of Property even more difficult in this economic battlefield.

All currencies today are in the form of money which is a kind of quasi-physical property circulating via trade. Money is too powerful. Operating as a measure of value and as Property or POM (physical object money), where each function conflates and corrupts the other.

Marc Gauvin of The Money Systems Transparency Alliance calls this: "Money's Core Misrepresentation: Common practice has adopted a notion of money where it is implicitly and explicitly assumed to be both a record/ measure of value AND a commodity/tradable good without noticing how these two notions (measure/commodity) are, by logic, mutually exclusive."[11]

The currency is also a commodity. It's both a measure of value— like miles or km for distances— and also Property itself with its own value relative to its quantity vs other currencies and all other Property in the game. That's all quite perplexing. Interestingly, the quantity of real Properties have real physical limits whereas the quantity of any currency, like the $, does not. Money is created by what they call fiat or ex nihilo (out of nothing). There are no limits to numbers in math.

So if money is man-made (flows into existence) and unlimited in quantity then how does it all flow as such and how does it become an object in the process? That's some real magic. Once transformed into Property, naturally, money thus circulates. Think about all the money out there swirling around right now.

Currently, there is much confusion and little consensus, if any, on exactly how all the valves of the money and credit system flow and who is

---

[9] Douglas Rushkoff, *Team Human*, p 193, 206

[10] c.f. Adam Smith: "a measure of quantity, such as the natural foot, fathom, or handful, which is continually varying in its own quantity, can never be an accurate measure of the quantity of other things; so a commodity which is itself continually varying in its own value, can never be an accurate measure of the value of other commodities." *The Wealth of Nations*, 51.

[11] Marc Gauvin, MSTA, https://www.moneytransparency.com/msta-resolutions

controlling these flows. Politicians make major economic decisions regarding flows of money yet they have almost no clue about what valves exist and how money flows. I don't entirely blame them. Circulatory money currency is confusing. And yet its numbers control the flow of all Property.

There is a finite amount of money 'in circulation' (with more added and deleted constantly) moving between players. All must participate to get some. People produce to consume. All to help the economy grow, otherwise no value circulates to the people. This is called the velocity of money: a measurement of the rate at which money circulates via exchange in an economy, or the number of times that money flows from one player to another. If enough money doesn't circulate with enough speed (equilibrium) then people can't participate in the market, causing recessions or depressions.

During the great depression, Pope Pius XI said "In our days not alone is wealth accumulated, but immense power and despotic economic domination is concentrated in the hands of the few… This power becomes particularly irresistible when exercised by those who, because they hold and control money, are able also to govern credit and determine its allotment, for this reason supplying, so to speak, the life-blood to the entire economic body and grasping, as it were, in their hand the very soul of the economy so that no one dare breathe against their will."

As the 'life-blood' of the market the currency system is all important. Game A's circulatory currency regime has never been nor can it ever be stable, efficient or fair. We've trapped ourselves playing the wrong game of value using the wrong kind of currency.

Now let's compare and contrast the two different currency systems: Circulatory vs Flow.

This is the heart of the matter and the most important thing I have to inform you about. Once you see how Flow works, it will forever change the way you see the world. You will have a new lens from which to look at Game A from a Game B perspective. Like Roddy Piper's character putting on his sunglasses in the movie "They Live."

Circulatory Currency: Money

"All the perplexities, confusions, and distresses in America arise, not from defects in their constitution or confederation, not from a want of honor or virtue, so much as from downright ignorance of the nature of coin, credit, and circulation."
— John Adams, August 25, 1787 in a letter to Thomas Jefferson.[12]

US Senate hearing, 4/14/2010:
Ron Paul: "Do you think gold is money?" Ben Bernanke: "...No."
Paul: "It's not money?" Bernanke: "It's a precious metal."
Paul: "Even if it's been money for 6,000 years, somebody reversed that, and eliminated that economic law?"
Bernanke: "Well, you know, it's an asset. I mean, it's the same... would you say Treasury Bills are money, I don't think they're money either…"
Paul: "Why do central banks hold it?"
Bernanke: "Well it's a form of reserves."
Paul: "Why don't they hold diamonds?"
Bernanke: "Well, it's tradition. Long term tradition."

Money is the most important tool in the world today. From an economic perspective, understanding exactly what money is and how it influences everything is crucial. In essence, money is merely a unit of account used primarily as a medium of exchange, or as a store of value.

Whether you have money ($, €, ¥) or not, it occupies way too much of your thinking and your life. You don't control your life, money does. How to get money is primary. Only then can you think about how you should live. The reason for this is simple, for without money you basically don't have a life. Without money you have nothing to exchange for the real things you need in order to live. You are only as free as your purchasing power permits you to be. And so you *live* mostly to get money. You can't make money, but banks can and do.

Most of us have to submit our lives to others for money. It's the only way it *circulates* to us. Welcome to Game A. Now get out there hustle and chase that money, *player*. We are all trapped and everybody wants out. The desire for freedom, to escape from this hamster wheel spawned the expression 'fuck

[12] The Works of John Adams, Vol 8, p. 447, Ed. Charles Francis Adams Little, Brown & Co, 1853

you money.' Everybody wants to get enough money so they can say 'fuck you' to this game and be free to live their life the way God intended.

What is money, this thing that we all must have in order to live? "Money isn't a material reality - it is a psychological construct" writes Harari in *Sapiens*. Money is a fictional super-duper multi-functional tool that is created 'out of thin air' by alchemists in finance. But it wasn't always like this.

Once owners and traders amassed money the game began to change. A new way to make money with money emerged. Interest. Because M=C it too could be rented out to others at interest, thus money produces more money M-M'. Interest was called usury and was made illegal by most of the religions because it led to unacceptable inequalities. So instead of lending the money outright they 'invested' in joint trading ventures which ultimately led to the Corporation. A fictional vehicle whereby people could share the risk and limit their personal liability.

This new trade had more complicated value flows requiring a more advanced accounting. The first recorded history of the description of double-entry bookkeeping was written by Benedetto Cotrugli in 1458: *The Book of the Art of Trade*. "The rise and metamorphosis of double-entry bookkeeping is one of history's best kept secrets and most important untold tales … Our world is governed by the numbers generated by the accounts of nations and corporations. We depend upon these numbers to direct our governments, organisations, economies, societies … Over the past one hundred years, Accounting has flourished to an astonishing degree, despite the many scandals it has left in its wake. The figures double entry generates have become a sophisticated system of numbers which in the twenty-first century rules the global economy, manipulated by governments, financial institutions and the quant nerds of Wall Street."[13]

Those with money have an advantage in trade, that much should be obvious by now. Double-entry accounting led to joint-stock or public companies and ultimately to stock exchanges. Some became so rich from trade that they waged wars, conquered continents and evolved into global empires. It was inevitable, according to the logic of profit. The Ambrose Bierce's Devil's Dictionary defines corporations as "an ingenious device for obtaining profit without individual responsibility." The Dutch East India Company was the world's first joint-stock company while the English East

[13] Jane Gleeson-White, *Double Entry: How The Merchants of Venice Created Modern Finance*, 2012

India Company is considered the birth of the modern corporation. It was the evolution of currency from coin to money that made it all possible.

Back when currency was still coin it had to be stored for safekeeping, because being physical meant it could easily be lost or stolen. Either it was stored with a goldsmith or eventually rich players who became bankers. What they would do is bring the gold in and get a note (signed receipt with a seal) and use that as money to buy things in the market. Others accepted these notes because they trusted the bankers. Anyone could at any time take their note and redeem it for its equivalent value in real coin. This became what money as we know it is today. It was safer because if someone stole it from you they still had to show their face at the bank to get the gold.

If a banker wanted to finance a ship to sail the seas to trade, suddenly they found themselves able to tap into multiple piles of money. They had their own gold they could use. They also had the gold of customer deposits. As just mentioned, it was not safe to carry gold. But now they also had this thing called money which they could create, and nobody except themselves knew how much gold they had so likewise nobody would know if they created more money than actual gold. The more trade one contributes to the more gold they get. As you might expect, these bankers then race to 'invest' money in as much trade as they can.

People aren't stupid though. They trust but verify. If someone began to distrust the banker, they would redeem their notes for their gold, and if too many people did that in a short period of time the banker could run out of gold and be ruined. Banks always lend more than they have. The history of banking is the history of bank runs. Since 1971, banks have simply issued these notes without convertibility to gold or anything at all. So in modern times, since people are depositing money not gold, and the banks lend money, then whose money are they lending, how and how much?

Isn't it strange how something so central to our lives is a tool that is hardly understood by anyone? You probably think you know how money *works*, but we'll see. Take a moment and reflect on what you know about money and how it flows; from whence it comes and goes. On the mysteries of money and the Federal Reserve, Henry Ford, Sr. famously opined: "It is well enough that the people of the nation do not understand our banking and monetary system for, if they did, I believe there would be revolution before tomorrow morning." I'm counting on it.

Most of us experience the game as individual players. How the money flows in our personal lives is all that we see and all that matters to us. The total picture, the macro view, of valves and how money flows is not in focus for most players and certainly beyond our control. From our perspective, the way we earn and spend money is simple but the mechanics of how money flows is said to be too complex for us mere mortals to even understand. In fact, it's easy to understand once we look at diagrams showing how the money flows. We are blind not because we're too stupid to understand or don't care, but rather by willful deception on the part of the bankers.

Here's some cliches we are constantly bombarded with about how our money system works. The Federal Reserve controls the money supply. The FED sets interest rates. When the government spends too much money, the FED turns on the printing press and then we have inflation. Sound familiar? That's what we hear daily on mainstream media.

All these crude generalities continue being either mistaken or too simplistic to describe the reality. The scientific pretensions of economics further confuses the public and politicians with language they can't understand and most economists don't dare translate for them. Unlike myself, *real* economists have to sound scientific to justify their pay, I mean *work*.

"The dominant mode of modern economic analysis mimicked the methods of Newtonian physics by presuming that economic behavior followed its own self-contained logic, rules and patterns as capable of replication as the natural laws that physicists discovered in the physical world. They cloaked their observations in dense, neutral-sounding terminology that was opaque to nonscientists. The neutral language masked the political content of economics and the social rituals of capitalism as if all economic players were simple molecules destined to behave according to the same natural order, regardless of their political values or wealth. All economic decisions were made not to reward one group or to punish another but simply to advance the universal objective of "sound economics."[14] As Galbraith drolly observed: "What is called sound economics is very often what mirrors the needs of the respectably affluent."[15]

By the end of this chapter, you'll know why bankers want us blind. Money isn't just some neutral source of power, it's an instrument which amplifies force and facilitates hoarding. As you learn about the flows the picture will come into focus and you'll see the complexity of the existing circulatory

---

[14] William Greider, *Secrets of the Temple: How the Federal Reserve Runs the Country*, Simon & Schuster, New York, 1987, p.55,56

[15] Galbraith, *Money*

currency (debt money) system. It will soon become visible to you how money is created and deleted all the time.

Do you know about the mechanics of how all money comes into existence from credit, or 'out of thin air'? Probably not. How many people can successfully diagram and account for how money flows? Even after I explain it, it might still be confusing and we will not have answered all possible questions and will not have diagramed all money valves and its flows. That's ok. We don't need to discuss every single valve of the circulatory money system because our ultimate focus is on the primary source of money creation itself: CREDIT. Credit is a faucet that literally creates the majority of the money in the world and yet most people don't even know it exists! "The process by which banks create money is so simple that the mind is repelled," wrote Galbraith. "Where something so important is involved, a deeper mystery seems only decent."[16]

How money is created out of credit is so simple and powerful, yet despite this valve being well hidden, it is not invisible. One more thing: it's called credit because when the faucet opens, free credit flows to bankers who wield this power and responsibility to distribute it as new money in the game.

Currently, most money in use is created by private banks whenever they extend credit. Nations and central banks too also issue some of the money supply (notes and coins). Try as they might, this cannot be made to work in the public interest and causes the following problems: concentrated wealth (inequality), financial instability (boom-bust cycles), ever increasing debt levels and unsustainable development. The power to create money gives banks an unfair advantage over all the other players. Money is the lifeblood of our economy yet how much money is created and where this new money gets allocated is primarily determined by private banks who, *naturally*, operate to maximize their own profits.

As discussed earlier, oil is valuable. The more extracted, the more money its owners collect. That money though, is valuable and represents wealth only if there are other goods to exchange it for. Without a market the money is worthless. If there is more money than goods in the market then prices go up; if too many goods flood the market then prices go down. It doesn't matter which came first, the Property coming into the market from extraction of the commons or Property in the form of money coming into the market from governments and banks. They are both an entrenched part of the existing circulatory flow of value. Where value is circulatory, it sometimes

---

[16] Ibid, p24

moves too slow or too fast and sometimes there are bottlenecks, clogs and restrictions and sometimes build up, bubbles and ruptures or popping altogether. It's all too complex and impossible to maintain any sort of 'equilibrium.'

"The ultimate test of soundness for any science was the ability of its rules and theories to predict outcomes, and by that standard, economics was a crude and underdeveloped discipline. When it's models failed, as they often did, economists grudgingly acknowledged that political impulses or human psychology had somehow disrupted the equations. These events were usually dismissed as "random shocks" - war or political intervention or social upheavals - that need not be explained since they were non-recurring aberrations. War and politics were not abnormal events in human society, only in economics. The reigning scientific perspective of economists, in addition to being severely limited in scope, was also outdated intellectually. Economics mimicked physics, but 20th century physicists had moved beyond the clockwork laws of Newton to the relativity of Einstein, a vastly richer and more supple conception of reality. Economists seemed unable to follow."[17]

The alternative we're introducing here is a new Flow currency system; which doesn't have all the unnecessary valves used in a circulatory system. Kinda like the difference between a gas powered engine and an electric engine. Ultimately, what's important is how currency flows and how it lubricates transactions of the real Property in the game. We'll compare and contrast the two currency systems so you can decide which is easier and better at the end. Now, let's examine how money is created, circulated, and deleted in Game A.

You'll find lots of language referring to money as some kind of liquid flowing, circulating and draining in and out of the economy. Author William Greider describes this perfectly:

> All in all, the financial system resembled the dynamics of a pump house, not an accountant's static balance sheet, and functioned according to physical laws that a hydraulic engineer might understand. It was like a fantastically complicated labyrinth of pipes and storage tanks and boilers, with pressure valves and plumbing and auxiliary pumps, all elaborately interconnected. Inside this system flowed the financial wealth of the nation, back and forth through many channels and tanks, always seeking higher return and less risk, searching out investments that best promised both. To grasp the larger action

[17] Greider, *Secrets of the Temple*, p.56

> of finance, one had to visualize its physics. Indeed, that is how financial analysts themselves spoke of it, using hydraulic metaphors to describe its conditions- the "liquidity" of banks, the "flow of funds" analysis, "circulation" and "float" and "velocity," the surge and ebb of "market pressures."
>
> The Federal Reserve Board stood alongside the system like a governor, like a supervising engineer who had the power to alter the flows inside the plumbing. Its decisions could slacken the pressures of the fluids or intensify them; its policies could stimulate the flow of lending or choke it off or nudge it toward different channels. The FED accomplished this, primarily, by injecting more fluid into the system or withdrawing it— that is, by creating or destroying money. The ability to create money was the power of sovereigns, almost magical in its simplicity. Central banks inherited the power from kings and, before them, the temple priests of ancient civilizations, leaders endowed by God with the authority to consecrate, en fiat, the currency their societies would accept and use. In the technocratic present, the process of money creation remained a powerful mystery to most citizens.[18]

Bankers create and control the flow of all money. "Few people are aware today that the history of the United States, since the Revolution in 1776, has been, in large part, the story of an epic struggle to get free, and stay free, of control by the European international banks. This struggle was finally lost in 1913."[19] Benjamin Franklin, in his autobiography, stated that the prime reason for the American War of Independence was a battle over who actually controlled and issued the money of the new colonies. The fight for power over money creation was at the heart of the French Revolution too, the American Civil War, War of 1812, Russia after 1917 and China after WWII.

Most currencies are now manipulated by a global cadre of central banks who enjoy an audit-exempt monopoly.[20] They continue to remain unaccountable to the public so far. That's by design and it's outrageous. "Permit me to issue and control the money of a nation, and I care not who makes its laws," Mayer Amshcel Rothschild, founder of Rothschild family international banking dynasty.

What a controversial game we're playing. So full of lies. Most people think that banks are merely just intermediaries of money when they are actually creators of it. Now it's time to look at how a modern bank really works.

---

[18] Greider, *Secrets of the Temple*, p.31

[19] Paul Grignon, "Money as Debt" video, https://www.youtube.com/watch?v=4AC6RSau7r8

[20] Cold Fusion, "Who Controls All of Our Money?", https://www.youtube.com/watch?v=mQUhJTxK5mA

Banks

A bank is a corporation that buys assets and securities for profit. It takes in investor money and customer deposit money and invests them. Then they 'lend' money out of credit. That's it. This money they 'lend' comes from credit and represents **new money** in circulation. Oops there it is. Magic money machine. Banks are apex corporations with power to create money.

Banking is so complicated that there are actually three different theories of what a bank is and how it operates. "Some things are hard to understand because they're complicated. Some things are complicated so they'll be hard to understand. The harder you look at the finance industry, the more evident it becomes that the complexity is deliberate, a means of baffling with bullshit."[21] So banking economist Richard Werner conducted an empirical test to find out. His presentation is quite illuminating.[22]

The first theory says they are just financial intermediaries (middlemen), taking in savings as deposits then lending them out at interest. The second, the fractional reserve theory or 'money multiplier' also says each individual bank is an intermediary but that also since many countries require deposit reserves be held at the central bank, in aggregate somehow collectively the banking system creates money. This one is complicated and many people think this is how it works. The third theory is the oldest called the credit creation theory. It says banks are not financial intermediaries but are creators of the money supply and they individually create money when they lend. Werner's test revealed that the third theory is the correct one. Banks are money creators.

The legal reality is that banks don't take in deposits and don't lend money. When you make a deposit at the bank you are legally lending money to the bank. It is now the bank's money. They do not lend out your money. Instead, they invest it for a profit in various assets and securities then share some of it with you. The bank records a credit on your behalf as the customer in the record of its debts. Your loan (deposit) to the bank is their liability. It is money they owe you. It sits on both sides of their balance sheet. On the other side it represents their asset to invest. Nice and neat.

---

[21] Cory Doctorow, https://doctorow.medium.com/a-weapon-of-mass-financial-destruction-f7fc5df7edc9

[22] Richard Werner, https://www.youtube.com/watch?v=KEfdlctvHH4

Nowadays most money is just numbers, but for whose convenience? For the depositor it represents liquid cash. It's always available to transfer or take out whenever you want. When banks go bust your 'deposit' is lost and you have to stand at the back of the line behind other creditors, and by then there won't be anything left for you. That's why the FED created the FDIC, to insure some of your funds and continue this illusion of customers 'depositing' money in the bank for 'safekeeping.'

The FED used to have a 10% deposit reserve requirement, whereby all member banks had to send 10% of their customer deposits to be held by the FED as reserves which could be used to prevent bank runs or in case any member bank defaults. It was because of this requirement that led many people to invent the fractional reserve theory of banking. This reserve system was little more than a clearinghouse for bank deposit reserves – that is, banks used the system to clear transactions within the system as customers moved money around. When money flows in or out of one bank to another such that the amount held at the FED was either too little or too much, these reserves could easily be borrowed by member banks to facilitate overnight smooth flows as needed. And since private banks create most of the money in the system a public clearinghouse is helpful for interbank payment clearing.

But as of March 26, 2020, the deposit reserve requirement is now 0%. You read that correctly: ZERO! It means banks got back their 10% the FED was holding, and they don't have to send any customer deposits to the FED going forward. Banks now have more customer deposits to invest. Strangely, this seemingly major decision by the FED got no attention in the financial press. The FED press release ends with this paragraph: "In light of the shift to an ample reserves regime, the Board has reduced reserve requirement ratios to zero percent effective on March 26, the beginning of the next reserve maintenance period. This action eliminates reserve requirements for thousands of depository institutions and will help to support lending to households and businesses."[23] Note: it doesn't support lending.

Suffice to say, banks do not lend customer deposits outside the banking system![24] This fiction that banks take in deposits and lend them is too ingrained in people's minds, but it's totally false. The internet is full of bank lies and misinformation, even among the major financial media and bankers

---

[23] FED, https://www.federalreserve.gov/newsevents/pressreleases/monetary20200315b.htm

[24] Paul Sheard, Chief Global Economist, Standard and Poor's, Aug. 2013, https://www.hks.harvard.edu/sites/default/files/centers/mrcbg/programs/senior.fellows/2019-20%20fellows/BanksCannotLendOutReservesAug2013_%20(002).pdf

themselves. By paying customers interest on their deposits, banks are able to continue the fantasy that they are merely middlemen, lending your money out for interest and sharing some of it with you. I want you to completely ignore customer deposits. Banks invest your money, they do not lend it out. It's just clearing your money transactions that banks are required to provide. They don't use any of your money for lending. They need it only so they can continue deceiving the public on what is really happening. Banks are running a mathematically rigged currency scheme. And just like in the game of tic-tac-toe, they can't lose.

If banks don't take in deposits and they don't lend money, what the heck do they do? By law, a bank is just another corporation following the Game A logic of profit through trade. It has investors or shareholders who put their money into it in order to profit. The Bank now owns this money called 'bank capital' and it can do whatever it wants with it. They invest it, buy Property (of various 'liquidity'), the same as they do with customer deposits, and as such so too is bank capital also a debt or liability on the balance sheet of the bank; it represents money it owes to others, the owners of the bank. Contrary to what you think, banks are not in the business of lending money. Instead, they are in the business of **buying** assets and securities for profit. And just like any other business, they are very careful on what they buy because it must be something that produces profit and not loss. They invest their bank capital in assets like stocks, bonds, real estate, commodities, treasuries, etc. That's all normal. Any corporation can do that. The real magic happens when they buy 'loan contracts' or others' promises to pay. This is what people typically call 'bank lending' but is a complete misnomer.

Legally, banks do not lend money, they create it. Banking rules allow them to issue new money out of credit based on a multiple of their bank capital (investor deposits, not customer deposits). Banks purchase securities by tapping into free credit. When you go to the bank to borrow $1M for a house, the bank first purchases your loan contract (security) that says you will pay them $1M (+interest), and then they simply create $1M into your account. They record the asset (the IOU, your promise and ability to pay as the security) on their books. They pretend to be loaning out already deposited money. It's an accounting trick but meanwhile $1M of **new money** just entered into circulation.

From the perspective of liquidity and circulation, if your deposit is loaned out to someone else then how could it also be available for you to withdraw all of it? If you lend a friend $100, you will have less liquid money and they will have more. Both parties' cash flow statements have changed, that's the reality of circulation. Only one of you can use this $100 in the game. But the accounting on the balance sheet shows that nobody's net worth changed. How's that possible? Because the $100 wasn't a gift or theft, it was a trade, an equal exchange called a loan, "money now for money later." A barter transaction occurred where you gave them $100 and they gave you an IOU of $100+.

"As the money of account represents the terms in which promises to repay or to engage in exchange are denominated, anyone can create money, so long as one's liabilities are accepted by a counter-party who is a willing participant in a forward contract. Thus, by creating money, one may "spend now, pay later," that is, one may receive something today merely on the promise to deliver "money" tomorrow."[25]

So you see, this $1M 'loan' doesn't come from bank capital or customer deposits, some of which are already invested in other assets and none of which belong to the bank. The $1M came from access to free credit that its bank capital affords and your signature promises. Banks use leverage, legal right of access to credit to purchase 'securities' which creates the money. So where does money come from? **It's all credit**. We do not have a fixed and stable currency system. We have a credit system in which money is created and destroyed by private banks constantly. Money is created as a deposit when the bank makes a loan and is deleted when the loan is repaid, as explained in detail by the Bank of England: "**Whenever a bank makes a loan, it simultaneously creates a matching deposit in the borrower's bank account, thereby creating new money.** The reality of how money is created today differs from the description found in some economics textbooks: Rather than banks receiving deposits when households save and then lending them out, bank lending creates deposits."[26]

This means banks don't need your money to extend loans since loans create deposits.[27] The NY FED, one of twelve private US regional reserve banks, made this clear in 1977: "Commercial banks create checkbook money

---

[25] L. Randall Wray, "Introduction to an Alternative History of Money", 2012, https://www.levyinstitute.org/pubs/wp_717.pdf

[26] Michael McLeay et al, "Money creation in the modern economy", https://www.bankofengland.co.uk/-/media/boe/files/quarterly-bulletin/2014/money-creation-in-the-modern-economy.pdf

[27] Cullen Roche, Pragmatic Capitalism, https://www.pragcap.com/loans-create-deposits-in-context/

whenever they grant a loan, simply by adding new deposit dollars in accounts on their books in exchange for a borrower's IOU."[28] Each and every time a bank makes a loan, the laws of double-entry accounting require them to create a new account for the borrower and make a deposit equal to the loan amount. It is reported that 97% of money comes into circulation through commercial banks extending credit while calling them 'loans.' Here's Richard Werner in his own words:

> When someone goes to a bank to borrow money the bank provides the individual with a promissory note. When the customer signs the promissory note the bank sees that note exactly as money. "An unconditional promise to pay is money". So the bank deposits this promissory note into a TRANSACTION ACCOUNT and from there the ENDOGENOUS FUNDS are produced to write the check for the loan. The endogenous money does not come from deposits. There is no fractional reserve lending. Presently there is 1.39 trillion exogenous dollars created by the government, and the banks create 12 trillion + of endogenous money. There is no multiplicity effect. What is wrong with this?
>
> 1) If a signed promissory note is exactly the same as money well… I could sign a promissory note and buy a new car, or a house. In fact everybody could do it. They don't need to pay it back because the promissory note is itself "money". Soon the entire economy will collapse because no one would want to work when they can simply issue promissory notes just like the commercial banks do.
>
> 2) Banks get rights to a house/car/business when someone signs for a loan but they have done nothing to get the house/car/business. All they did was an accounting trick.
>
> 3) The media and schools are controlled by bankers, otherwise this would be common knowledge.
>
> 4) Banks do not tell "borrowers" that they are providing the funds for the loan. In a proper contract full disclosure is required.
>
> 5) Most of our money is created by debt; It is a promise to pay. So we will never get out of debt. Most people won't have enough capital to start their own business and savings will be dismal.
>
> 6) The bankers control the housing market and will price homes out of the reach of most people.
>
> 7) When a promissory note is paid off, it loses value. Fulfillment voids the value of a promissory note. This causes the money supply to shrink. It means that we are going to be forever in debt if we are to have money.

---

[28] Federal Reserve Bank of New York; Friedman, David H. (1977). *I bet you thought …* p. 19

> Signature. It is your signature that creates new money. The minute you sign the loan for anything, a brand new deposit is created. ("every new loan is a new deposit" Bank of England). No, the bank did not loan you their money or money from any of their customers, they're not allowed to do that. Brand new money is created from your signature, from your valuable energy that eventually you'll pay back but the bank doesn't have to wait till you do, it's insured anyway, another sleight of hand (scam).[29]

For economists, endogenous means from within. In Werner's example, he is saying that the money customers borrow doesn't come from outside the bank (from investor or customer deposits), but rather from within the bank itself. It comes from credit or 'out of nothing.' Remember when Tom took free clay from the commons, molded it into pottery and sold that to Sam for an IOU? Here we have the bank getting free credit (fictional property from the commons), doing absolutely nothing to improve it and selling it to borrowers for an IOU.

Congressman Charles Lindbergh Sr., former banker and member of the House Banking & Currency Committee, said of this monetary system in 1913: "The banks have been granted the special privilege of distributing the money, and they charge as much as they wish... This is the strangest, most dangerous advantage ever placed in the hands of a special privilege class by any government that ever existed."[30]

When more loans are being created than are being repaid, the money supply inflates. When fewer loans are being created than are being repaid, the money supply shrinks, a phenomenon called 'debt deflation.' Either way, our money supply is in a chronic state of deflation, due to the way money comes into existence. Banks create the principal but not the interest needed to repay their loans, so more money is always owed back than was created in the original loans. Thus debt must always grow faster than the money supply.

They're able to do this because banks are allowed leverage to lend much more money than they have. Not to get too technical so I'll explain briefly. Let's use the fictional Apex Bank as an example. It has $1M in bank capital. The Central Bank sets the capital requirements for the private banks based on their size; it might be 8%, 6% or 4% today, but let's say it's 10% for simplicity. Apex must have bank capital assets of at least 10% relative to the size of

---

[29] Richard Werner, https://professorwerner.org/

[30] Congressional Record: 63rd Congress, 2nd Session, Vol, LI .Pg. 1450, Washington DC, 1914.

credit (loans) it issues. That means Apex, with $1M in bank capital, is leveraged to buy securities called 'loan contracts' worth at least $10M. Or said another way, it can 'loan' out up to $10M in new money out of credit. Notice, this amount of how much leverage (credit the bank can tap into) is based on actual investor bank capital.

Here's how that works in practice: A customer comes in and wants $1M to buy a house. Apex does due diligence to make sure the house is valued correctly and the buyer has enough income to pay off the loan. The more creditworthy the borrower, the less risky the 'loan', the less 'bank capital' is required.[31] The correct way to look at this transaction is as if Apex itself is buying the house and renting it out to the buyer until they pay it back plus interest. If the borrower defaults, Apex still owns the house. All loans are 'secured' one way or another because banks are not in the business of losing money, especially money that they don't even have. Imagine if they didn't secure the loan and lost $1M. All investor bank capital would be lost, bankrupting them with just one loss.

Banks use leverage when they issue more loans (credit) than actual investor capital in the bank. The same access to leverage is given to regular people too in brokerage trading accounts. With a $1M margin account, you get 4-1 leverage, which means you can buy up to $4M worth of stock like Nike or Apple. And if you were to open a currency trading account, you can get 100-1 leverage, which means you could control up to $100M of money to buy and sell currencies. Whenever leverage is used, it's not borrowing existing money from someone else, but rather new money 'out of thin air.'

Out of free credit banks create money, a real Property they rent out for interest. By getting free credit and issuing it as secured debt, the bank is the ultimate owner of everything belonging to the debtors. In America, people who buy homes with bank credit are counted as 'homeowners' but that's obviously a lie. The bank still owns the home while the borrower owns the risk. As long as debtors are repaying, the bank collects the interest from their labor. If the debtor defaults, the bank is entitled to claim their possessions. Banks don't lose. Tic-tac-toe.

If the borrower puts down 20% or more, it's less risky and so that 'loan' costs them only half of their capital requirement which uses only 5% of their

---

[31] FED, https://www.federalreserve.gov/newsevents/pressreleases/bcreg20130702a.htm, "Banks and regulators use risk weighting to assign different levels of risk to different classes of assets--riskier assets require higher capital cushions and less risky assets require smaller capital cushions."

bank capital according to banking regulations. Meaning, Apex can issue up to $20M of AAA rated mortgage loans. The risk of the loan determines how much leverage they have. For example, loans to local, state or federal government entities have either low capital requirements or none because presumably lending to the government is risk free. If the government can't pay its debt then really the whole thing has collapsed anyway. This is why municipal bonds of cities and states in America are highly coveted by banks. It's like free interest collection at no risk and at no cost.

Think back on what happened in 2008 when home loans originally rated as AAA were found to be Junk and thus had to be re-rated. All of a sudden the capital requirements of banks needed to be adjusted and uh oh, many banks were found to not have enough bank capital because they lent out more than they were supposed to. To make matters worse, the value of their investments (assets) also began to go down, further reducing their bank capital. This caused major currency flow blockages throughout the banking system which required some unusual FED maneuvers. Since the FED makes its own rules and it too has access to unlimited free credit, this was not a problem it couldn't solve.[32] What they did is to tap into free credit to buy up all the 'toxic' or under-capitalized assets of their member banks, thereby relieving their bank capital requirements. This was called 'quantitative easing' (QE) and they are now back at it once again.

On March 15, 2020 screenshot of my phone: Since QE is money that reads: FED announces unlimited money. QE comes from credit and credit is just numbers and numbers are unlimited.

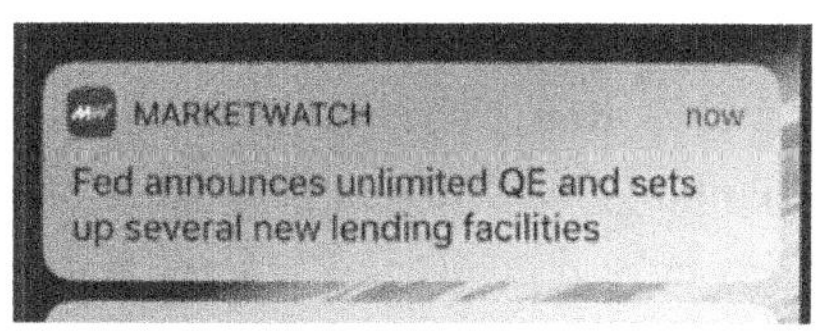

The FED says right on their website that "The Federal Reserve System is not "owned" by anyone," however its profits flow to the US Treasury.[33] "In addition, decisions of the Board— and the Fed's monetary policy-setting body, the Federal Open Market Committee — do not require approval by the President or anyone else in the executive or legislative branches of government." None have the power to audit them. The FED does pay independent accountants and makes available to the government reports of its finances. Are they telling the truth? Nobody

---

[32] Modern Monetary Theory (MMT)— espoused by Randall Wray, Bill Mitchell, Warren Mosler, Stephanie Kelton et al— describes how national and global monetary systems actually work in practice. Telling the truth is controversial.

[33] FED, https://www.federalreserve.gov/faqs/about_14986.htm

knows. The original powers of the FED were to set rules and monitor private bank reserves and to control the interest rates. Nowadays, they actively buy Treasuries, Bonds, and, like the central bank of Japan, probably stocks too. Again, nobody really knows.

Did you know there is a global bank for central banks? That's what the Bank for International Settlements calls itself. It is owned by 63 central banks representing 95% of all GDP according to their website.[34]

Just so you know, when the US spends more than it taxes, the FED pretends to get money by selling Treasury Bonds or as is primarily the case today, it buys them itself from money it gets as credit (out of thin air). It pays interest on these bonds to itself and to its member banks, other Nations and rich players. Risk free interest. Thomas Edison observed in 1921: "If our nation can issue a dollar bond, it can issue a dollar bill. The element that makes the bond good makes the bill good also… It is absurd to say that our country can issue $30,000,000 in bonds and not $30,000,000 in currency. Both are promises to pay… If the currency issued by the Government were no good, then the bonds issued would be no good either… If the Government issues bonds, the brokers will sell them. The bonds will be negotiable: they will be considered as gilt-edged paper. Why? Because the Government is behind them, but who is behind the Government? The people. Therefore it is the people who constitute the basis of Government credit. **Why then cannot the people have the benefit of their own credit by receiving non-interest bearing currency?**"

U.S. Rep. Wright Patman (1893–1976) Chair, House Committee on Banking and Currency said in 1942: "I have never yet had anyone who could, through the use of logic and reason, justify the Federal Government borrowing the use of its own money. ... I believe the time will come in this country when [the public] will actually blame you and me and everyone else connected with the Congress for sitting idly by and permitting such an idiotic system to continue."

Why does the FED continue to pretend it needs to borrow money? Like Bernanke said, "long term tradition." In a 2006 interview famed economist and winner of the 1976 "Nobel Prize" in Economics says, "The difficulty of having people understand monetary theory is very simple: The central banks are good at press relations, the central banks employ a large fraction of economists. So there is a bias to tell the case, the story, in a way favorable to

[34] Bank for International Settlements, https://www.bis.org/bcbs/basel3.htm

the central banks."[35] Of course they don't want the public to know that all money is bank made and that it all comes from credit. They need us to believe that money just is and that banks are just neutral agents. Because if we knew that all money is credit, we might demand democratic control and take away their power. Banks are apex corporations and they like it that way.

"The modern banking system manufactures "money" out of nothing; and the process is, perhaps, the most, astounding piece of "sleight of hand" that was ever invented. In fact, it was not invented. It merely "grew". ... Banks in fact are able to create (and cancel) modern "deposit money", just as much as they were originally able to create, or call in, their own original forms of private notes. They can, in fact, inflate and deflate, i.e., mint, and un-mint the modern "ledger-entry" currency."[36]

What we do know is that all new money created always impacts the economy. This is massive power. "In both subtle and obvious ways, the national monetary and financial systems influence nearly every aspect of our lives. The volume of money influences the inflation rate and cost of credit. The very design of the financial system, particularly the profit motive that drives it, influences which businesses receive funding, what they make, and how their workers and the environment are treated. To the degree that the financial system produces extreme wealth for some, it also affects politics; political and financial power are deeply intertwined. Very few aspects of modern life remain untouched by the monetary and financial systems."[37]

This power of banks to manipulate the economy is not new but it seems that the average person today doesn't even know this power exists. Many really believe banks are mere middlemen. "Keeping the public divided along racial, religious, ideological and partisan lines does nothing but serve the interests of the money power by distracting the American people from the underlying causes of social and economic despair. Monetary reform provides a critical unifying metanarrative for those concerned about addressing injustice and expanding American prosperity beyond the financial elite," said Reverend Delman Coates, senior pastor of Mt. Ennon Baptist Church, Clinton, Maryland on October 1, 2016 at the American Monetary Institute.

---

[35] Russell Roberts, "An Interview With Milton Friedman," Recorded Interview, July 2006, published August 28, 2006 for the Library of Economics and Liberty, https://www.econtalk.org/milton-friedman-on-money/

[36] Lawrence Lee Bazley Angas, 1937, *Slump ahead in bonds*, Somerset Pub. Co. pp20-21.

[37] John C. Boik, *Economic Direct Democracy*, 2014, p. 110

People in the 1700s all the way to the mid 1900s knew all too well about bank credit. A couple of weeks before he was assassinated in 1881, then President James A. Garfield observed similar: "Whoever controls the volume of money in our country is absolute master of all industry and commerce, and when you realize that the entire system is very easily controlled, one way or another, by a few powerful men at the top, you will not have to be told how periods of inflation and depression originate."

Every assassination, every war and everything terrible in the world is because of banking and the power of currency, especially in the form of debt based circulatory money. "And I sincerely believe with you, that banking establishments are more dangerous than standing armies; & that the principle of spending money to be paid by posterity, under the name of funding, is but swindling futurity on a large scale."[38] Senator Bronson Cutting summarized this when he said in 1934 that, effectively, "the bankers are collecting tribute [profit] from the community on the community's credit."

Why don't the bankers and the financial regulators recognize and change this system? Most are specialized engineers too busy operating the pump house and they probably don't even recognize the machinery for what it is. "The few who understand the system will either be so interested in its profits or be so dependent upon its favours that there will be no opposition from that class, while on the other hand, the great body of people, mentally incapable of comprehending the tremendous advantage that capital derives from the system, will bear its burdens without complaint, and perhaps without even suspecting that the system is inimical to their interests," wrote the Rothschild brothers of London to associates in New York in 1863. Indeed, our central bank employs over 1,000 economists.

And that concludes our lesson on Game A money and economics. Hopefully you have a better understanding of how money and economics works so now we shift our focus to our proposed alternative. The questions before us are how to reimagine the ownership and control of all Property (the means of production) and the currency (the unit of measure). Next I reveal the details of the common planet approach to both of these.

Even us outsiders trying to reimagine a new system have to contend with psychology. Gabrielle Adams at the University of Virginia and colleagues asked people to complete several tasks where solutions involved either adding or subtracting parts. All of the experiments were designed so that subtraction

---

[38] Thomas Jefferson, 3rd US President, in a letter to John Taylor in 1816, https://founders.archives.gov/documents/Jefferson/03-10-02-0053

would be one of the most efficient options, yet participants still preferred adding. She said that this tendency to add complexity may cause us to miss potentially superior options and designs. "Addition may be culturally valued. It's easier to demonstrate your contribution with an addition than a subtraction, and additions might get more praise."[39] You will find this alternative currency system much simpler— even a child can understand— and for this reason I suspect almost all high-paid (credentialed) 'economists' will call me a crank or some variation of that. The higher up these folks the louder will be their howls.

Graph from Subir Grewal's 2020 book *Struggling Amidst Plenty:*

[39] New Scientist, "People are bae at spotting simple solutions to problems.", https://www.newscientist.com/article/2273931-people-are-bad-at-spotting-simple-solutions-to-problems

Common Property

It is believed that someone must own a thing. This is why we have our dominant ideologies today split along this question of who should own and therefore control things. Capitalists on the one side championing that of private ownership and Socialists on the other championing that of collective ownership. The Capitalists insist that socialism distorts the allocation of resources causing market deficiencies and the Socialists in turn insist that capitalism distorts the allocation of resources causing market disruptions. So who is right? They are both right and they are both wrong. Neither was able to separate the value of people from the prices of things in a game where the things are the primary source of value.

Leo Tolstoy believed that, "Solving the land question means the solving of all social questions... possession of land by people who do not use it is immoral - just like the possession of slaves."

Communism thought it had the right formulation to solve this problem, recognizing that all revolution is Land, but it did not change where value derived from and it couldn't evolve away from commodity currency without the existence of secure databases to produce the trust as the glue to hold it all together. It too merely concentrated power in the name of claiming all the Property as 'the peoples', took over Corporations and what remained was just the State, still playing Game A against other players.

The assumption that capitalism or socialism (or some combo of the two) are the only possible economic order is unquestioned in academia and society in general. "Neither system, however, empowers and liberates every person within it. Both systems are structured to concentrate opportunity, ownership, and power in a few hands— whether in private hands (as in capitalism), or in the State (as in socialism). Such concentration inevitably breeds poverty, corruption, and conflict. What few academics, politicians, or media gurus have considered seriously is whether there can be a moral and truly democratic alternative—a "Just Third Way"—that transcends both capitalism and socialism," says the Center for Economic and Social Justice. I very much admire the work of Norm Kurland and his team at CESJ.org.

If I hadn't imagined a new currency system I'd be promoting their proposal in combination with Henry George's Land Value Tax as the best possible version of Game A. Their model of 'own or be owned' (citizen ownership of the central bank and ½ stock of public corporations) would distribute wealth from production fairly to citizens and in combination with a more fair taxation of excessive wealth from land ownership, it would produce a more equitable Game A.

But we can move beyond that now with the help of modern computers, into global Common Property. "The equal right of all to the use of land is as clear as the equal right to breathe the air—it is a right proclaimed by the fact of existence. For we cannot suppose that some have a right to be in this world, and others no right," proclaimed Henry George.

Kai Heron encapsulates this problem and solution for us in his brilliant Twitter thread from October 2021:

> Sometimes the obvious needs saying. Common land ownership and #LandBack aren't just moral necessities to address prior (and ongoing) injustices of settler genocide, slavery, dispossession, enclosure, and clearance. They're an urgent ecological and social necessity. Here's why. Right now the ecological and social harms of capital accumulation are socialized. Think, for example of pollution, poor health, hunger, biodiversity loss, government subsidies to fossil fuel and agro industries, soil erosion, desertification... and, of course, the climate crisis. While the social product — accumulated wealth, knowledge and infrastructures — is privatized to be used or put back into circulation as capital in pursuit of further private accumulation (causing further social and ecological harms in the process). The fight for common land ownership reverses this. Our accumulated wealth, knowledge and infrastructures are socialized, while the price for socializing them is privatized: expropriating the expropriators, as Marx put it. When land is managed as a private asset in the pursuit of capital accumulation, short-term profit maximization is prioritized over long-term land stewardship. Capitalists are compelled to act this way or go out of business. The result is dispossession, exploitation, domination, and ecological deterioration. Everything we know and suffer from today. No amount of ethical consumption or investment, no amount of greening capital accumulation or planting trees can reverse this. In contrast, when land is managed as an intergenerational commons, to be maintained, repaired, and passed on to future generations, we are empowered to manage it in ecologically benign ways to deliver what Ariel Salleh calls 'eco-sufficiency' for all. Or socialized wealth. As Indigenous, African and Asian scholars, militants and organizers have argued, this way of managing the land accords with many non-European traditions of land management. But it's also present in the communist tradition — even the European one. Italian communist Amadeo Bordiga, for example, wrote explicitly about the need to treat land as an intergenerational commons. This is one reason why anti-colonial Marxists and Euro-American internationalists put the land and agrarian questions at the forefront of their struggles. As Fanon says: "For a colonized people, the most essential value, because it is the most meaningful, is first and foremost the land: the land, which must provide bread and, naturally, dignity."

> Collective care, repair, and management of land, in accordance with a democratically determined plan of (re)production is therefore essential to both the struggle for reparations and the struggle for a world in which human and non-human life can flourish. Anyone paying attention to COP26 in the coming weeks will see these questions fastidiously avoided. Already governments are working with landowners to ensure their private interests are placed above social and ecological necessities. It's a disaster made and in the making.[40]

Table 1: Cosmo-Local Production. Source: Ramos (2017): [41]

Table 1: Cosmo-Local Production. Source: Ramos (2017)

	Traditional manufacturing enterprise	Distributed manufacturing enterprise (neo-liberal global factory)	Cosmo-localization
IP / knowledge sharing regime	Held by one company	Held by one company or consortium (e.g. Apple)	Shared under open or CC or Peer Production licence etc.
Location of manufacturing	A single of local manufacturing center	Global factory, wherever the product can be most cheaply and effectively produced, elements of product can be produced	Globally distributed networks of localized manufacturing, depending on take up and use of global design commons
Transport and trade	Product sent from local manufacturing centers to other places	Parts move across many countries and once assembled are shipped for trade	Requires development of localized production ecosystems for complex manufacturing, Micro-manufacturing clusters
Enterprise model	Publicly Listed Corp., Family Owned Corp., Nationalized Corp..	Corporation or consortium with complex supply and distribution ecosystem	Open value network model, Platform Cooperatives, Maker spaces, Phyles / Transnational collectives

Flow Currency - Credit

What if instead nobody owned the value of common things and the currency just flowed to people directly? Those who manage the things collect currency directly for their contributions. Everybody gets currency as UBI then earns more currency for putting things into the fridge. When the currency flows to all, everybody can enter the fridge because everybody will always have currency. Things will still have value. Some things will still have a price. People will still compete to produce things, not because they have to, rather because they want to. People will use their currency to select things from the fridge. Those items then become private personal possessions and the currency simply deletes; it has nobody to circulate to because nobody owns the value of the things in the fridge. They came from the Commons.

---

[40] Kai Heron, https://twitter.com/KaiHeron/status/1450525673890648067

[41] Michel Bauwens, Jose Ramos and Rok Kranjc, "P2P: Towards a Commons Economics", https://wiki.p2pfoundation.net/Mutualizing_Urban_Provisioning_Systems

The currency flows into existence, is used in the market and deletes. We account for things in the market, rewarding more currency to those whose items are the most popular or the best on multiple metrics of our choosing, and likewise can send stop signals (shut off currency flows) to producers whose items suck.

So what is Common Planet? It is two things:

1 All common Property becomes the common heritage of all humans It will be 'owned' by nobody and everybody. Everything is accounted for in open, transparent databases. We the people make democratic decisions, managing the commons (what to put in the fridge). From there, the people produce whatever they and their fellows want.

2. Flow currency: Credit flows to all and does not circulate as Property.

Money as Property is definitely one of the core Game A features that is a major problem and can finally be changed today only because we can use computers to create trusted, unalterable, indestructible records for the currency system. "Money is so defining of our civilization that it would be naive to hope for any authentic civilizational shift that did not involve a fundamental shift in money as well," says Charles Eisenstein. But this time, the currency must be only as a unit of exchange, not Property itself. This way, the currency can be distributed fairly, transparently and it doesn't ever require re-distribution.

With this new formulation of Flow currency there is an opportunity to create a new economic equation: one that creates value directly in people and not based on values of Property... basically, if we issue the currency directly to each person and stop competing and extracting for value from prices of Property, we can then use this currency to compete for the limited resources that are extracted/produced from the Commons, in a fair game which would neuter our 'natural human nature' to amass power which has historically always been represented by Property (land & money). Property becomes distributed fairly thus its power is neutered and the concentrated power of currency issuance (banking) is eliminated altogether.

Common Planet is a new equation that begins value with humans and it would enable, finally, implementation of the Universal Declaration of

Human Rights.[42] It is a new game of value, where the value (Credit currency) flows to all. Credit is a Flow currency, not circulatory like money. Credit is infinite. Credit is distributed equally as UBI, as well as directly to people when they learn, play and work. Credit flows to all and all use it in the open market.

No longer will humans be valueless or useless; always having Credit currency means always having access to a true free market. Individuals and their community get to determine together, for themselves, when, where, or how they want to participate or produce in the market. Then, this value, this Credit currency, is used in the open market of goods produced from the commons whose prices determine allocation of how the real Property is managed, for once. Here, the prices alone do not determine the real value. Prices are just market information to value production not to value people.

Here's what we propose: Delete all debts. Give every person a new digital Credit account with a guaranteed personal starting balance based on an equal amount times their age. Let people convert most of their current net worth over too. To recognize that all humans have value, give every person a monthly UBI and allow anyone to collect more Credit when they provide more value. A Proof of Value (POV) game so when people learn, play or work, they collect the Credit directly.

Credit is created to recognize and incentivize real value. Individuals and local communities decide amongst themselves— using the global protocols— to determine what is valuable. Credit flows in when earned and deletes when used in exchange for limited goods or activities.

This new economics makes individuals sovereign. It gives everybody the agency with which to control their identity, to become present in society. Today, having to compete, we find ourselves in a disconnected set of disparate spaces in the digital world. Using different online identities for social media, financial, shopping, gaming and all kinds of pay-for accounts (rentierism). There is no connection.

Instead, we can provide a real sense of belonging to a community populated by real people with real agency, real recognition and real accountability. Decentralized and distributed. No single organization will build it. It will be constructed collectively using something like Holochain technology: an interlocking set of interoperating parts using Credit currency as the standard global unit of value.

---

42 United Nations, https://www.un.org/en/about-us/universal-declaration-of-human-rights

On the positive, humanity is so lucky right now to have access to incredible technological tools and capabilities once shifted morally. The population we have could be an asset, instead of the liability it is seen as today, since the new game will allow each person to self actualize with maximum opportunity. Smart, creative people are the best hope we have to solve the problems already baked in. Game A does not flow value to all humans so they can't exercise their abilities and reach their potential. Instead, far too many are not allowed to even participate.

Credit is not a finite *thing* or circulatory like the money system we just described. When Credit is created it doesn't come from someone else's pile. Credit is direct currency creation when you earn it in a true meritocracy. There are no taxes or redistribution schemes necessary either. Just simple standard fair distribution. Anyone is free to do and to collect directly. There is no limit to how much Credit can be produced in the world; just as there is no limit to money in a circulatory regime. You can create work that you wish gets done, and anyone who does it collects the Credit for it. **The Credit is designed as a unit of exchange for your personal use only and deletes upon use so there are no banks, taxes, stocks, insurance, no inflation, loss, theft, corruption, or coercion. None of those complicated and useless value flows exist in a Flow currency system.**

Credit flows to all and all use it to buy things made from the commons, or to trade personal possessions. That's it. It'll be that simple for most people. As per Enterprise accounting (detailed in chapter 5), Credit transactions reveal the accounting, with price information used to allocate resources based on signals from our needs and desires for the limited goods in the open market. Credit currency also facilitates trade of existing private goods (and art), but it is created by the contributions of the people themselves, not via profit from trade.

You get credit for doing things (living) and then it is deleted when you spend it on things in the market or on limited activities and events like sports or concerts and the like.

Credit is like a token currency. It is not property like money, so it cannot be transferred to another directly without an exchange of some other real property. This non-transferable feature strips away the evil power of money as it exists today. It eliminates almost all coercion, corruption and robbery. What it means is: you will not be able to use your Credit currency to control other people. It is only a unit of account to acquire or trade personal possessions. Nobody can and nobody will any longer attempt to take your

Credit or your possessions. For if they ever could and did, it would show up in your account and in their account because Credit and Property have digital records. Besides, nobody will ever run out of and be desperate for Credit because they get more every month as UBI and more every time they participate in society. Credit just flows into your life periodically. How much depends on how much you contribute.

Life becomes one long game of you deciding when and where to contribute your time and your life and this new transparent economic protocol makes it all work, seamlessly. No more stressing out over how you're going to get money in order to live. Instead, your challenge will be how to live or rather, what to do with your time. It will be like Jean-Paul Sartre said: "Everything has been figured out, except how to live." Instead, you will pay attention to what really matters to you personally, and to the stuff and activities your community has, needs or wants. We will finally pay attention to managing the real resources behind the numbers used to represent value, and not just the numbers like we do today.

"...humanity then will have recognized and organized itself to realize effectively the fact that humanity can afford to do anything it needs and wishes to do and that it cannot afford anything else. As a consequence Earth-planet-based humanity will be physically and economically successful and individually free in the most important sense. While all enjoy total Earth no human will be interfering with the other, and none will be profiting at the expense of the other. Humans will be free in the sense that 99.9 per cent of their waking hours will be freely investable at their own discretion. They will be free in the sense that they will not struggle for survival on a "you" or "me" basis, and will therefore be able to trust one another and be free to co-operate in spontaneous and logical ways."[43]

There is incentive to create, invent, work and produce still. Not by force. You don't have to, but you can if you want to. Individuals join or form cooperative Enterprises to produce products or services for two reasons: first, they get to collect Credit for the value of their labor directly, and second, they are awarded more Credit based on new metrics of profit, which is no longer based on only the differential of prices from trade. Instead, we can reorient Enterprise incentives (currency flows) towards competing to

---

[43] Buckminster Fuller, *Operating Manual For Spaceship Earth*, 1969, p. 34

produce based on *Cradle to Cradle*[44] metrics like those of *Doughnut Economics*[45]. The workers run and *own* the Enterprise[46], so-to-speak, and they split these Bonus Credit allocations for their direct contributions. The new accounting is information used to determine allocation of resources and which Enterprises people actually need and want becomes our new reality.

This kind of equation places value creation where it belongs, in people, and not to incentivize simple value extraction from the commons like today. Edward Snowden lamented recently: "Sometimes I try to imagine a world where scientific young minds enjoyed greater rewards for revolutionizing, like, farming methods, manufacturing, or energy, rather than the dark patterns used to optimize ad-clicks at Google and Facebook. How did we get here?"[47] We got here because we confuse prices for real value.

In professional sports, it doesn't matter if the score ends 1-0 or 7-0, the teams are awarded the *real* points based on outcome of the game, not on the differential of the score. Winners get 3 points, losers get zero, and each gets 1 point for a tie. That is standard protocol in many sports. And none of those points come at the expense of the other teams: they are created 'out of thin air' the same as currency. They exist only in our collective minds or as records if stored in databases. But the currency points which circulate in Game A are serious. They are possessions. Individuals and teams compete forever to capture more of the money from each other, even though all money is actually created out of thin air, just like points are in sports.

And like sports teams, companies too have differential powers. Just because they are able to manipulate the accounting to produce the most profit— like the score of a game— shouldn't result in them getting the most currency. Profit should be based on the real value of the result of their production or service.

Should a company be rewarded only for being able to trade as much as possible, at maximum price differential? That's the equation of Game A. Or should they be rewarded based on other more important metrics? Do you want companies to produce the most profitable product— which mostly rewards already rich owners— or do you want them to produce the best

---

[44] William McDonough and Michael Braungart, *Cradle to Cradle*, 2002

[45] Kate Raworth, *Doughnut Economics*, https://doughnuteconomics.org/

[46] Michael Albert, Participatory Economics (Parecon), https://participatoryeconomy.org/, https://participatoryeconomics.info/

[47] Edward Snowden, Twitter, https://twitter.com/Snowden/status/1451342274667876353

possible product for the real stakeholders: the workers, consumers and society? Products with the best quality, sustainable, reusable, upgradable, recyclable, etc. Game A makes no distinctions and in fact it does not allow for any other metrics besides profit as measured by the result from crude accounting of trade.

This often leads to planned obsolescence, where products are made intentionally to not last, to be thrown away so more transactions and more production and more trade can be taken advantage of because profit is the only measure incentivized today. What in the hell are we incentivizing?

Maybe these bad externalities were tolerable with fewer people, but today it's downright suicidal. It's all about consumption for the sake of production. That's totally backwards. Growth for the sake of growth is cancer. You know what really pisses me off, it's calling these things externalities as if they aren't the direct result of the existing game. They are external only to current owners of business, but they directly affect all life on Earth.

Bret Weinstein warned about the dangers of profit seeking in a 2012 TEDx talk:

> The central flaw in our system… our global system, with the US at its head, what we have here are feedback loops that interact. Wealth that is made in the market is capable of increasing one's power over regulation. Power over regulation allows increased opportunity to make money in the market. This is a positive feedback loop that should scare any engineer or biologist because positive feedback loops that are not bounded by some negative feedback force are unstable, they detonate, they explode. In our case this feedback loop has re-engineered our system cryptically and turned it into an engine for the concentration of wealth and power. It has installed, amongst us, an unelected group of very powerful and wealthy people, effective veto power over any attempt to change from the status quo. So, many people I know from experience can accept this logic when it comes to corporations. What happens though when you try to explain that this logic actually is not sensitive to scale, that it applies equally to nations, and even more troublingly, to people is that the mind wants to repel, it doesn't want to believe it."[48]

Nowhere is this for-profit measure of Game A producing more disgusting incentives than in healthcare. Research goes into drugs that can treat illness but not cure them. When drugs are discovered, their knowledge is kept secret, not shared, sometimes even quashed altogether as patents get bought

[48] Bret Weinstein, TEDx, "The Personal Responsibility Vortex", https://www.youtube.com/watch?v=SjNRtrZjkfE

and technologies are left to die and never see the light. It costs almost nothing to produce most drugs yet they are sold at maximum price and withheld from those who need them, leaving people to suffer and die.

And then there is the equally, if not more, deadly energy sector. How much dependence on oil is due to this profit incentive we have? Do you really believe we couldn't have more or better energy options by now?[49] Why do you think they burned down Nikola Tesla's lab? Is our transportation infrastructure built efficiently or to further production, consumption and waste? Is all this burning of fossil fuels and CO2 even necessary? Yes, it is, according to Game A profit dictates. It's in the game!

It does not allow *investment* toward solutions that can't be *profitable*. It does not allow solutions if they reduce profit, reduce consumption, reduce waste, increase efficiency, reusability, or any solutions that benefit consumers or society because it interferes with the total necessity and zeal of individual players to pursue profit, or be rendered useless. Profit is the multipolar trap.

A bank has to *invest* its credit in profit making enterprises. It can't invest in people who want to invent cures for diseases or for a sustainable, free energy system. People would benefit tremendously yet the economic game of circulatory money would collapse. It's all about the money honey.

We have the most miraculous machines, yet how come most of our products don't seem to last very long? You know why. The need to constantly sell more shit. These are not fake conspiracies. This is happening more than we know. Have you heard of the Phoebus Cartel[50] (lightbulb manufacturers), who, almost 100 years ago, monopolized the markets in their global regions, got together (conspired), met and set prices and standards so nobody produces long lasting light bulbs.[51] The cartel lowered the life expectancy of light bulbs to 1,000 hours— down from 2,500 hours at that time— and raised prices without worry of competition. The cartel tested their bulbs and fined manufacturers for bulbs that lasted more than 1,000 hours.

Are today's global monopolies any different? Apple's slogan was 'think different' but is Apple any different? Of course not. They are the epitome of planned obsolescence, waste and greed. Apple's entire business model is

---

[49] The Guardian, "Oil and coal-rich countries lobbying to weaken UN climate report, leak shows" , https://www.theguardian.com/environment/2021/oct/21/oil-and-coal-rich-countries-lobbying-to-weaken-un-climate-report-leak-shows

[50] Why All Lightbulbs Are Designed To Break, https://www.youtube.com/watch?v=-kIpX4MkMOs

[51] NPR, https://www.npr.org/2019/03/27/707188193/the-phoebus-cartel

designed to make products that need replacement so they can sell more again and again because that is what the current *profit* metric rewards. Profit incentives drive behavior, full stop.

There is no doubt that the oil cartels (US, Russia, Saudi Arabia, and gang) are among the most damaging and dangerous group of people to ever walk this Earth. They may not know or care who are the ones pulling all the strings, the ones at the top of this shit pile, stand the bankers. In just five years since the Paris Agreement, the world's 60 biggest banks flooded fossil fuel projects with $3.8 trillion of financing, according to a report from the Rainforest Action Network and the Sierra Club.[52] This 1970s newspaper cartoon captures this predicament perfectly:

Even the famous American 'father of modern linguistics' and philosopher Noam Chomsky can't describe these psychopaths: "I don't know what word in the English language— I can't find one— that applies to people who are willing to sacrifice the literal existence of organized human life so they can put a few more dollars into highly overstuffed pockets. The word 'evil' doesn't begin to approach it." They can't help themselves and they're not even trying to understand or change the system. "The sociopaths who rule our world," laments Caitlin Johnstone, "are no more conscious of their own inner processes than your average serial killer."[53]

Bill Burrough expressed this same sentiment in his poem "Ah, Pook Is Here": "The rulers of this most insecure of all worlds are rulers by accident, inept, frightened pilots at the controls of a vast machine they cannot understand, calling in experts to tell them which buttons to push."

In the sports world, nobody would agree to play a game where the winners of last year keep their points in the table and start ahead of everyone else, year after year, making it impossible for any other team to compete fairly.

In April 2021, twelve European soccer clubs— all of which are *owned* by oligarchs— tried to form their own breakaway league of 20 of the top

---

[52] Laurel Sutherlin, https://www.bankingonclimatechaos.org/

[53] Caitlin Johnstone, "We Are Ruled By Apes With PR Firms", https://caitlinjohnstone.substack.com/p/we-are-ruled-by-apes-with-pr-firms

European teams. It was gonna be called the Super League except for just one problem, it wasn't set up to be a fair league. Similar to how the UN was formed to maintain the power of the founding members, so too the 12 founding teams would automatically forever stay in the top league without ever having to lose their spot. No matter if they aren't a top team anymore. The other 8 teams, though, would only remain in the *top* league based on actual results and standings. That's not how most soccer leagues in the world are set up. Every team competes for rank based solely on their performances that season. If you win your league you move up, likewise, if you lose you move down. It's the most fair method possible. Imagine finishing in 6th, 7th, and 8th place in the league and being demoted because the other 12 loser teams were *founding* members? The oligarchs of the 12 founding teams didn't want their teams to ever have to compete. They wanted to lock in guaranteed profits for themselves. Our monopolized Enterprises are the same. It took less than two days for these teams to backtrack and abandon forming the new league because fans and players wouldn't stand for it.[54]

Where participants form games, they must be set up fairly or nobody will ever play. After all, you can't force people to play or watch when they have a choice. Game A today is forced, but only because we've not come up with a new game of value that people can choose to play. When Margaret Thatcher said TINA, she wasn't kidding. Our goal is to give the world a choice of which economic game to play.

> Whichever way we look at it, this pandemic and crisis requires an unprecedented transformation of economics as we know it,' said Vinod Sekhar, Chairman and Chief Executive of environment and biotechnology conglomerate, The Petra Group. Sekhar, who has made it to Forbes' Asia rich lists, recently set up the Good Capitalism Forum to promote responsible business. 'We need a true form of capitalism premised not merely on private profit but dedicated to social purpose and public good,' he told me. I asked him whether such a paradigm could still be called 'capitalism'. Sekhar's answer was that some of the best innovations are still happening in the private sector — the challenge is to ensure that the benefits accrue to society, rather than being hoarded by an ever-tightening network of elites. 'We need an approach which protects planetary boundaries, not one which ignores them to make money. This is now the urgent mission of our times,' he said. 'To understand that to create wealth we need to lift society as a whole. All business leaders that want to remain relevant, if not survive, must be

[54] NPR, "Super Collapse: Plans For New Elite Soccer League Implode" https://www.npr.org/2021/04/21/989409263/super-collapse-plans-for-new-elite-soccer-league-implode

> attentive to it. The world has changed permanently and the economic order must change with it. This is a fact we must accept.[55]

Today, it doesn't take much money to get people to do anything, moral or not, and incidentally, it's so obvious that the key to any Game B future is right there: the ability to control people with money is the root of the problem. Leo Tolstoy noticed, "Money is a new form of slavery, and distinguishable from the old simply by the fact that it is impersonal, there is no human relation between master and slave." Your life is worth nothing unless you serve somebody, on their terms. So, if we flip that on its head and say from now on everyone's life is valuable, and anyone can collect more currency directly, then our actions become truly our choice and not some fake semblance of freedom to do the bidding of some master. Then we are onto a better game of personal sovereignty and responsibility. From an amoral game to a moral game. Or, we will continue screwing over each others' lives and this planet in pursuit of the same old tired profit dictates of Game A.

Common Planet changes the currency system from a circulatory system to a Flow system, along with Enterprise accounting itself. I'll give you a quick overview of the rest and then we'll get into the details in the next chapters.

Every adult becomes a guaranteed caretaker of housing, free with no debts, no insurance, no rent and no taxes... none, not ever! A house will be yours for free for as long as you want, and you can move to a similar quality anytime, almost anywhere on the planet. When you select a new house the previous house becomes available for someone else to choose. Credit is used to improve housing and to compete for higher quality housing.

Electricity, water, internet, tv and mobile are mostly free. Products and services that are almost unlimited, like medicines and healthcare, can be free as can things with zero production costs like digital music, movies, games, books, classes and more all at no cost. Recall, producers claim their work time and Credit directly, then receive Bonuses on back end for the most popular, inventive, efficient, productive, etc. Everybody earns, then collects, then uses Credit in the market where it's deleted in exchange for some good or activity. Simple. Each and every person has direct access to Credit (interest and inflation free currency). For your personal use only. Or would you rather banks issue you credit as debt instead?

---

[55] Nafeez Ahmed, "Will Covid-19 end the age of Big Oil?", https://mondediplo.com/outsidein/covid-19-oil

All commercial land, properties and resources become the commons, accounted for and listed in local city distributed databases. Corporations, Clubs and government agencies transform operations into co-ops with free lease to their equipment and properties. Anything unused can be leased out for free from the city like a library today so that anyone can start a new Enterprise. There is no more debt, rent, taxes, or labor costs for any of these Enterprises. Here, labor is an incentive, an opportunity to earn Credit. It is not an expense. No one pays for it. It's earned. Their only *costs* to account for: prices of real physical resources in the market (fridge).

Starting an Enterprise will be open and easy, but success will depend on cooperation from others and the market. No more patents, secrets or any of that kind of bullshit. Accounting of market activities is now just information and can be used to allocate resources and determine some of the Enterprise value, but trade is no longer the sole deciding factor of value to humans. Similar to how sports teams don't get points based on the score, but on the result. In this way, we can issue Credit based on competition for Enterprise results we wish to see from them. If one cooperative Enterprise, say Apple, doesn't want to make a better product, too bad for those workers because others will be able to make use of 'open everything' to make a better product and they'll get the bonus Credit for doing so. That's what win/win competition will be like. The new Enterprise game is to make the best stuff in the most efficient and sustainable way possible. Those become the new 'profit' metrics which receive the Bonus Credit; with consumer, producer and community groups setting the goals and the standards based on the moral needs of the community and not individual profit incentives.

Chapter 4
Sovereignty

"We have the power of Gods but not the wisdom of Gods."
– Daniel Schmachtenberger

Sovereignty is having supreme authority of oneself. Being empowered, conscious, purposeful and responsible to the world. Here, it begins with empowerment for all. With everybody getting a Personal Credit (PC) account.

Upon start, **everyone** gets 3,000 Credits **x** their age (up to age 50 then -3,000/yr after 50). A 10 year old **x** 3,000 gets 30,000 PC, a 50 yr old gets 150,000 and a 70 yr old gets 90,000. The fact that every person gets this lump sum starting amount of global Credit currency means that the new game can begin at a chosen future date whenever the world is ready. Plus, there's no advantage or disadvantage for any person on when to start playing.

For the majority of us who don't have any Game A money, this will be our starting amount and for others, they'll have ample time to confirm existing 'net worth' in exchange for more Credit.

Opening an account will be easy and immediate, via mobile or stations, however, the process of proof of identity (POI) will be employed to make sure nobody creates more than one account.[1] We're talking about easily verifiable data here. You will be living in a house with a specific address on digital mapping records after all.

The folks developing the technology like Holochain and Mattereum are already building the tools for everything in this book. Please don't confuse this for the 'social credit' score that China is using, or the credit scores used in America. The Credit currency we're discussing here is a market currency, a unit of exchange for goods and services only.

---

[1] Only a limited amount of PC is made available upon immediate account opening until the account is fully verified.

Once an account is opened with all the basic information— name, age, address, biometric?, etc. We could offer an incentive of 10 PC to confirm an identity, with each person able to confirm up to 100 people. That might be fun or not. Is all this verification even necessary? Probably not. Once the game begins, transactional data could reveal abnormal patterns. Having trust right from the start is key.

Once your account is confirmed, you will receive more Credit every month as a universal basic income (UBI); let's say it's 300 PC per month for now. Whatever the actual amount, this will always be the same for every person!

It should go without saying that all existing currencies and debt become obsolete. Everyone will earn more Credit when they learn, play, create, invent, or work. Using an open proof of value (POV) architecture, the Credit goes directly into your account. You decide where to participate in what is necessary, worthy or valuable to you. And Bonus Credit to reward all kinds of special achievements to make life more rewarding.

Here's how people get Personal Credit:

1. UBI, everyone gets the same amount every month
2. POV, standard: every-time you learn, play or work… voluntarily.
3. Bonus, for exceptional individual, Club or Enterprise achievements based on new value metrics

Personal Credit is used in the marketplace for personal access to limited goods or activities. PC cannot be given or transferred to another person by itself. This way, nobody will ever be able to bribe, coerce, steal or 'rob' you of your PC. Flow currency is not a physical *thing*, it's just a digital currency.

As a currency of exchange, Credit is used to buy things like food, clothing, furniture, products, and more. After you buy something, the product is added to your record of personal property. Because it is yours, you can use it, give it away or even sell it. Up to you.

When you buy goods or spend it on an event like a sold out concert, your PC deletes; it does not circulate into some other person's account. It doesn't need to, everyone gets UBI. Besides, nobody is 'paying' for the labor of others anymore. Labor collects Credit for its value using the POV system. We as a society recognize and reward contributions right then and there, not based solely on the final sale price of whatever good or service they produced. The value of the good or service can be judged afterward, and that's where Bonus Credit comes in to better reflect the total contribution of labor and to determine what to produce more of or less of.

Although many things will have a market Credit price, many things will also be free. Utilities such as energy, water, internet, TV and mobile service will mostly be free. Anything with a production cost of zero, will be free, of course. This includes all digital content: music, books, movies, games etc. No more monthly fees and password nonsense. Go ahead, download and share whatever you want. The producers don't need you to 'pay' them anymore since they get to collect Credit directly for their time already and for a chance of more as Bonus if the market likes what they are doing.

As we build and improve technologies, 'costs' will go down, and eventually more and more 'things' will become free, like food, clothing, products, even transportation; maybe this can lead society toward that elusive dream of the Resource Based Economy (RBE).

Events like a showing at a movie theater, a concert, skiing, hotel or air travel have the potential to be free as well. For example, if an artist is unable to fill the arena, everyone attends free. Why would we need to put a price to restrict access when there is no scarcity of seats? The artists collect Credit for their performance just the same, and probably even some Bonus depending on metrics used. But still, all the PC they earn is collected directly. It does not come from your account. Generally speaking, the use of Credit is more to compete for limited resources and activities, with the goal of production being to produce quality and abundance.

When demand exceeds capacity, though, the order of who gets to go can be arranged in a number of different ways to accommodate everyone in a fair manner in an open market, with individuals and the Community all having input. They'll come up with many exciting ways to handle this. People are creative and we'll learn from each other.

Your PC deletes when you buy physical things like bikes or cars, however, these kinds of items still retain some exchange value for years to come and so you can sell them for their present value in the Private Market, or gift it to anyone you want. Although, you will not be able to sell your private goods for more Credit than you paid for them. Either you need or want to use something or you don't, but we shouldn't incentivize any kind of hoarding or trading behavior which is unnatural and wasteful of resources.

If your friend gives you a bike for free, since you cannot sell it for more than you paid, that bike is now worth zero in the Private Market to you. The bike might still have a present value of 50 PC in the Private Market and will cost a buyer 50 PC, but the seller receives up to what they paid, unless they add more labor or parts to improve the bike. In any event, you can keep the bike, gift it to another or place it for sale in the Private Market.

If gifts of physical goods were allowed to be given away for free and then simply resold by the other person, well then, that's just another way of one person giving Credit to another. That's why private goods cannot be sold for more than was originally paid for them. Even though gifting something makes its exchange value worthless for the receiver, most items still have use-value and so we must still limit the total amount of gifting from one person to another to prevent abuse. I don't have a number in mind yet but there should be an annual limit for gifting between individuals.

Every person has access to collect Credit at will. There's only one Personal Credit account per person so we trust people to enter their Credit activity directly into their account to claim their currency. Consider, most activities are group based, easily confirmed and verifiable. Worst case scenario, a person or enterprise lies to collect a little more Credit than they deserve. If caught, their gains reversed and maybe fined. Are you gonna tell me that the thousands of billionaires in Game A earned their wealth? Bezos, Gates and Dimon *earned* that much? Theirs is not merely 'wealth' that affords access to needs and desires like Credit does in Common Planet; theirs is wealth of the commons and control of our productive labor and physical world. Lying or cheating for a bit more Credit is nothing compared to the horrors of Game A concentrated power and wealth; not to mention theft, robbery, kidnapping, bribery, coercion, sexual predation, murder, poaching, etc.

"Bill Gates made his money by extinguishing free software and forcing us to pay him a tax just to turn our computers on. This was only possible because the State was ready to violently enforce his "intellectual property". He didn't create a computer revolution, he destroyed one. Zuckerberg made his money in the exact same way, of course – by destroying a free social network. A social network was bound to emerge, what Zuckerberg did was prevent it from following open protocols, like email, so just anyone couldn't set up a server to socialize with anyone. To say these people added value to the world and therefore "deserve" their billions is absurd. They subtracted value, an enormous amount of value, and stymied progress to seize control and extract wealth. Computers and the internet would be more advanced if they had never existed."[2]

---

[2] Twitter, https://twitter.com/existentialcoms/status/1192893342905815040

What's someone going to do in Common Planet? Steal your car or kidnap your son? In exchange for what? Your digital Credit currency? Can't. It's non-transferable without an exchange of goods and even if it were technically possible the transaction would show up on both accounts; would be self incrimination. All exchange creates digital records. The only reason someone might steal something is to use it, that's it. They'll never be able to sell it in the market for Credit.

Same goes with unauthorized or illegal activities like overfishing or poaching for profit. Are you gonna claim Credit for killing a Rhino that your community told you is not to be touched. Good luck. The only reason all of these illegal activities are possible in Game A is because transactions use circulatory currency. Besides, most people don't poach because they want to, they do it because they have to, in order to get money to live. Not anymore.

Community & Community Credit

There are three communities every person belongs to: Local, Regional and Global. As a sovereign global citizen, you get to vote and participate as much as you like in every club, enterprise, local, regional or global community in which you belong.

Your Local community is where you live. Your Region is where your Local is located. And all Regions make up the Global. Each Local is autonomous and self managing. That's right. You and your fellow citizens decide how to run the place. I imagine there might be lots of experimentation and hopefully diversity. We can learn from each other's successes and mistakes this way.

Each Local gets a Community Credit (CC) account funded automatically every month with an equal amount of CC x number of citizens. Let's say it's 50 CC every month per citizen. Think of it like a direct UBI for the Locals, replacing the need for taxes. Citizens organize themselves, make plans and allocate their Community Credit to fund clubs and enterprises in their City, buying resources for housing, buildings or whatever they need or want.

Each Region also gets a Community Credit account. Because it contains a much larger population, this one is funded with a lower amount of CC x number of citizens. Let's say it's 10 CC every month per citizen. Once again, the citizens decide where to spend this currency for their Region.

We do the same for the Global community. Maybe this one gets only 3 CC per citizen monthly. I remind you, the numbers I'm using need to be modeled but you get the gist. The purpose of the CC is to be able to buy resources for projects that are bigger in scope, that benefit more citizens than just those of a local or regional area. It wouldn't be fair for one Local community to spend their CC on something that benefits the Regional and likewise it wouldn't be fair for the Regional to use their CC to build something that benefits the Global even if it's located within their borders. For example, it's determined that a specific geographic region is best suited for a massive Solar farm, but the Locals don't want to use up their CC to pay for the materials. That's where Regional and Global funds come in.

Community Credit has the same 'value' as Personal Credit (1 CC = 1 PC) so all goods are priced in Credit, however CC can only be spent by fictional entities like communities, clubs and enterprises.

I have some good news: everyone also gets their own Community Credit account too. Funded from the start with a lump sum of 1,000 CC **x** your age. Plus a monthly UBI of 100 CC for you to direct this personal allotment of CC to fund anything of your choosing anywhere on the planet. It's kinda like crowdfunding. You can give your CC to a person, you can bet CC, maybe casino games or lotteries and the like for CC but eventually it will find its way to one of the fictional entities to be spent. You can't personally use Community Credit to buy things in the market for yourself. You have Personal Credit for that. That's why it's ok and safe to allow transfers of CC between people because it's a different kind of currency. It's one that is used by communities and enterprises to support their needs and ultimately what they buy becomes owned by the Local community.

Between all these various CC funds, we can be sure to fund essential services that may not be 'popular.' For example, a school might request an annual budget of 200,000 CC to buy supplies. If they are unable to raise all the funds from the people, they can request funding directly from the Local CC account. With adequate support, they can buy all the supplies they need.

Harari reminds us, "All humans share some core experiences, values and interests, and that no human group is inherently superior to all others. Cooperation is therefore more sensible than conflict. All humans should work together to protect their common values and advance their common interests. And the best way to foster such cooperation is to ease the movement of ideas, goods, money and people across the globe."

The current town or city borders can be used as the Local and country as the Region at the start or whatever the people decide. It doesn't matter where we draw the borders of the Local and Regional areas because we can apply simple math based on the population numbers to make it equitable and fair.

Vitalik Buterin: "The economist's utopia would be one where kind of everything is an incentive aligns in the sense that there aren't inner conflicts between what satisfies your goals and kind of what is good for everyone in the world as a whole."[3]

Common Planet has decentralized both 'political' power and the issuance of currency. There is no longer a small group of people making decisions for the whole on either political or economic decisions. Instead, everything is open, democratic and participatory, and, most importantly: fair.

Housing

Every adult becomes a guaranteed caretaker of housing, free with no debts, no insurance, no rent and no taxes. Your house will be yours for free for as long as you want, and you can move to a similar quality anytime, anywhere on the planet. When you select a new house, the previous house becomes available for someone else to choose. Credit is used to improve housing and to compete for higher quality housing.

Humans have always built shelter. It is a primary necessity. Today, many people own multiple housing units as 2nd homes, vacation or investment property. Rich players have been 'real estate investors' for some time but now corporations and Private Equity firms are using massive amounts of leverage from low-interest bank credit to snap up and drive up the prices all over the world. Housing is built not for purpose, as shelter, but to invest, rent and make more money. The amount of resources used for housing is huge. Forests are cut, land is mined and earth blasted to extract all these resources. All of this production drives GDP growth but is it producing what we need and want? No.

Now there's AirBnB exacerbating our problems. People convert housing into vacation rentals thereby removing them from the housing market altogether and making them into mini hotels for the rich to enjoy while the locals get squeezed into sharing overpriced housing. You don't need me to tell you about how messed up the housing markets are right now so let's focus on the Common Planet solution.

If you currently 'own' your primary home or have a mortgage, you become an instant Title holder. Whatever 'equity value' you have in the property is

---

[3] Lex Friedman interviewing Vitalik Buterin, https://www.youtube.com/watch?v=3x1b_S6Qp2Q, min 23

converted into additional Credit currency in your account. The house is now yours for as long as you want it— no more mortgage, insurance, rent or taxes. If you own more than one house, those Titles are added to your list of property too, and debts deleted, but you'll have some decisions to make. If they are 2nd or vacation homes, you might choose to keep them for yourself. If you decide you don't want them any longer you can release yourself from the Title and convert any 'net equity' into PC from these properties too. You'll also have the same decision to make with any rental properties. Since you can't rent them out, you will either keep them for use or release yourself from the Title in exchange for its 'net equity.' Your choice.

Would you want to be a caretaker for something that is no longer of any use to you? Because it is still your property, you might have the option to grant first right to Title to a family member or friend if you want or choose whichever for your primary house.

Do you currently rent? If so, then you will be first in line for Title selection should the 'owner' release the house. The 'owner' gets more PC and you get the Title for free. Housing that is currently owned by banks, investment funds, REITs, Private Equity, Insurance, or Public companies becomes part of the Commons under open direct-democracy control by the locality in which it exists. The 'investors' of those companies are exchanging their 'equity assets' into Credit, thus have no more claim to these housing units. They become available for real people to select as caretakers.

Using open mapping technologies like OpenStreetMap.org and the dozens of Geographic Information Systems (GIS) like Regrid.com we have a shared, open Property architecture already in existence. Extensive data also exists on the various real estate sites like Zillow.com. By using these applications we can rate and choose housing as well as map out and account for all the other real world Property data too. I can't even begin to describe how amazing this is gonna be. Real life SimCity.

Every house will be assigned a rating from 1-10, with 10 being the best. For the initial rating we can just base it off existing prices and convert them into a rating to start. Then, we allow anyone to rate a house from 1-10, similar to how people rate movies on IMDb.com. You'll earn 10 PC for every house you rate, with some limits of course. After enough votes a rating is produced, 6.3 for example. There will still be professional inspectors and appraisers whose reports and ratings will matter more, and of course those folks are all collecting PC for their time and labor as part of their work.

Everyone will receive a personal Housing Level (HL) from 2 – 10, based on various factors like your age, previous addresses, current home net value, demand, current inventories among other factors. It will be based on a universal algorithm with value inputs by people. For example, once you fill out all the dates and addresses where you've ever lived, it calculates your Housing Level based on what you've experienced (and presumably earned/ deserved in Game A).

Your Housing Level will determine which housing units you can choose from as all houses will be rated from 1 to 10. Don't worry about where you start because this number will increase throughout your lifetime and you can always 'buy' up in levels using your Credit currency.

If you get a personal Housing Level of 6.5, what does that mean? It means you have qualified to select any house with a value up to 6.5. You will use the App to find available housing anywhere in the world, choose the date you wish to move, then select a Title to a home. As a result, your previous home becomes available for someone else to choose from. The App will even allow you to get in line for a house you really like should it ever become available. We can build in functions like temporary swaps, other uses too.

There are three ways to increase your Housing Level. The first is to directly 'buy-up' using your PC; for example, the market price could be 50,000 PC per 1 HL increase. We imagine the algorithm will be a sliding market scale that may cost more as Level increases, factoring in supply/demand. Whatever the numbers, it will be the same for everybody.

You could also use your Credit to upgrade your house, which also upgrades your Level. For example, your personal Housing Level is 6.5, but your house has a rating of 5 and you decide to spend 50,000 PC on a major renovation. In this example, your HL will increase +1 to 7.5, and the house value also increases +1 to 6. That way, if you move, you didn't just spend all of your Credit on a house that is no longer yours. Perhaps we allow 'cashing out' Credit thus reducing your HL too if you're content with less access.

If you don't maintain your house and it loses value it will affect your HL too. Say it's rated at 5 when you move in and after 10 years, you didn't replace anything. No new appliances, flooring, decking, or roofing. Nothing at all. At that point newer ratings produce a lower value, let's say 4 and so that will reduce your personal HL too because you're the one who let it happen. Same if you damage the place, it's gonna cost you.

What about fires? If it's not your fault, no worries, no cost for you, but if you are responsible then it will likely end up costing you some. It may be your house to live in but it still belongs to the local community. If you merely maintain the house and value neither decreases or increases then it doesn't affect your Housing Level.

How many houses should people be allowed to 'own'? It depends on the reality of the locality. Perhaps we start with a modest limit, say no more than 3 per person. That way, those who have dozens of rental properties can't decide to keep them after the transition as a form of protest from not being able to collect rent anymore. Of course they would still get extra Credit based on their 'net equity' when they release the Title but the choice to keep them all will not be an option if there's not enough for everybody else.

If you only have 1 house now and wish to buy another you will simply use your Credit to choose a 2nd or in partnership with others. As newer, better housing is built and inventories become more plentiful, everyone's HL can be adjusted upwards.

In all cases, the Local communities decide which houses can be private residences and which are for short term needs or for vacation purposes. This will make it easier for communities to tear down and rebuild housing based on more modern and appropriate methods. No more cheap insulation and ugly giant rectangular boxes consisting of smaller boxes.

Chapter 5

Opportunity

"Production without possession, action without self-assertion, development without domination." - Lao-Tzu

"By mutual confidence and mutual aid – great deeds are done, and great discoveries made." - The Iliad, Homer

Now that you have guaranteed housing, a Personal Credit (PC) account with a monthly universal basic income, and you know a little bit about how the Flow currency is created, used and deleted in market exchange, what is the new game of life and work like?

The answer that started this whole thing came after I asked this question: can we remove labor as an expense from Enterprises (Corporations)? In Game A, if an enterprise can't be 'profitable' then it dies, unless it is funded either by donations or taxes. Someone has to *pay* for the labor, but there is always a finite amount of currency in circulation and it's used mostly when and where it's profitable, with less regard if it's socially necessary or desirable. The incentives are restricted to simple selfish profit and growth. This worked great to impel work and production in a world with minimal technology and machines, but today efficiency and sustainability are more important, critical actually. And that means we have to change the incentive structure of how we work and produce.

Instead of banks getting free credit and issuing that as debt money to fund enterprises, who then *pay* labor, why not just issue the credit as pay to the laborers themselves directly? **Currency is created when it's earned. Interest free, tax free, inflation free and theft free.** And production changes from for-profit to for-purpose. You do the work and you collect the reward. Simple. This way, labor is voluntary, purposeful and moral rather than forced and amoral. From win/lose to win/win. It becomes a game where each person has equal opportunity to access and manage Property for use and purpose. When some win through fair competition, it creates something that benefits and elevates the whole. We all win. Win/win/win.

How you choose to spend your time is an opportunity for you to earn more PC. When you work any job; go to school; read; teach; write; take classes; create art; play music; exercise; play sports; care for children, the needy, or elderly, you will earn more PC.

No person, enterprise or community has to 'pay you' for your time, thereby eliminating the biggest 'expense' most groups face in society today: labor costs. A school is no longer limited by how many teachers it can have due to a lack of money. It is only limited by how many people are able or willing to teach— this is at NO cost to the school. The school needs only to collect enough Community Credit to fund the purchase of real supplies like paper, computers and renovations— not for labor.

The same goes for any group. Labor is now an opportunity for people to earn Credit rather than an expense the group has to pay for. This eliminates most coercion and corruption that is rampant and built-into today's system. This also allows more flexibility in the 'labor pool' in cases of emergencies. Right now, if there is a fire, flood or hurricane, there will be a limited supply of labor because first you'll need the money to pay for it, and it has to come from someone else. Whereas here what needs to get done can get done quickly because those that do the work collect the Credit directly. There is always Credit to pay for any necessary or socially desirable labor. That's how it's created. The only limits are real labor and real resources. Here, money doesn't rule us, money serves us.

Labor is more than an industrial input. It is people. And it is the only way to turn raw materials into finished goods and services. Capital can't do that by itself. It's immoral to heavily reward the 'risk' taken by fictional capital when it's real humans in the labor pool who are truly taking on all the risk.

Here's what Abraham Lincoln had to say in his first annual message on Dec. 3, 1861:

> there is one point, with its connections, not so hackneyed as most others, to which I ask a brief attention. It is the effort to place capital on an equal footing with, if not above, labor in the structure of government. It is assumed that labor is available only in connection with capital; that nobody labors unless somebody else, owning capital, somehow by the use of it induces him to labor. This assumed, it is next considered whether it is best that capital shall hire laborers, and thus induce them to work by their own consent, or buy them and drive them to it without their consent. Having proceeded so far, it is naturally concluded that all laborers are either hired laborers or what we call slaves… Labor is prior to and independent of capital. Capital is only the fruit of labor, and could never have existed if labor had not first existed. Labor is the superior of capital, and deserves much the higher consideration.[1]

Needless to say all work is done on a volunteer basis. You work where you want to work and you help to create work too. This can be a free market of labor. Finally, society can reward people for doing good instead of allowing masters to coerce and force people to do bad. How many poor people alive today have the potential for genius? Potential that isn't today being fulfilled but could. Imagine if we gave them that potential. When life opens its resources to each person, and offers them healthy living conditions of food, education and opportunities for growth, how many millions will become eminent scientists, doctors, teachers, engineers, writers and artists building us a glorious world. I want to live in that world please.

In a long Medium post titled "A simple plan for repairing our society," Vinay Gupta says: "We need a *trans-ideological consensus* to allow people with incompatible world models to tolerate each other well enough to work together to combat climate change and preserve and expand our rights as human beings… Civilisation in its deepest core is a pact between adults to make a better place to raise their children. There is no reason planetary civilisation could not work that way too."[2]

Flow currency is a universal alternative currency system that can be used if or when the people need or want to evolve. It's a plan for a new game of life,

---

[1] Abraham Lincoln, https://www.presidency.ucsb.edu/documents/first-annual-message-9

[2] Vinay Gupta, "A simple plan for repairing our society", https://medium.com/@vinay_12336/a-simple-plan-for-repairing-our-society-we-need-new-human-rights-and-this-is-how-we-get-them-cee5d6ededa9

but this time, without debt, without taxes and without Masters. It's time for supreme rule of oneself. With these steps, we can unite humanity.

These new economic protocols produce "**A transparent, open, information sharing world.** Where all the information that could empower people is readily available; all interests are aligned with what is true and systemically positive; disinformation is identified and discarded, etc. Choice making (governance) can only be as good as the relevant information fed into the process (sense-making). [Partial and/or corrupted information make good choice making impossible.]"[3]

The game starts after the deletion of all debts and currencies. Since there will be no need for banks, insurance, investing, tax or debt collecting, real estate agency, manipulative advertising, sales, other middlemen or any financial 'services', all of their equipment and properties like houses, offices and buildings currently in use will become titled to the Local community and available for its citizens, clubs or enterprises to use however they choose. Plus, those and any other workers in jobs that feel their job is 'bullshit' become free to contribute to society in new ways of their choosing.

Just imagine, you'll be able to answer your phone calls again because there won't be any more stupid scam phone calls about the IRS coming to arrest you or your car warranty expiring soon. Nobody is gonna try to sell you shit cuz there ain't nothing in it for them any more. Influencers? Gtfo. Not to mention all the 'legitimate' invasive advertising bombarding us everywhere we look. I'm sick of it. What is advertising but psychological warfare to induce trade. Fuck YouTube and their hours long ads.

Michael Parenti pointed out that "The goal of a good society is to structure social relations and institutions so that cooperative and generous impulses are rewarded, while antisocial ones are discouraged. The problem with capitalism is that it best rewards the worst part of us: ruthless, competitive, conniving, opportunistic, acquisitive drives, giving little reward and often much punishment -- or at least much handicap -- to honesty, compassion, fair play, many forms of hard work, love of justice, and a concern for those in need."

Neale Donald Walsch has good advice for us on this journey: "The deepest secret is that life is not a process of discovery, but a process of creation. You are not discovering yourself but creating yourself anew. Seek therefore, not to find out who you are, but seek to determine who you want to be."

---

[3] Schmachtenberger, https://civilizationemerging.com/new-economics-series-3/

Jeremy Rifkin in his 2004 book, *The End of Work*, speculates that on account of recent and continuing developments in information technologies, automation, and telecommunication it is quite possible that "...as little as 5 percent of the adult population will be needed to manage and operate the traditional industrial sphere by the year 2050. Near-workerless farms, factories, and offices will be the norm in every country."

In *Bullshit Jobs*, David Graeber posited that the productivity benefits of automation have not led to a 15-hour workweek, as predicted by economist Keynes in 1930, but instead to "bullshit jobs": "a form of paid employment that is so completely pointless, unnecessary, or pernicious that even the employee cannot justify its existence." He wrote, "I would like this book to be an arrow aimed at the heart of civilization. There is something very wrong with what we have made ourselves. We have become a civilization based on work - not even 'productive work' but work as an end and meaning in itself. We have come to believe that men and women who do not work harder than they wish at jobs they do not particularly enjoy are bad people unworthy of love, care, or assistance from their communities. It is as if we have collectively acquiesced to our own enslavement… This is a disastrous state of affairs. I wish it to end." Let's do this for David.

Just because a job becomes useless in the new economics, that doesn't mean I'm inferring that you as a person are useless. On the contrary. You are an incredibly valuable member of our global family and there is no reason for you to engage in an activity just for the sake of collecting money in order to live. That's why everyone gets UBI. "Doing nothing is better than being busy doing nothing," said Lao Tzu.

Lori Summers got it right on her Twitter thread where she says: "When discussing Universal Basic Income, inevitably the retort comes: "So you just want people to not have to work, is that it?" Accompanied by a smug smirk, expecting me to backpedal and hem and haw, say "Of course not, that's silly." Except...yes. Yes, I do. People shouldn't HAVE to work. People should WANT to work. Sharing in the labor of building and maintaining a society because it benefits everyone should be desirable, not forced. It shouldn't be something we do because we'll die otherwise."[4]

"And you ought not to tell me about people who don't work, and you can't give people money without working, 'cause if that were true, you'd have to start stopping Rockefeller, Bobby Kennedy, Lyndon Baines Johnson, Lady

---

[4] Lori Summers, https://twitter.com/madlori/status/1153729750738833414

Bird Johnson, the whole of Standard Oil, the Gulf Corp, all of them, (applause) including probably a large number of the Board of Trustees of this university. (applause). So the question, then, clearly is not whether or not one can work, it's who has power? Who has power to make his or her acts legitimate? That is all."[5]

John Vervaeke calls our existing conundrum "the meaning crisis" and he has an incredibly illuminating series with that title on YouTube. In another of his YouTube posts "Going Post Paradigmatic w/ Jordan Hall & Gregg Henriques" he says, "So [in] our culture, we have been reduced to; i) citizens of the state, and ii) consumers of the market: We are not participant persons within the culture anymore."[6]

That is the crux of a Flow currency system: it wrests the power over our lives away from masters and gives it to each and every one of us. It puts individuals in the decision making driving seat. Sovereignty. Self-rule. This is our demand. Public ownership and local stewardship/kinship of our energy, food, water and so on is the future or there will be no future. This is how we'll find meaning.

Work today can and should be conscious and significant. It should improve the experience of life. We'll all have to get involved. Life is hard. It just is. Yet we are lucky because we can use our gifts and abilities to make it a little less difficult for ourselves and everyone else. Work can be the way to an easier existence. It can be what it has always been in Game A: the unleashing of human potential.

Imagine you wake up tomorrow, your company is now run democratically by all the workers, who can choose to continue to work there or not, because wherever and whatever you choose to participate in, you get the Credit. You are free to 'work' wherever you choose, or not. Cooperative groups perform what the people need and want, rather than something that can be done because there is profit in it. Do you really believe capitalism fosters innovation?[7] Could we have already come up with better energy alternatives to oil? or automobiles? Go talk to any city planner and they'll tell you how insane our 'development' has been. So many things that are good for the

[5] Stokley Carmichael, "Black Power", 1966, p. 4, 5 https://atribeofthemiddlepassage.voices.wooster.edu/wp-content/uploads/sites/213/2019/04/Stokely-Carmichael-22Black-Power22-Speech-Text-Voices-of-Democracy.pdf

[6] John Vervaeke, https://www.youtube.com/watch?v=Ft_7n3eUytQ, min 20:36

[7] Arash Kolahi, https://twitter.com/ArashKolahi/status/1225940422855290880

world are not appreciated because there is no money in it. Or worse, sabotaged so others can continue to extract and profit.[8] Let's escape that.

What we need is a model of use and responsibility rather than ownership and rent extraction. I'm so excited for the future. The explosion of advancement will be epic once we transition to a society of participation and co-operative competition. We will slow down and speed up at the same time. Douglas Engelbart says, "The better we get at getting better, the faster we will get better."

"Where the driving imperative and mode of being of our complex social-economic-political systems (and our dominant cultural stories) shifts from surplus wealth accumulation with a rivalrous and consumeristic mode of being to one of co-operation, co-creation and universal participation in the value creation process where the dominant mode of being is anti-rivalrous. All work is aligned with true value creation in support of the collective and the planet, and all work is voluntary."[9]

Proof of Value (POV)

In addition to collecting 300 PC and 100 CC per month as UBI deposits, every person can collect more personal Credit for participation. An example:

Personal Credit Protocols		
1.	**Personal/Amateur: 1 to 10 per hr**	
	Group Activities	Fun Work
	Class or School	Coaching
	Sports	Teaching
2.	**Professional: 10 to 20 per hr**	
	Advanced Study	Teaching
	Semi-Pro	Coaching
	Mid/Advanced Work	Teaching
3.	**Expert Level: 20 to 30 per hr**	
	Professional	Pro Sports
	Experts	Top Leadership

	Pay Rate	Annual Increase
Kids (age 3-10)	1	0.25
Kids (age 11-14)	3	0.5
Kids (age 14-18)	4	0.5
College (any age)	6	0.5
Grad/Advanced Study	8	0.5
Job - Entry Level	10+	0.5
Non-desirable Jobs	15+	0.5
Emergency Work	15+	0.5
Sports Adults - Amateur	1-5	0.5
Sports - Semi pro	6-15	0.5
Sports - Pro	16-30	0.5

---

8 Veblen viewed capitalist production as sabotage, that profits for capitalists are not based on enhancing productivity but 'subverting' it.

9 Unknown source from my research notes (a mix of words from the Game B community?).

Using an open proof of value architecture, you get to participate and decide what is necessary, worthy or valuable in society and the Credit goes directly into your personal account. It's wonderful that we have the technology to manage all of this data and more. And it's secure, incorruptible, verifiable, open, and so much more, plus this is easy because everyone only has two accounts: a simple ledger for Personal Credit and one account for Community Credit.

The new game of life won't so much tell you how to live or what you must do, but rather assure that you can live, play, learn and work. The how and what is whatever you want it to be. As it should be. "You are under no obligation to remain the same person you were a year ago, a month ago, or even a day ago," said Richard Feynman, "You are here to create yourself, continuously."

Even people from inside Game A have spoken out about the flawed monetary system. Richard C. Cook, working in the US Treasury Department from 1986 to 2007 as an analyst, examined the monetary system's role in why, despite our civilization's many technological advancements, the economic demands on the average worker are getting more burdensome, not less. He wrote of the problem in 2007:

> Why can't mothers have the choice of staying home with the kids like they could a generation ago? Why can't some people choose to do eldercare? Why can't others comfortably go into lower-paying occupations like teaching or the arts? Why can't some just opt to study or travel for a while or learn new skills or start a business without facing financial ruin as they often must today? Why can't retirees enjoy their retirement instead of having to stay in the job market or worrying about Social Security going broke?... [It is] due to the lunacy of the financial system, not because we can't produce enough... Fundamental monetary reform implemented to restore economic democracy is what America's real task should be for the twenty-first century. One thing is for certain. The out-of-control financial system that has wrecked the U.S. and world economies over the last generation cannot be allowed to continue.[10]

[10] Richard C. Cook, "The Crashing US Economy Held Hostage", July 7, 2007, Centre for Research on Globalization, https://www.globalresearch.ca/the-crashing-u-s-economy-held-hostage/6239

A Vision of Life in Common Planet, a story

On the day I was born they gave me 1,000 of this new digital money called personal Credit, and another 1,000 of something called Community Credit. Plus I get 300 PC and 100 CC more every month.

In the beginning, my parents buy things from their personal Credit accounts, not mine. After a few years, I'm enrolled in school at no cost to me or my parents. In fact, I get to earn PC for going; that's right, I get to earn money for going to school. I'm just a kid, so I'm paid only 1 PC per hour in my first year, but at 20/hrs a week that's 80 PC per month. In the 2nd year, I'll be getting 1.25/hr and so on according to the standard global protocols.

By my 5th birthday, I've got almost 20,000 PC and 7,000 CC. I can use this money to pay for food, games and activities with parental help and permission, or my parents can pay using their PC accounts.

My parents enrolled me in some activities. I joined the Cub Scouts, played soccer and took music lessons. The Scout leaders and the soccer coaches that used to be just volunteers, now get to earn PC for their time directly, and I don't have to pay for any of this. It's kinda like I created an opportunity for them to earn PC money and they still get the personal satisfaction that comes from helping and teaching others. Also, can you believe it, I get to earn more PC per hour to do all of these things. This is so cool.

My parents told me that years ago, just after the transition, there were supposedly not enough soccer fields and only enough space to build two more fields in town and that it was still not enough, because they were all using the fields only on weekends and a few hours at the end of each weekday that they realized they had a scheduling problem, not a limited resource problem.

It turned out this same 'problem' existed for many other resources in town. We had enough of everything: roads, cars, gyms, theaters, fields, but we had created a world in which everyone was doing the same things at the same time. This was easy to change using the new accounting protocols.

Now I'm 11 years old, with a PC balance of almost 40,000 and a CC balance of 14,200. The educational system has now completely been transformed. What was once a stale, boring, repetitive jail-like system for kids is now more dynamic, fun and rewarding. Every day I get to learn new things, meet new people and interact with my peers and the community on the things that interest me, and I earn PC money for doing this. I love school. I love this life.

Because I'm older and more experienced at some of the classes and activities that I've been doing, I'm receiving 3 PC per hour now. There are also all kinds of individual and group achievements and competitions that allow me to earn Bonus PC too.

I recently bought a bike. It's amazing, one of the newest light weight models. I paid for it myself. It cost me just 100 PC. The money was subtracted from my account and now the bike shows up on my list of private possessions. No one steals bikes anymore. If someone were to steal my bike, the only thing they could do with it is use it. They wouldn't be able to sell it because I have the digital Title, they don't. In fact, if they did try to sell it, at the listed market rate, the money would get credited to my account, not theirs. And if they got caught with a stolen bike, well, let's just say that the fine for something like that is small, but the social stigma could really sting, and might cost them some loss of respect or friends. So yeah, stealing is no longer a problem.

Most of my friends have now tried and have experience with many different subjects, activities and sports that we're beginning to find what we really like and what we're really good at. Some of them are really good soccer players and they're on more competitive teams in more competitive leagues and they're earning more PC per hour than I do for playing, but that's ok because I enjoy watching them play. Besides, it's a good outlet for competition and it's great for the body and mind.

Some of them have become really good at music, art, programming, video editing, science, math, engineering, farming and all kinds of things. Most of us speak multiple languages now, even though we have applications that translate in real time. We are encouraged to occasionally join the adults in their clubs and enterprises to expand our knowledge and experience beyond just the classroom. For this we usually get paid more PC per hour, and the adults like it because we not only help with their workload, but teaching us teaches them too. It's a win/win.

Allowing everyone to self-maximize is better for the whole of society now and people prefer that than in the past Game A where you didn't want people to better themselves because then they might outcompete you and render you useless. What a shit game you guys were playing back then. How mental were you people? You sick bastards.

In a Capitalist run system, kids joining the labor pool led to less jobs and lower pay for adults so they had to ban kids from working, which is why they put them in school jails for the first 18 years of their lives learning how to memorize things they didn't care about. It was a monumental waste of time for most of them, when they were obviously quite capable of contributing and benefiting their communities. Kids should be allowed to pursue their passions while immersed in the community, not locked up in rote repetition.

"The goal of teaching should not be to help the students learn how to memorize and spit out information under academic pressure. The purpose of teaching is to inspire the desire for learning in them and make them able to think, understand, and question," said Richard Feynman.

Here's some of the things we're learning in school that you didn't: how to grow food, composting, seed saving, food preservation, medicinal herbs, native plants, no-till permaculture, fermentation, water filtration, foraging, mushroom ID and First Aid.

Now I'm 15 and both of my accounts have continued to grow. I'm also earning more PC per hr for school now and have already gotten a chance to attend multiple camps away from home. I recently applied to go to a prestigious Academy in another city. If I get accepted, that means I'll be living away from home for the next year or more for the first time in my life. It also means I'd be earning more PC in pay because of all the work I've put in to reach this honor.

When I turn 18, I become fully autonomous. I get complete control of my accounts without needing parental approval anymore, and I get to vote on so many more things in my city and my planet. I also get my first Housing Level, starting with level 2. That means I have access to residential housing anywhere on the planet. There's not much available for me at my Housing Level to get a place on my own, but I could always join others to share a house if I want. But I plan to apply to some colleges, just not sure where yet.

As a College student, I earn more PC. Some of my friends plan to stay home for a few more years, since they do work that interests them and still take classes at various local universities. There's not the same societal stigma to have rigid schedules like the past, so I'm told.

There are some geniuses and talented kids in any group, and this new currency system really opens up opportunities for them to pursue their passions and contribute like never before, and they get to personally earn the Credit and the recognition from their peers, rather than some bank, CEO or capitalist 'owner' taking all the credit and profit from others' work like before. I still can't believe that people put up with that system for so long. It's just crazy. None of you even understood it and it makes no sense.

They used to allow men to create these Corporations, to buy resources, land and buildings all in the pursuit of profit. Thankfully that's all ended. Now, anyone can start a club or enterprise, lease out land, buildings, equipment and resources that are owned by the City that are not being used by anyone at the moment. It's kinda like a Library but instead of just books, magazines and videos, the City is flush with all kinds of resources.

My City has warehouses and distribution of all manner of shared resources like maker spaces, tools, equipment, and even boats, bikes and cars for anyone to use. All Transportation is now free. My parents said everyone was surprised how quickly the City was able to transform after the transition. We did have an advantage though, because being one of the wealthier cities with more resources gave us a head start. My parents used some of their CC to help their homeland overseas because they needed it more.

The groups don't need money to pay for the workers anymore because everyone is allowed to earn PC money directly, it doesn't come out of anyone's pocket. They still have resources and other physical materials they need to operate so this is achieved with Community Credit. I have a CC account, and I can give this money to any group anywhere in the World. I can fund the things that I want or need. If you recall, I get 100 CC every month, as does everyone else. Also, my City gets 50 CC every month per citizen, and we have various local government groups that work together to make sure all the necessary clubs and enterprises in our City are funded so they can buy what they need in the open market. The groups create budgets and request money from the people and the City. Those that are either the best or necessary get funded, and sometimes others fold. When groups end, they simply return all the land, buildings, equipment and supplies they were using back to the City, along with any CC remaining. This way, others in the community can come up with ideas to create, design, build, or provide services and they will have access to the buildings, land and resources they need to fulfill their visions.

The best thing is, the Groups compete to create the best, environmental, efficient, long lasting, desirable products and for the winning groups get a Bonus PC for all their workers. These workers sometimes also get Bonus PC for completing the work contracts, like teachers who complete the year get a year end Bonus, as do workers for production quotas or quality levels. All manner of Bonuses have been set up to incentivize the labor that needs to get done.

You should see how the engineers have transformed Cities all over the world because that is what happens when you let the people decide how and what to build rather than private 'owners' who only seek a profit. What a disgrace and an embarrassment the previous system was. Y'all should be ashamed.

My parents tell me how when people owned things privately for profit, everyone mistreated houses, buildings and property. Now it's different. Everyone has a sense of pride and acts like they own everything, which in a way, we kinda do. I feel like everything is for me, and that I should help take care of it. Everyone takes care of everything now because it is all ours. After all, we do live on a Common Planet.

Proof of Value continued

Level 1, Amateur: 1 to 10 Credit per hr

These are any Personal & Amateur Activities School, Class, Sports, Fun Work, Entry Level Jobs, Coaching, Teaching

Level 2, Professional: 10 to 20 Credit per hr

Activities requiring more commitment or experience
Mid to advanced level jobs, Advanced Study, Semi pro sports, Undesirable work, Coaching, Teaching

Level 3, Expert: 20 to 30 Credit per hr

These are experts, professionals, and top leadership roles.

You'll notice that the more you continue to contribute to a particular activity, the more experience, skill and your hourly pay rewards and reflects that. Keep in mind this is individual based. A 50 year old with no previous experience in carpentry doesn't start at the higher hourly pay just because they are older. Experience and skill earns more, not age.

You can be as greedy as you like but the reward for greed has a limit of how much you can get paid, so it's fair and equitable while still allowing for bonus, advancement, achievement; however much the individual wants is made available using standard rules and in the control of the individual and communities.

Bonus allocations could be based on total PC collected by the citizens of the Local community. For example, simply issue a fixed percentage, say 30% extra PC (perhaps annually?) based on that number and let the individual clubs, enterprises and community set and decide some of the Bonus metrics themselves. Yes, there could be some standard metrics for some of the larger clubs and enterprises but the idea here is to defer Bonus allocations to the groups themselves, since democratic participation is standard. Who knows better which teams or individuals deserve it than the participants themselves? They might simply divide the Bonus equally, give some members more or some less.

Bonus also has multiple incentive functions besides as a reward for superior performance. Bonus can be tied to commitment. The last thing any group wants is people who are flaky and don't show up when they should. A school or enterprise could tie Bonus to fulfill their time commitments. You get paid your standard hourly rate based on your experience but also a Bonus if you complete a term of work, like a coach, teacher, or worker for the year or whatever. A 30% or more Bonus might be a big incentive for many.

"As to the childish question, repeated for fifty years: "Who would do disagreeable work?" frankly I regret that none of our *savants* has ever been brought to do it, be it for only one day in his life. If there is still work which is really disagreeable in itself, it is only because our scientific men have never cared to consider the means of rendering it less so. They have always known that there were plenty of starving men who would do it for a few cents a day."[11]

When work is appreciated by society one doesn't get the same sense of shame that is common with today's game where we tell workers they are 'essential' but pay them and treat them like shit. If a job is truly essential the amount of Credit available for the volunteer can be raised until someone steps up or Bonus can also be offered. Any kind of recognition events like dinners, awards, names on buildings, statues or parades even. Ok, maybe not statues and parades but you get the idea.

Look, let's be honest, lots of people are doing work right now they would love to abandon and go enjoy their lives. One of the things we can do when

---

[11] Peter Kropotkin, "Anarchist Communism: It's Basics and Principles", 1887, https://www.fourmilab.ch/etexts/www/kropotkin/ancom/

we start the game is to figure out which jobs, clubs and enterprises are truly 'essential' and ask those people what their plans are. How many plan to continue and how many plan to leave. If too many want to leave, we can offer them or others something crazy like 2x or 3x hourly pay for the first year or two. Whatever we need to get things done to make the transition as smooth as possible. Keep in mind that possibly 50% of existing jobs are useless or 'bullshit' and those individuals will be looking to do something too.

I'm willing to bet that many cities are gonna find out they have overbuilt infrastructure due to all those bullshit jobs and the cars used to get to work. Reducing our dependence around cars is an obvious design priority. "It's not that I'm trying to do social engineering around people using bikes, walking & transit," said transport expert author Gabe Klein, "I'm trying to undo the 60+ years of social engineering around the complete reliance on the automobile."

Because everyone in the community has data on what is happening and how their community is doing, it makes participation and competition different than today. If there is a need for more work in one area it will be known. If too many people open bakery shops relative to the size of the community perhaps the community doesn't make space available for that purpose. I just got a funny idea. Maybe we do promotion relegation for the various groups in their 'industry' where space and resources become stretched. Which brings us to how we account for enterprises.

Clubs & Enterprises

All corporations, community agencies, sports teams, schools, police, etc are either a club or an enterprise. They all function as co-operatives where the members run everything democratically. People may be owners of their private possessions, but all clubs, enterprises and communities are caretakers of resources and property, they are not owners. A caretaker is responsible and answerable to society, whereas an owner is master and answers to no one.

Clubs and enterprises do not have to 'own' Titles to property or equipment to have right to access and use. All things are owned by either individuals, Local or Regional communities. These groups exist and are formed only to produce products or provide services as deemed desirable by the individuals in their community. This way, anyone can start a group, find available land, property, equipment and request 'use' by loaning it out free from the

Community, like a lease. A budget is created and Credit is requested so they can buy whatever they need to operate. Upon dissolution, all property and Credit balance is returned to the Community and available for other Groups to use.

Recall that every person has cashed out their equity holdings on all land and buildings in exchange for more PC, thus they have no more 'ownership' claims to those; the Local is now Title owner. The original 'owners' become caretakers and directors of their business group (if they want) and for this extra responsibility they will earn more pay in Credit. There are no rent, tax or insurance costs to pay anymore. The land and building can continue to be used by the same business simply by registering to lease free from the City. The business group is run by existing workers cooperatively and/or new workers who choose to work there for Credit.

Another way to earn Credit is Bonus. Individuals or groups earn Bonus through competitions or simply from executing or producing extraordinary feats in society. Bonuses could be awarded to a student, teacher, scientist, doctor, farmer, writer, artist, musician, inventor, police officer, firefighter, pilot, or athlete depending on the accomplishment.

When you go to the gym, exercise, or play rec sports, you might earn 1-3 Credit per hour. If you're a serious athlete who has spent years training and the more you advance in competition, the more you would earn per hour, like you would in the professional leagues, in addition to bonuses for championships and other tournaments.

Through participation, by contributing directly to proposals and projects of various enterprises, or performing myriad other services and adding value to the network, users will collect PC and build ranking reflective of competency in everything they choose to do. Even within enterprises there might be rankings of all sorts of measures, like we do in sports, so as to encourage, reward attention and Bonus PC. As your deeds add up, so do rankings. Some of these rewards can be within an enterprise network, giving its users access to features that are not otherwise available without the ranking. It's an earned level of trust, based on the value of your reputation, thus can be acknowledged even by those who have never interacted with you. An open system of measuring contribution to the common good helps us to trust each other. Trust is the lifeblood of society.

Jobs Ending	Jobs Expanding	Jobs Reducing
Banking	Science	Lawyers
Financial	Medical	Judges
Insurance	Engineering	Police
IRS, DEA, CIA, etc	Farming	Prisons
Real Estate Agency	Community Service	Gov't Agencies
Weapons Manufacture	Teaching/Coaching	Middle Managers
Most Sex 'Work'	Child/Elderly Care	Sales/Advertising/PR

Any club or enterprise that no longer needs to exist will cease operation and all owner(s) are compensated for the value of their portion of assets with personal Credit. All of their equipment and resources then become part of the Local or Regional commons. If they were small owner operator type businesses then some of their possessions might well be those of the current owner. The owner(s) can decide to keep these items for themselves (added to their private property account), or donate or sell them.

Existing clubs and enterprises transform operations into co-ops registered in their Local community. Larger enterprises might belong to the Region instead. They get free use of all their existing resources which are accounted for in the Local databases too. Each maintains their own private Community Credit account. Accounting of all purchases of inputs and sales of goods is done in the normal traditional manner. They are just numbers after all. How much they 'pay' for labor and all raw materials and other 'expenses' are accounted for just as they are today. However, all of this accounting here is just information (like the score during a sports game), and is used mainly to compare similar enterprises. So the accounting of auto manufacturers is compared against similar consumer industrial manufacturers to determine which is more efficient or desirable in the market. Some enterprises will always produce 'profit' and some will always produce 'losses' but they are compared with their peers, not with dissimilar enterprises. An engineering firm is different from a bakery and different from a manufacturer. An enterprise is either succeeding or failing only in relation to their peers, compared likely on an annual basis.

It doesn't matter if too many enterprises are producing losses and creating more Credit than they are 'deleting' because ultimately most Credit will get deleted when we compete for the limited activities and on housing. This is why we say there is no inflation. Once we model these numbers we'll learn more.

Any enterprise or club that is failing and breaching their limits runs out of Credit and is unable to buy more stuff to continue; unless consumers or the Local community decide to allocate their CC to them. When they fail and close, all 'assets' remaining flow to the Local database and CC account. Those resources can then be selected by existing or new Local enterprises at no further cost since they've already been 'paid' for. Likewise any that are succeeding and increasing their CC levels can use it to grow as needed.

When Bonus is dished out, it too is issued directly to the workers. It does not come from anyone's account but unlike the cost of labor, in this case, it does not count as a cost or expense in the enterprise accounting.

Opening a new enterprise is as easy as registering it with your Local community. You and your compadres can set it up however you wish. You make the rules for your own place. This way, the organizational structure can be made to suit the purpose or desires of its members. You can see everything that is available to you not only in your Local area but in other areas you wish to operate and request use.

In the example of a movie theater, it already exists, the workers work, they all have a say and they can organize it however is best to run it. They will have some expenses, they'll need to buy cleaning supplies, bathroom items, and generally repair and replace things over time. For this they will have a Community Credit account. Any person or the community can give them the CC they need. The drink and food at concession could be paid for by user personal Credit rather than from Community Credit in this case.

You and some friends are decent chefs and you just found the perfect space available for a restaurant. There's some existing restaurant equipment already in the space but you need more. You request to register the space and equipment as McLovin Cafe. Once confirmed the CC account is open. You can fund it with some of your own CC, request it from other people or even ask your Local for a direct CC allocation or CC allowance. You and your friends put up 1,000 CC and your Local approves you for a CC allowance of up to 4,000. In this example, your Local did not give you the CC from their account yet, they only authorized you to use up to that amount, knowing that whatever you do buy with it, that if you fail, then they will have to use their

CC to pay for the cost. But in the meantime, it's like a credit debt for your new business.

You post job openings in the online board, spend 5,000 CC on equipment and food, then finally open your doors with a balance of -4,000 CC in your account. You make your menu, set your prices and customers start coming in. You can charge customers PC item by item like restaurants do today or you can offer a flat fee for each type of meal, breakfast, lunch or dinner with drinks separate (unless all your drinks cost about the same then include it in the 'price fixe'). Since you have an account deficit, you might have to charge more to cover the difference. If your food is good and customers are willing to pay then you will succeed and if not you will fail. The better you are, the more CC you'll earn to update the place and more Bonus you get.

Right now you're thinking: "Who the hell would want to work at a restaurant?" I don't blame you, considering how they are treated today but people do enjoy cooking and we all like eating and hanging out. The place isn't going to be set up and run like they are today. One thing is for sure, there will be lots of experimentation and much more informal arrangements. Here's Rushkoff's ideas about this:

> Another commons-derived idea "subsidiarity," holds that a business should never grow for growth's sake. It should only grow as big as it needs to in order to accomplish its purpose. Then, instead of expanding to the next town or another industry, it should just let someone else replicate the model. Joe's Pizzeria should sell to Joe's customers. If they need a pizzeria in the next town, Joe can share his recipe and let Samantha do it.
>
> This is not bad business - especially if Joe likes making pizza. He gets to stay in the kitchen doing what he loves instead of becoming the administrator of a pizza chain. Samantha may develop a new technique that helps Joe; they can even federate and share resources. Besides, it's fun to have someone else to talk with about the pizza business. They can begin to develop the collaborative abilities instead of their competitive ones.
>
> Bigger isn't necessarily better. Things in nature grow to a certain point and then stop. They become full-grown adults, forests or coral reefs. This doesn't mean they're dead. If anything, it's the stability of adulthood that lets them become participating members of larger, mutually supportive networks.
>
> If Joe has to grow his business bigger just in order to keep up with his rising rent and expenses, it's only because the underlying economy has been rigged to demand growth and promote scarcity. It is this artificially competitive landscape that convinces us we have no common interests.[12]

[12] Rushkoff, *Team Human*, p. 112-113

Let's examine landscapers. Most already have their own equipment already but what if you're a new group wanting to get started with nothing. It is quite likely that many homeowners will either donate or sell some of their equipment that's just sitting in their garages to Tool Libraries or equipment storage places. That way any group can take out as needed. No more renting from Home Depot or buying new items for rare use, or one time use and returning them.

Individuals waste more time and require access to more tools, plus cost of transportation of said tools from place to place. Specialized workers in groups are more efficient/productive. Small groups of landscape people come into my neighborhood with trucks loaded with all the various mowers and tools and just go from plot to plot, checking off all the tasks that homeowners have requested, completely freeing up people from that responsibility. End up doing all the landscaping for the folks who can't or don't want to do it themselves. This same principle applies to many labor tasks, which are all interconnected and necessary in current production and distribution globally.

Imagine you go to a Beauty Center, a big place of everything beauty related: makeup, hairdressing, facials, nails, perfume and even makeover artists. The cost of many of these goods will be minimal because mostly they are plentiful. The only reason they cost so much today is because of salaries, marketing and of course profit. Perfumes that cost $100s or $1000s today would be almost free, and their formulas and ingredients no longer secret. A consumer would be able to know everything that went into making it, how it was made and even who made it. The entire supply chain record is open. And no more 'luxury' brands throwing away brand new items because they don't want to hurt the image of the 'brand' by selling more cheaply. Go to hell.

Did you hear about the European airlines flying 1,000s of planes completely empty so they could maintain their routes because of arcane Game A accounting nonsense?[13] Go straight to hell.

I could give a lot more details and examples of what's possible using this new currency accounting but for sake of brevity and getting this book out as fast as possible, I'll spare you. Besides, it's not my area of expertise anyway but there are plenty of people with the knowledge and experience, 'Parecon' for example, and Michel Bauwens with the P2P Foundation:

---

[13] Wired, https://www.wired.com/story/airplanes-empty-slots-covid/

Some of our readers may be familiar with the 'calculation debates', of the 1930's, which pitted liberal pro-market economists, like Hayek, who favoured pricing mechanisms, against the socialist economists like Bauer, Neurath and ultimately, Polanyi, who argued the benefits of planning. In our industrial societies, this lib/lab discussion has obscured a third dimension: that of the commons and their self-management through mutual coordination. Today, large capitalist firms certainly plan, but they do not plan for balance with humanity and natural beings, it is extractive planning. The market allocates resources, but without any knowledge of impact. And finally, we see a substantial amount of commons-based mutual coordination occurring in the production of so-called (but not really!) 'immaterial resources' (knowledge, software, design), but has hardly touched the coordination of material production yet. Through shared accounting, which sits between transactions in the material world, and our human decision-making, this now becomes possible.

So what we are describing here is a 3-layered economy, and its infrastructure, that is able to coordinate production, by transcending and including the 3 great methods of allocating resources:

1. Mutual coordination through shared logistics and shared accounting

2. Ethical, generative market mechanisms for the fair exchange of resources

3. A planning framework, indicating the planetary resources available for human choice, so that we can produce while preserving the planet and its beings, and even regenerating them.[14]

"The ability to invent something new is resident everywhere, The ability to take that idea and actually build it and then to distribute it. What's literally different today is the world of the Internet and crowd creation. We are living in a time where the idea is the most important part. The ability to fund it from the crowd, the ability to use computers out there to design, test it, distribute it as more and more people are connected to the internet as the exponential tools for manufacturing things, designing thing, modeling things, are coming online, the ability for more people to innovate and to create, is itself growing exponentially."[15]

"The idea here is, again, that richer, larger and more complex societies offer much greater opportunities for people to develop unique experiences,

---

[14] Michel Bauwens, Commons Transition, "P2P Accounting For Planetary Survival", http://commonstransition.org/p2p-accounting-for-planetary-survival/

[15] Unknown source in my research notes

skills, ideas, relationships and perspectives. Societies that integrate larger quantities of human activities, natural resources and flows of information create fertile soil for the growth of a myriad of human perspectives and experiences. Greater economic and social integration spur higher dividuation: People are finding and recasting their "selves" and their relation to life on new, higher and more subtle levels."[16]

Resource Management

All existing resources within the Local community are accounted for, entered in shared databases for all to see, with some restrictions on data based on permissions where appropriate. "The commons is not a winner-takes-all economy, but all-take-the-winnings economy. Shared ownership encourages shared responsibility, which in turn engenders a longer term perspective on business practices. Nothing can be externalized to some "other" player, because everyone is part of the same trust, drinking from the same well."[17]

The idea is for everyone to contribute to 'managing' this shared data to produce what is now called a circular economy. It's not a new idea. Bucky wrote about this 50 years ago: "So, planners, architects, and engineers take the initiative. Go to work, and above all cooperate and don't hold back on one another or try to gain at the expense of another. Any success in such lopsidedness will be increasingly short-lived. These are the synergetic rules that evolution is employing and trying to make clear to us. They are not man-made laws. They are the infinitely accommodative laws of the intellectual integrity governing universe."[18]

As more and more data is input, eventually we'll have a stock of everything on the planet. We'll know how much of any specific item is being extracted, produced, consumed… everything. Much of this data already exists but is scattered and held privately. One of the necessary functions of a Common Planet is to determine how much resources can be extracted safely and sustainably. What is sustainable development? The Brundtland definition

[16] Unknown source in my research notes

[17] Rushkoff, *Team Human*, p. 110

[18] Fuller, *Spaceship Earth*, p. 44

(1987) is "Sustainable development is development that meets the needs of the present without compromising the ability of future generations to meet their own needs."

Data Visualization (DataViz) will help us to analyze and understand all the data. It can be used to present complex information or ideas in a clear, precise and efficient way. DataViz is both an art and a science, as the saying goes "a picture is worth a thousand words." Here's an example:
Near-real-time global gridded daily CO2 emissions[19]

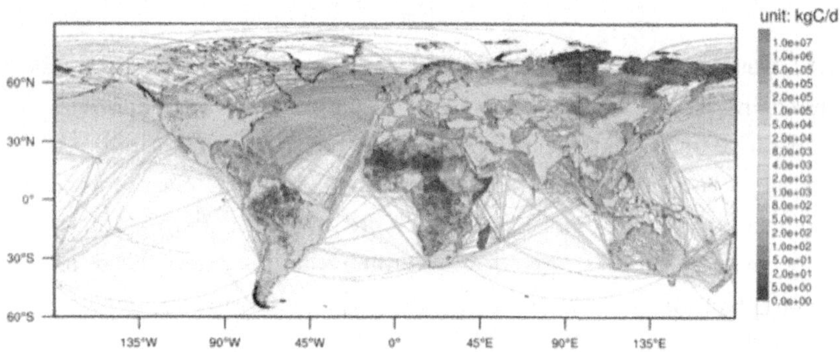

"The true source and measure of value and wealth is not money or any kind of human currency. Rather, it is the resources and ecological integrity of the Earth. At the same time, whatever (derivative) value and measure of wealth that money carries is backed solely by earth's ecological integrity, and comes fully and directly from the earth and the resources of its ecosystems. This is the most radical and universally ignored economic truth. Money, and all of economics, has no function, no reality outside of ecological reality."[20]

Vinay Gupta is building his company Mattereum.com specifically to power a circular economy, "Yes, it envisages a World Computer with nearly infinite computing power *but that is coming…* Imagine that all manufactured goods have digital twins on the blockchain. As the assets change hands and experience wear and tear every repair is logged. Soon we can see what is repairable and resellable, what can be patched and mended, and what is just dead-loss scrap. If every single thing we buy has a unique ID and a

---

[19] "Near-real-time global gridded daily CO2 emissions", Nov 2020, https://www.cell.com/the-innovation/fulltext/S2666-6758(21)00107-7

[20] David Haenke, "Bioregionalism and Ecological Economics", 1996, "Gaia, Economics, Money, and Wealth", https://medium.com/age-of-awareness/david-haenke-on-bioregionalism-ecological-economics-77be911685ce

permanent place to store its records, things will change. Manufactured goods cannot fail to improve in every way when exposed to the harsh light of transparency. Nobody wants to buy junk. A property rights transfer is as simple as having a neutral third party check that the item matches the blockchain record of the object, and an NFT is transferred to move the legal ownership."[21]

Credit currency is designed to flow, to always lubricate the movement of goods in society rather than to hoard and waste them as circulatory currency produces. Flow currency is composed of two parts, Personal Credit and Community Credit. Together they form an integrated monetary/financial system that embodies the ideals of transparency, fairness, democracy and cooperation. Real life Sim-City. It produces what Cynthia Bourgeault and others call "Autopoiesis":

> The term *autopoiesis* itself comes from the Greek roots "*auto*" (self) and "*poeisis*," creation. **Self-creation**, or in other words, a system capable of reproducing and maintaining itself. The popular shorthand for this is a "self-specifying system." A system exhibiting *autopoiesis* is a self-regulating whole. It has an inside and an outside, a diversification of function within an overall unity, and a capacity to self-monitor, rebalance internally, repair or replace damaged internal structures, and to reproduce itself. It also demonstrates so-called "emergent properties," capabilities that belong only to the whole and are not assignable to any of the component parts.
>
> The traditional aphorism here is that "the whole is stronger than the sum of its parts." But this is not just on account of "fellowship," or "strength in numbers," but because "greater degrees of relationship" really do create "greater degrees of information flow"—i.e., more manifest consciousness. There is a systemic intelligence that resides only in the whole, in which the individual members participate "severally"—or as we would say in the more technical language of our own time, "holographically."
>
> My growing suspicion is that the common good as it plays out within the Integral structure of consciousness is exactly that: *an emergent property of the whole*, in which the individual members participate holographically through their common belonging to the whole.[22]

Whether we change the economic system or not, change is already happening. Futurists James Arbib, Tony Seba and Deepak Chopra™ MD

---

[21] Vinay Gupta, https://medium.com/humanizing-the-singularity/can-the-world-computer-save-the-world-part-3-building-an-economy-with-a-future-5d4156f06a04

[22] Cynthia Bourgeault, "Autopoiesis", https://cynthiabourgeault.org/2021/08/20/autopoiesis-a-continuing-blog-series-on-the-common-good/

wrote an article on LinkedIn titled: "To Survive Our Technological Transformation, Civilization Needs a Cognitive Revolution" where they warn: "Over the next decade, industrial civilization will experience a scale of technological disruption never before seen in the history of humanity. Converging across the five foundational sectors of information, energy, transportation, food and materials, this disruption will drive massive transformations across the economy. But while this disruption is inevitable due to fundamental economic drivers, only by transforming our very core way of seeing and understanding the world will we navigate this transition in a way that elevates humanity to new heights while avoiding societal breakdown."[23]

By changing our currency system we will be able to avoid the coming chaos and instead harness the power of our exponentially growing technologies. In the same article they alluded to Common Planet: "Together, these disruptions will facilitate a breakthrough production system making old extractive systems obsolete. In their place, we will see a decentralized model of localized ownership and creation alongside a global model of product design and technology development. This creation-based system would enable the abundant, local and cheap production of energy, food, knowledge, tools and materials for the benefit of all, rather than a few. We call this potential new epoch, in which human beings for the first time in history could be free of concerns around material survival, the 'Age of Freedom.'" If you want more info on what kind of technologies are coming, be sure to check out their research at RethinkX.com.

Robert Conan Ryan calls this synthesis of using information with conscious intent the Fifth Great Magisteria, saying it "should be both a revolution in global information commons as well as global environmental commons, and that the two sides of this revolution should, in many ways, provide stewardship of all the world's basic resources. Furthermore, this new way of combining the inputs of all global citizens will help to stabilize the world without killing the engine of creative destruction that has driven us this far… By working in an orchestrated effort, the global citizen will provide an oversight that restores balance to the relationship between humanity and environment. Certainly, some degree of expertise and job hierarchy will be required to administer the system, and it won't be a pure paradise all the time.

---

[23] James Arbib, Tony Seba and Deepak Chopra™ MD, May 4, 2021, https://www.linkedin.com/pulse/survive-our-technological-transformation-civilization-deepak/

Feelings get hurt, tempers flare, and differences of opinions will continue - however, we will enter a new era where we can manage complexity on an order of magnitude never before, while also reducing the risks by a similar order of magnitude. The Fifth Great Magisteria can, and will, carry us forward into a Post-Industrial Era."[24]

Sounds to me like Mr. Ryan is describing Common Planet. Because Credit currency flows to each person and from each person, this produces what James Gien Wong wrote in a November 2021 email to Ryan: "A global superorganism-type coordinating system for bottom-up actors is desperately needed, something that can provide the efficacy of a circulatory, nervous, digestive system to millions of separately metabolizing local actors and create the cohesiveness required at this time."

"We have to plan what can be planned, according to our common decision. But the emphasis of the idea of culture is right when it reminds us that a culture, essentially, is unplannable. We have to ensure the means of life, and the means of community. But what will then, by these means, be lived, we cannot know or say," wrote Raymond Williams in his 1958 book *Culture & Society 1780-1950*.

---

[24] P2P Foundation Wiki, "Fifth Magisterium of the Commons", https://wiki.p2pfoundation.net/Fifth_Magisterium_of_the_Commons

Chapter 6
Liberty

"Freedom means the opportunity to be what we never thought we would be."
- Daniel Boorstin

Liberty was defined best by Ben Franklin: "Liberty is freedom, with responsibility." Freedom is the beauty of choosing for oneself and acting on one's initiative. Man's nature is that of a finite, social being. Therefore, his freedom must be limited. Freedoms have some obvious limitations so that they cannot be extended so far that they present a danger either to social relations or to values that allow the society to function in harmony. Freedom has a special use as a moral and a social concept, usually referring to situations arising within personal or social relations. There are important differences about the meanings of some particular aspects of the term.

Bertrand Russell once wrote, "Freedom in general may be defined as the absence of obstacles to the realization of desires." This definition is too broad.

Rulers have always controlled and manipulated information flows to citizens and what views they encounter. Educators for these regimes have molded the minds and views of the young. Consequently, citizens ultimately desire exactly what their rulers want them to desire. It rarely occurs to the citizens that there are alternatives to their accustomed actions or that their personal freedom has, in any way, been limited. They are unaware of any obstructions to their desires because obstructions may not exist to the satisfaction of any desires they experience.

The brilliant bastard Edward Bernays, the 'father of Public Relations', revealed to us in his 1928 book *Propaganda*: "Society consents to having its choice narrowed to ideas and objects brought to its attention through propaganda of all kinds." This case illustrates conditions that still exist more or less in all societies today. Would we say that the members of such a society enjoyed any or much freedom?

"In regard to propaganda the early advocates of universal literacy and a free press envisaged only two possibilities: the propaganda might be true, or the propaganda might be false. They did not foresee what in fact has happened, above all in our Western capitalist democracies - the development of a vast mass communications industry, concerned in the main neither with the true nor the false, but with the unreal, the more or less totally irrelevant. In a word, they failed to take into account man's almost infinite appetite for distractions," lamented Aldous Huxley. The MSM long ago zeroed in on this obvious fact of human nature to capture our 'eyeballs' for advertising money.

How much control of your beliefs and behaviors do you think you have? In this new book by Robert H. Lustig, MD, MSL, *The Hacking of the American Mind: The Science Behind the Corporate Takeover of Our Bodies and Brains*, he reveals how food manufacturers and electronics companies both capitalize on the biology of dopamine versus serotonin to get us addicted to their products. My friends, we are constantly being manipulated. Our dopamine rush, that feel good or reward-generating impulse is the same no matter what our source of pleasure is. It can be a thing like nicotine, alcohol, drugs or junk food; or it can be behavior, like social media, shopping, gaming or porn.

Another definition of freedom is a condition characterized by the absence of coercion or constraint imposed by another person (Encyclopedia of Philosophy). By this definition, people are free to choose their goals, available alternatives and consequent actions. No other person, nor the state, nor any other authority can compel a person to choose a course of action or prevent him from choosing a course of action. This definition is also too broad because it allows a person freedom to lie, steal or kill.

In clarifying the definition, freedom is the absence of obstacles to the exercise and satisfaction of specific interests and forms of activity which are accepted as possessing especial moral and social significance (Encyclopedia of Philosophy).

This definition allows for freedom of thought, speech, assembly, worship, use or disposal of one's property, etc. In every case there is a reference to individual choice and to the absence of coercion or interference with that choice. And this choice is not unlimited but specifically bound to some social activity within which the right to make one's choice must be of particular importance in the moral and social life of the individual.

Therefore, freedom can be said to be a claim to a particular liberty. The late Ezra Bowen, Journalist and Professor, wrote:

> For despite the formal words of the Bill of Rights, what the Constitution, the First Amendment grants the press, is not freedom at all, but liberty. Benjamin Franklin defined the difference between freedom and liberty, thus: liberty is freedom, with responsibility. Understand the difference. With complete freedom, I could override the law, destroy your life— or your wife or husband. But no, I may not do so, with impunity, with no regard for law, honor, for decency and ethics, or for the other person's side of the story. I may not do so, for I function under the permission of liberty, not freedom. As do all Americans.

Is there any person who doesn't value personal liberty, if not someone else's, then at least their own? I would think not.

Liberty is the essence of life.

In American grade school, every morning we stood up, put our right hand across our chest and recited the "pledge of allegiance" out loud in unison: "one nation, under God, indivisible, with liberty and justice for all."

Freedom and liberty is not just an American thing, it's a human thing. Everybody dreams of the freedom to be able to live their life how they want, but most don't have it.

If liberty was always *the* goal of humanity, then how did we ever come to value material possessions more? Consider the promise of the American Dream, where if we *work* hard (play Game A), we can have everything we desire: a house, car, family and a pleasant retirement. Since wealth affords freedom then the pursuit of wealth is the pursuit of freedom, right? But wasn't it always the ultimate goal to have more leisure time to enjoy life? To be in control of our own time to choose our own experiences?

Writer Oshan Jarow calls this 'time inequality': "Time ownership is a new phrase draped over an old idea. In Ancient Greece, they called it freedom. In the early days of industrial capitalism, leisure time. During the 100 years between 1830 and 1930, leisure time for all was seen as the highest dividend, the greatest promise of economic progress."[1]

---

[1] Oshan Jarow, "Against Time Inequality: A Framework for Progress", https://www.musingmind.org/essays/time-inequality

Reading books about 'money' only magnifies the connection of money to time freedom. Let's examine a few quotes from Morgan Housel's March 2021 best selling book about money *The Psychology of Money: Timeless lessons on wealth, greed and happiness.* "Money's greatest intrinsic value—and this can't be overstated—is its ability to give you control over your time… Controlling your time is the highest dividend money pays… The freedom to do what you want, when you want, with whom you want, for as long as you want, is true freedom…. Independence, to me, doesn't mean you'll stop working. It means you only do the work you like with people you like at the times you want for as long as you want… More than I want big returns, I want to be financially unbreakable… Using your money to buy time and options has a lifestyle benefit few luxury goods can compete with."

Housel clearly understands that there is no such thing as freedom without money. If that is true, and it is true in any market system, then the only possible way to freedom would be to make sure everyone always has money. That is exactly what the design of a Flow credit currency does. Decentralize and democratize money to ensure everyone has the freedom to access and participate in the market on their terms. Common Planet is literal time freedom for each and every person on the planet.

Historian Benjamin Hunnicutt wondered why, after 100 years of shorter working hours, did America abandon the pursuit of leisure? These are the main topics of two of his books - *Work Without End,* and *Free Time: The Forgotten American Dream* - which chronicle America's history of the pursuit of leisure time for all. "We have forgotten what used to be the other, better half of the American dream. In our rushing about for more, we have lost sight of the better part of freedom - of what Walt Whitman, with so many others throughout American history, called Higher Progress."

The path to freedom is paved with money. In his new book *Creating Freedom,* Raoul Martinez talks about historical capture of and abuse of the word freedom. "In the scramble to define it, the ideal of freedom has been pushed, pulled, twisted and torn; expertly moulded to suit the interests of those with the power to shape it."

Everybody knows we're not free. *We are Anonymous* message: "Far too many of us struggle in this cacophony of deceit that our corporate owned government institutions force upon us. We are indeed not free, but servile to financial institutions that have their webs cast upon every facet of civilization. The money those in power use to propagate your slavery is a mere illusion.

They create your worth, your fiber of being and the majority of us are kept under heel. This needs to change."

Human Rights struggles have always been a part of the human experience, with a notable explosion in the 1700s which shaped the American & French Revolutions. Most recently, in 1948, the United Nations Universal Declaration of Human Rights attests that "freedom of speech and belief and freedom from fear and want has been proclaimed as the highest aspiration of the common people." They got this very right.

To aspire means to hope, to desire and to set one's sights on achieving. I ask you, have we achieved these declared human rights? No. Have we seen an increase in these rights among the people? No. In fact, we've seen the opposite. It's been over 70 years, how much longer is it going to take? It'll never happen because Game A makes a mockery of these rights. "Freedom is measured by the amount of control you have over the things upon which you are dependent," wrote C. Wright Mills. We are dependent upon the natural resources of the Earth and have NO RIGHTS TO and NO CONTROL over them anymore. When you give rights to one group to 'own' all the resources for private profit, and keep them from others under the threat of violence, you have just denied everyone else freedom from fear and want forever. It's built into the game.

"Cannibalism, as I define it, is the consuming of another's life for one's own private purpose or profit. Imperialism and exploitation are forms of cannibalism and, in fact, are precisely those forms which are most diabolical," writes Jack D. Forbes in his 2008 book *Columbus and Other Cannibals.*

It's not just that the commons have been privatized but also more sinister and diabolical is the money, the token needed to access those privatized goods. The fact that a small group of men control its issuance is insane power, antithetical to and nullifies any possibility of personal freedom.

"Liberty, finally, is not a box into which people are to be forced. Liberty is a space in which people may live. It does not tell you how they will live. It says, eternally, only that we ***can***," wrote Karl Hess.

Democracy

We've shown how freedom is much talked about, much lauded but completely non-existent and unattainable for most in Game A, but what about democracy? America is said to be a democracy and surely we have functioning democracies all over the world in 'modern' times right? What is a society where huge tax-evading, profit driven multinational Corporations run by an oligarchy rule the Planet? It's not democracy. It's a plutocracy. "Under capitalism, we can't have democracy by definition. Capitalism is a system in which the central institutions of society are in principle under autocratic control," says Noam Chomsky.

Sheldon Wolin called the rise of a new and terrifying configuration of corporate power an 'inverted totalitarianism', a dictatorship of capital. "One cannot point to any national institution[s] that can accurately be described as democratic, surely not in the highly managed, money-saturated elections, the lobby-infested Congress, the imperial presidency, the class-biased judicial and penal system, or, least of all, the media."[2]

This is different from past forms of totalitarianism; there is no State dictator or authoritarian figurehead that maintains this oppressive system. Instead, it finds its expression in the faceless anonymity of the corporate state, which has captured all of the mechanisms of power to render the citizen impotent.[3] If we can't vote out Monsanto, Facebook or Lockheed Martin, who rule our politicians who rule our lives, well then, that's a dictatorship.

Once we become free with sovereignty and liberty restored to all, we also need a sort of new social contract. Like a global Bill of Rights.[4] Here's what I suggest for a Common Planet. The following rights are not subject to restriction by any person or community.

Freedom of Mind:

A person's mind is their personal sacred spirit. All information is to be free, never subject to restriction.

---

[2] Sheldon Wolin, *Democracy Incorporated: Managed Democracy and the Specter of Inverted Totalitarianism*, 2010

[3] Arash Kolahi, https://twitter.com/ArashKolahi/status/1294322016086941699

[4] Bill of Rights, https://www.law.cornell.edu/constitution/billofrights

Freedom of Speech:

This includes freedom of opinion and expression.

Freedom of Body:

A person's body is their sacred vessel. It cannot be coerced, controlled, enslaved, violated, injured or imprisoned by another; any such act is intolerable and illegal. All people have complete control of their bodies without limitation; what a person puts in their body, or on their body is personal and their decision alone. All physical violations such as assault, abuse, rape and murder are illegal and subject to arrest and punishable by law.

Freedom of Assembly & Participation

All persons have the right to assemble peacefully toward the advancement of their personal, group or societal needs and desires so long as they do not violate the rights of any person or group as stated above. All people have the right to participate in society, to exercise their vote in a Direct Democracy.

"The majority is wrong. Always were. Then again, what else should we expect? The point with democracy isn't that the majority is always right. The point is that there is a process of free and sufficiently systematized truth-seeking and dialogue going on for small groups to be able to prove the rest of us wrong, again and again, so that values, opinions and laws can evolve and adapt. That's how democracy works—you can't "vote" about the truth; the idea is that the truth offers a powerful attractor point so that, in the long run, more truth than falsehood will win out, and that this, on average, will have better consequences."[5]

"Democracy is self-government at scale, and that requires decision-making at scale. Good decision-making depends on good information… If we have no shared basis for making sense of the world, we have no shared basis for governing ourselves. To save democracy—and repair the damage to our epistemic commons—we need a new cultural movement that values high-quality reasoning and open dialogue in an open society."[6]

---

[5] Hanzi Freinacht, *Nordic Ideology: A Metamodern Guide to Politics, Book Two*, 2019, https://www.facebook.com/permalink.php?story_fbid=958068228041479&id=100015149321507

[6] The Consilience Project, "Democracy and the Epistemic Commons", https://consilienceproject.org/democracy-and-the-epistemic-commons/, https://www.youtube.com/watch?v=cMnD2kYLVGw

In order to move forward, we'll need a shared, open and trusted information ecology. "Democracy depends on the individual voter making an intelligent and rational choice to what he regards is his enlightened self interest in any given circumstance," said Aldous Huxley.[7] This is not possible in a rivalrous economics where information is power. Power is not shared. It's used to win at the expense of the 'others.' Information is power, and we've already discussed how our information ecology is poisoned and polluted beyond all recognition of what is true or real today.

Imagine having the right to vote on all matters in your local community, in all the places you play, learn and work. Imagine further voting on regional and global issues too. The type of democracy I'm talking about is called "Democratic self determination" by Arash Kolahi:

> If a decision only affects you, only you get to have a say (self-determination). Only once others are affected do they get to have a say (democratic) and only to the degree they are affected (fair). Freedom means being able to use our own cognitive abilities to make decisions for ourselves… Democracy is more than voting. It's more than majority vote. It's more than even consensus. Real democracy means those AFFECTED by a decision get to have a say in that decision. How much of a say? A say proportional to how much the decision affects them. The corollary to true democracy is that those who are not at all affected by a decision should have no say in that decision. If a decision only affects me, only I should have a say. If a decision only affects you, only you should have a say. If a decision affects us both equally, we should both have equal say. If a decision affects you a lot & me only peripherally, then you should have more say. If a decision only affects your neighborhood, only people in your neighborhood should have a say. If a decision only affects your community, only your community should have a say, etc. When we say we want freedom & democracy, what we really mean is we want to use our cognitive abilities & have a say in decisions that affect our lives. We want the same for others. So that means we want a say in decisions proportional to how much the decision affects us. Some argue this definition is too idealistic. Perhaps. But we are not saying it's 100% attainable in every situation. We are saying that this is the ideal we are striving for: People having a say in the decisions that affect them, proportional to how much it affects them.[8]

---

[7] Aldous Huxley on Technodictators, https://www.youtube.com/watch?v=oIgjujAI6cE

[8] Arash Kolahi, https://twitter.com/ArashKolahi/status/1125471207086649346

According to Engage2, a Sydney consulting group, these are the 5 main models of democracy:[9]

1. **Direct** – everyone votes / decides on everything.
2. **Liquid** – like direct, but you can pass on your vote to someone else.
3. **Representative** – people vote to elect officials who represent them and make decisions on their behalf.
4. **Deliberative** – a demographically representative group of people discuss an issue and decide on everyone's behalf. These mini-publics are randomly selected.
5. **Participatory** – people actively and openly discuss matters of state and decide together. Everyone has equal authority, and the majority rules.

There are now organizations all over the world building technology to offer us these new forms of democratic decision making. Many are open-source, so there's a lot of room for you to join and contribute to building these technical and social frameworks if you want. Here's some of the leading organizations involved in this space. I'm sure there are many more.

Democracy.earth - - Horizon State - - VoteFlux - - Democracy at Work
The Co-intelligence Institute's Wise Democracy Project - - FairVote
Represent - - One Global Democracy - - Our Global Justice Movement
Democracy Collaborative - - Democracy Club

[9] Engage2, https://engage2.com.au/models-of-democracy/

Governance

If our goal is to have a resilient commons-based society, then we need to listen to people.[10] People are ready to play a role in participating and solving problems. I've found many organizations already doing the work, thinking about how we can organize the decision making processes utilizing a commons based approach. Many of them identify the exact same root problem as I have in this book: economics. You now know what Game A is and mostly know what Game B is supposed to be like but during my research I was unsatisfied with others' proposed solutions for Game B economics. These ideas of a 'Resource Based Economy' or 'Post-Capitalism' or 'Fully Automated Luxury Communism' allude to this 'other' and 'new' but I was left unsatisfied with the details of their monetary alternatives.

Despite lacking some of the monetary details, many of these people and organizations have been able to map out ideas and plans that build on the commons foundation. In almost every plan, the solution revolves around transparency and accountability which leads to trust. "Trust is like the oxygen that a free society needs to breathe, and we are like the trees that can emit oxygen."[11]

I'd like to introduce some of them here since my expertise is specifically on currency systems, not really much of anything beyond that, except for soccer. I shouldn't diss myself. I've spent over 7 years researching these things so I have more than a few insights I wanted to share and intended to but for expediency, I'm not including them in this first version of the book.

One of my favorites is a collaborative effort led by Robert Schram called the World Summit Movement.[12] They describe themselves as "a peaceful (r)evolutionary movement connecting and unifying thousands of groups and individuals worldwide who are converging now to create a new operating system, including entirely new self-governance and regenerative economic models, by 2020. We have already partnered with over 50 different groups from all sectors of society including universities, NGO's, social justice and

---

[10] Ted Rau, Sociocracy For All, "Sociocracy meets Listening At Scale", https://www.sociocracyforall.org/sociocracy-meets-listening-at-scale/

[11] Mike Lowe, GameB FB group, https://www.facebook.com/groups/gamebcore/permalink/2779866815576694/

[12] HackHumanity, https://hackhumanity.net/worldsummit-movement/, https://www.facebook.com/groups/worldsummit/

environmental movements. We are gathering the critical mass support to flip the paradigm to a better world that meets everyone's basic needs."[13] They have a few nice presentations available online. The 3 Pillars of Activism, an Integral framework, the mother of all hacks, Transition Tactics, and a video Humanity's Phase Shift - A New Story.[14]

In 2017, The Global Challenges Foundation organized a competition to reimagine global governance for the 21st century. Naveen Srivatsav and a group of friends submitted their proposal called ComplexCity:

> In essence, we are proposing to harness civic participation for global governance through grassroots-level collaborative complexity engineering... To do this, we propose to have a platform for global citizens to: 1) **learn** how to appreciate complexity and thus engage constructively with it; 2) **apply** a socio-scientific framework to identify community problems, structure pilot experiments, measure outcomes and thus enact systemic sustainable change within a complex environment; and 3) **build** toward long-term civilizational goals via decentralised initiatives that improve and grow the commons.
>
> While we do not believe that such peer-to-peer interactions through virtual platforms will be a one-size-fits-all panacea for global problems, we do argue that forward-looking solutions to global governance can and should leverage them instead of ignoring this untapped human capital. We thus propose to leverage collective intelligence, introducing the open-source mantra that "given enough eyeballs, all bugs are shallow", in the arena of global governance itself.[15]

Trainer, facilitator and writer Miki Kashtan offers her powerful framework of Convergent Facilitation, which is a model of group decision making that is both efficient and ensures that all voices are heard. Here she is talking about "Exiting the Either/Or Trap - Beyond Consensus vs. Command and Control" with the East Point Peace Academy on May 11, 2020, as part of their "Where Do We Go From Here" series. Kashtan says "we either have a nonviolent future or we have no future because the kind of present that we

---

13 World Summit, Unity Paper, https://drive.google.com/file/d/1l91_GLXHufpKYEhewIEqOiVI1ML9gFkc

14 World Summit, https://docs.google.com/presentation/d/e/2PACX-1vSpwyTsZdpRXGWssUflsNwsBHIl65tE30YkcWH9o-ZMiajJv70VDa1arzOuS_SPUJyOKEhrD6ke8K5W/pub?

15 Naveen Srivatsav et al, https://issuu.com/sumergoconicio/docs/complexcity_-_white_paper

have is the way of living that is based on scarcity, separation and powerlessness that comes from 7,000 years of patriarchy. I see in patriarchy our control and either-or thinking and that is what I'm gonna try to show how we approach decision-making. We can exit those and go to a nonviolent future of choice, togetherness and flow so that control is replaced by purpose and either-or thinking is replaced by integration."[16]

Another is Humania, a human-centric resource based proposal whose "research shows that groups make better decisions than individuals so, in collaborative communities, would it not make sense to try and tap into the collective intelligence instead, without resorting to potentially parasitic authority/hierarchy?"[17] Their proposal contains quite a bit of thought and specific details also helpful for the transition.

Law, Police & Military

Humans have been making rules of behavior before we even started speaking. When language was finally invented the first thing said was "stop fighting," followed by a club to the head. Bad joke, sorry. Records from Mesopotamia reveal The Code of Ur-Nammu is 4,100 years old, and the more influential and more clearly defined Code of Hammurabi is about 3,800 years old. Clearly, rules are important.

In his 1994 book *Order without Law*, Robert Ellickson shows that law is far less important than is generally thought. He demonstrates that people largely govern themselves by means of informal rules, or social norms, that develop without the aid of a State or other central coordinator. Indeed, this is how it was for my people. The Albanian Kanun is an old customary law and likely the reason we've been able to survive the relentless Game A genocides of Europe for thousands of years despite being located in the geographic center of the battle between Catholic Romans and Muslim Turks. These are ancient oral traditions that have served us well. Everybody wanted to and tried to annihilate or dominate my people, and none could. It's because we adhered to the concept of Besa, our word or pledge of honor to each other.[18]

---

[16] Miki Kashtan, https://www.youtube.com/watch?v=Qvmqeeme42M

[17] Humania, https://docs.google.com/document/d/18r9iCYR5ZJVODkXw5sm0jHELEIC1hNcGaeaKO0WM9U

[18] https://en.wikipedia.org/wiki/Besa_(Albanian_culture)

Most people instinctively know all the formal and informal rules of social behavior. However, do you know all the laws in your city, region or country today? Of course not, nobody does, yet ignorance of the law is no excuse. Even lawyers spend years then end up specializing in only one branch of law. When we learned about law in grade school, I remember the first question that popped into my head was "how can a person be held liable for a law if they don't even know it exists?" I always found it odd that knowing the rules of the game of life weren't a prerequisite to play. It makes no sense at all.

"Ignorance of the law is no excuse" only makes sense if the law is simple enough to learn before one makes meaningful actions in the game. It makes much less sense when law is as complex as it is today.

Why is law so complex and the laws so numerous? Because laws are more about Property than behavior. How many of our laws today revolve, in one way or another, around Property? The majority. Most of today's laws exist on account of Game A. If you go to any American courtroom (other countries likely similar), much of what the judges are deliberating on has to do with Property of one type or another. Contract disputes over business, sales, purchases, employment, theft, rent and marriage. These have everything to do with the constant warfare that is Game A 'ownership' of Property.

Here's a list of lawyer types for Property: Business, Bankruptcy, Tax, Divorce, Labor, Estate Planning, Immigration, Personal Injury, Intellectual property, Entertainment, Medical malpractice, Contract, Social Security Disability, Mergers and Acquisitions, Environmental, Finance and Securities, Real Estate/Property, and Digital Media.

Now here's a list of lawyers about behavior: Criminal, Constitutional, Family, Public Interest and Civil Rights.

That's a short list. It's short because a Flow currency makes Property relations clear, transparent and fair.

When and why were police invented? The below article shows the creation of the first police forces in England and the US, within a few decades in the mid-19th century, were not created to prevent crime or protect the public, but primarily to control crowds, especially the working class:

> The new institution was not a response to an increase in crime, and it really didn't lead to new methods for dealing with crime. The most common way for authorities to solve a crime, before and since the invention of police, has been for someone to tell them who did it.

> Besides, crime has to do with the acts of individuals, and the ruling elites who invented the police were responding to challenges posed by collective action. To put it in a nutshell: The authorities created the police in response to large, defiant crowds. That's — strikes in England, — riots in the Northern US, — and the threat of slave insurrections in the South. So the police are a response to crowds, not to crime.[19]

So local police were created to protect the Property of the rich from crowds. For the same reasons, national military forces were created to protect the interests of Property owners from foreign players or other States but more so to protect and capture Property within other countries too.

The US cities and states spent over $118 billion on policing in 2018 according to US Census Bureau data. Not to mention the $ billions in extra military equipment that got funneled for local *security*.

Have you ever heard of 'civil asset forfeiture'?[20] You're never going to think about the police the same way again. To understand the scope of this problem, you should know that cops take more money from people in civil asset forfeiture than all burglaries combined in the U.S. The cops at the local, state and federal levels across the country have taken almost $70 billion in civil forfeiture in the past 20 years![21]

It's the same thing with national policing. Over $1 Billion in settlements have been paid out over the past decade by US police departments for beatings, shootings and imprisonment. These settlements are not paid by police departments though, they don't cost the police anything, they are paid by city and state taxpayers. Meanwhile, bankers profit from local bonds issued to cover the costs because they are unable to tax the citizens enough. It is a vicious cycle of racism, brutality and greed.

Even criminal 'justice' has more to do with money than actual crime. "The death penalty is fundamentally a poor person's issue. Over nearly 40 years of visiting death row facilities across the United States, I have never met a single

---

[19] David Whitehouse, "Origins of the police", https://libcom.org/history/origins-police-david-whitehouse

[20] Alec Karakatsanis, Twitter, https://twitter.com/equalityAlec/status/1412428329806860288

[21] J. Justin Wilson, Institute for Justice, https://ij.org/press-release/new-report-finds-civil-forfeiture-rakes-in-billions-each-year-does-not-fight-crime-2/

person with money or resources. Capital punishment means 'those without the capital get the punishment.'"[22] wrote Sister Helen Prejean on Twitter.

Who wants this?: "VICE: Killer Robots are Coming."[23] This shit has got to go. Gabrielle Blair wrote this fantastic Twitter thread full of ideas on what's wrong with US policing and how to reform it.[24]

Mariame Kaba in an interview talking about the abolition of policing:

> How are we going to deal with the rapists and the murderers?" This is the question that always gets thrown at anybody who identifies as abolitionist—and my question back is "what are you doing right now about the rapists and the murderers?" That's the first thing: Is what's happening right now working for you? Are you feeling safer? Has the current approach ended rape and murder? The vast majority of rapists never see the inside of a courtroom, let alone get convicted and end up in prison. In fact, they end up becoming President. So the system you feel so attached to and that you seem invested in preserving is not delivering what you say you want, which is presumably safety and an end to violence. Worse than that it is causing inordinate additional harm. The logics of policing and prisons are not actually addressing the systemic causes and roots of violence.[25]

"In capitalist culture, if you sign up to kill & die for the rich, you're a hero. If you kill and die while fighting against the rich, you're a terrorist. This is masked as nationalism/patriotism, but it's really about where you stand in relation to the capitalist power structure."[26]

If you pay attention to mainstream media you will hear them banging the war drums wherever they can. China, Ukraine, Iran, Afghanistan, Syria, Venezuela, Chile and even in our homeland. Look at this nugget on the Cybersecurity & Infrastructure Security Agency (CISA) website: "**Malinformation** is based on fact, but used out of context to mislead, harm,

---

[22] Sister Helen Prejean, https://twitter.com/helenprejean/status/1350334166819241984

[23] VICE, "The Killer Robot Takeover is Inevitable", https://www.youtube.com/watch?v=0M4JMhXNNOg

[24] Gabrielle Blair, https://twitter.com/designmom/status/1270038204754919424

[25] Mariame Kaba, interview with Next System Project, https://thenextsystem.org/learn/stories/towards-horizon-abolition-conversation-mariame-kaba

[26] Hampton Institute, https://twitter.com/HamptonThink/status/1182484383233642496

or manipulate."[27] By this definition, anyone can be classified as a terrorist according to the terrorist State of the 'United States of America.'

Independent reporter, and my mental doppelgänger, Caitlin Johnstone cuts right to the point in her blog post full of resources and links, "US Troops Die For World Domination, Not Freedom":

> This is all US troops have been fighting and dying for since the Berlin Wall came down. Not 'freedom', not 'democracy', and certainly not for the American people. Just continual uncontested domination of this planet at all cost: domination of its resources, its trade routes, its seas, its air, and its humans, no matter how many lives need to risked and snuffed out in order to achieve it. The US has killed millions and displaced tens of millions just since the turn of this century in the reckless pursuit of that goal.
>
> And, as Smedley Butler spelled out 86 years ago in his still-relevant book *War is a Racket*, US military personnel have been dying for profit. Nothing gets the gears of industry turning like war, and nothing better creates chaotic wild west environments of shock and confusion during which more wealth and power can be grabbed.[28] War profiteers pour immense resources into lobbying, think tanks and campaign donations to manipulate and bribe policy makers into making decisions which promote war and military expansionism, with astounding success.[29] This is all entirely legal.[30]

This is how much is spent annually for Military by Country:

S. Korea:	$42 billion	Sa. Arabia:	$62 billion
Japan:	$48 billion	Russia:	$65 billion
UK:	$49 billion	India:	$71 billion
Germany:	$49 billion	China:	$261 billion
France:	$50 billion	USA:	$768 billion

As you can see, the US is the head of global policing and they work to enforce the interests of global capital. The financial oligarchy depends on investing excess capital to indebted war making nations.

---

[27] CISA, https://www.cisa.gov/mdm

[28] Naomi Klein, *The Shock Doctrine* documentary, https://www.youtube.com/watch?v=B3B5qt6gsxY

[29] RepresentUs, Corruption is Legal in America, https://www.youtube.com/watch?v=5tu32CCA_Ig

[30] Caitlin Johnstone, "US Troops Die For World Domination, Not Freedom", https://caitlinjohnstone.substack.com/p/us-troops-die-for-world-domination

Author John Perkins exposed a lot of these tactics in *Confessions of an Economic Hitman*, his 2004 best seller: "Economic hit men (EHMs) are highly paid professionals who cheat countries around the globe out of trillions of dollars. They funnel money from the World Bank, the U.S. Agency for International Development (USAID), and other foreign 'aid' organizations into the coffers of huge corporations and the pockets of a few wealthy families who control the planet's natural resources. Their tools include fraudulent financial reports, rigged elections, payoffs, extortion, sex and murder. They play a game as old as empire, but one that has taken on new and terrifying dimensions during this time of globalization. I should know; I was an EHM."

In the more recent 2018 book *Giants: The Global Power Elite*, author Peter Phillips tells how most US action is disguised and sold as 'humanitarian intervention', just as Perkins experienced and wrote about. Phillips details how the financial oligarchy promotes military actions "ideologically justified as peacekeeping or humanitarian missions," especially in cases where other States are "viewed as unfavorable to the TCC's capital interests [thus] resistance forces will be supported and encouraged toward regime change, as in…Libya, Syria, Iraq, Yemen, Somalia, Ukraine, Venezuela, and Yugoslavia."

Phillips' main argument is that the protection of transnational capital is the reason for "failed states, manufactured civil wars, regime changes, and direct invasions/occupations." History is full of States whose apparatus of force is used by the other players for personal profit and especially by banking cartels wanting to issue more debt.

What would an army look like in Common Planet? Game B explorer Jason Stone calls his idea 'The Holographic Army', an outline for how to form a fighting force to protect the land from those who would control it under more coercive, exploitative terms.[31]

Since poverty will be eradicated, violence will go down. "Poverty kills far more people than all the wars in history, more people than all the murderers in history, more than all the suicides in history, not only does structural violence kill more people than all the behavioral violence put together, structural violence is also the main cause of behavioral violence."[32]

---

[31] Jason Stone, Holon group, https://www.facebook.com/groups/251257168752681/permalink/651634522048275

[32] Dr. James Gilligan, Former Director: Center for the Study of Violence, Harvard Medical School. *Violence, our Deadly Epidemic, and it's Causes"*

Chapter 7
Transition

"Optimism is a strategy for making a better future. Because unless you believe that the future can be better, you are unlikely to step up and take responsibility for making it so." – Noam Chomsky

"Not everything that is faced can be changed, but nothing can be changed until it is faced." – James Baldwin

We didn't choose or vote for Game A. Nobody wants oligarchs to own and control all the Property in the world for their advantage. They didn't ask for our permission. It's time we have our say. It's time to open the untapped potential of all humanity to build a society that allows, enables and empowers all people to push the boundaries of their abilities.

So how do we seamlessly move to something that is more capable and stable without the current one coming apart? How do we go from Leavers to Takers to Makers?[1]

Our choices are politics or some form of direct action. Can we get our politicians to help in ushering in these changes we seek? Do we protest? "Protest is like begging the powers that be to dig a well. Direct action is digging the well and daring them to stop you," said Graeber. Would it be possible to vote for politicians who could lead the transition? Doubtful, since politicians represent the interests of the State which is captured by the oligarchs. Don't for a minute think we actually live in a democracy. Utsa and Prabhat Patnaik told us: "Democracy requires that alternative visions of society be placed before the people, from which they can choose. But if all political parties have the same policies, namely those approved by capital, then the choice of the people becomes meaningless."

---

[1] A nod to Daniel Quinn's 1992 book *Ishmael* references to leavers and takers.

Perhaps it would be possible to replace existing politicians with random citizen volunteers to help during the transitory phase. "I personally call the type of government which can be removed without violence 'democracy,'" said Karl Popper, "and the other, tyranny." Does that mean we must resort to violence since we live under the tyranny of oligarchs? Not this time. Lucky for us, I have discovered dragon glass: Flow currency. When we are ready, in one synchronized movement all concentrated power in the world can be instantly destroyed, decentralized and distributed among all the people.

Unfortunately, Flow currency doesn't fit into the circulatory regime of Game A. It's not like the existing circulatory currencies. We're not interested in merely replacing the currency with another only to continue playing the same wrong game of value. That's what all so-called prior revolutions have done. That's what all existing crypto currencies want to do and it will change absolutely nothing. A Flow currency is an entirely different system and therefore will require approval and planning prior to implementation.

The key to major societal change is getting enough people to alter their behavior at the same time. It's not enough for individuals to act alone. It's possible to change things on a large scale if we are able to communicate on a much greater scale. When everyone knows that everyone knows, changing what we do is much easier.

As Michael Suk-Young Chwe writes in his 2013 book, *Rational Ritual: Culture, Coordination, and Common Knowledge*, "Successful communication sometimes is not simply a matter of whether a given message is received. It also depends on whether people are aware that other people also receive it." According to Suk-Young Chwe, for people to coordinate on the basis of certain information it must be "common knowledge," a phrase used here to mean "everyone knows it, everyone knows that everyone knows it, everyone knows that everyone knows that everyone knows it, and so on." The more public and visible the change is, the better.

John Bunzl thinks it can be done using governments, with his idea for simultaneous action: "The campaign we're talking about is called the Simultaneous Policy (or SIMPOL, for short). As one politician who signed the Pledge commented, 'The compelling logic of Simultaneous Policy is really collective common sense – it's a campaign to find out how common sense really is!'"[2]

---

[2] John Bunzl, Simpol, https://simpol.org/

> If we want to help and heal the world, we must realise that we are all in the same boat; that no one is really to blame, and that global problems are caused by the absence of cooperative global governance. Not a world government, simply cooperative global agreements that solve global threats and are designed to be in every nation's self-interest. "Designed", because we are now at a stage in human evolution where global cooperation will have to be planned and established consciously and intentionally. Precisely because we are all in the same boat, there is no longer any out-group that might compel us to cooperate. So global cooperation will not happen all by itself. Instead it will have to be consciously planned and chosen. So what might such a plan look like? What might its design criteria be?
>
> Any solution must be implemented simultaneously by nations. If all or sufficient nations act simultaneously, no nation, corporation or citizens need lose out to any other: global and simultaneous – everybody wins. But since dominant nations may not see global cooperation as in their interests and would seek to free-ride and undermine global cooperation, our solution must give citizens the power to compel their governments to cooperate. Our solution must not just be global and simultaneous but also be driven by citizens.[3]

We believe Common Planet is such a global plan, and indeed, can only be driven by the people. What I like about Bunzl's proposal is that it doesn't require any violence or force. "Force is divisive and through that divisiveness, weakens, where as power unifies... Power serves others, where as force is self-serving. Power appeals to our higher nature, force to our lower nature... Force is limited, whereas power is unlimited."[4]

"So this abolitionist movement is not about using force to fight the powers-that-be. That is the old story of separation and divisiveness. That's how the bloody American Civil War weakened us. We cannot use force as a self-serving mechanism for the few. This time it will be based upon power, for the greatest good of all of us. In not fighting, in simply dissolving the corrupt powers and brute force, this is how we can break the patterns that have shackled humanity for many millennia. Now we can use the true power of firm love to achieve our unlimited potential."[5]

The 1960s and 70s were a period of great social change in America with calls for revolution echoing throughout the land and then nothing substantial came of it. Everything achieved has long since been reversed. Protests

---

[3] John Bunzl, *The Power is Ours*, https://www.consciousevolution.co.uk/blog/the-power-is-ours

[4] David R. Hawkins M.D. Ph.D, *Power vs. Force*, 2014

[5] Troy Wiley, *The Next Copernican Revolution*, 2016, p. 165

proved to be of limited short success. Even MLK changed his mind about the tactics needed. "King abandoned the incremental approach to social change of his civil rights protest days in favor of pursuing "a reconstruction of the entire society, a revolution of values," one which would "look uneasily on the glaring contrast of poverty and wealth with righteous indignation." And his condemnations of American militarism and gross disparities in wealth and opportunity still echo, though to little more effect than he was able to achieve 50 years ago."[6]

The people must be offered a voice and a choice, but have we the power to act once we've expressed our voices? How can we get power to change the world? According to John K. Galbraith in his 1983 book *Anatomy of Power*, there are 3 sources of power: personality, Property and organization.

Forget about personality. I'm a nobody and have no plans or desire to build anything around me or any other person. They could, and probably will, target and squash me like a bug. This is about global systemic change, not some scheme to elevate people into positions of power like all previous revolutions. Using celebrity will be an effective use of power to advance our cause but not to advance any person into power themselves.

I have no personal Property so I lack any power to buy attention or influence in the market.

That leaves us with only the third option: we need to build an organization to more quickly advance our interests and values in the world. An organization can combine the support of personalities and property to then wield greater power of influence in the world. That's the goal of the Common Planet Foundation. Please support us if you can so we can begin what Joe Brewer calls a 'design pathway'.

> A design pathway is a developmental trajectory—filled with design choices along the way—that moves toward a sequentially derived outcome that cannot be achieved in a single step. This is best explained using an example. When John F. Kennedy declared that the United States should place a man on the moon by the end of the 1960's, he was advocating for a design pathway to fully enter the space age. A trajectory would be needed that (a) identified all of the necessary steps involved; (b) outlined the obstacles to success for each necessary step; (c) progressed sequentially (or in parallel) through the resolution of all obstacles as each step was completed; until (d) the final outcome was achieved.

---

[6] James C. Cobb, Smithsonian Magazine, https://www.smithsonianmag.com/history/why-martin-luther-king-had-75-percent-disapproval-rating-year-he-died-180968664/

> How each of these steps is understood at the beginning of the process may have very little resemblance to what the actual trajectory looks like in hindsight after it has been walked together by all of the people involved. This is because the purpose of a design pathway is to hold intentions for navigating toward a North Star beyond the current horizon of knowledge. We will need to make efforts to comprehend the obstacles and opportunities involved so that we can navigate to the best of our abilities, but this is quite different from what we will learn along the way as we actually walk the path.[7]

Our goal is to upgrade the world's socio-economic infrastructure. To transition from a world run by inefficient bureaucracies and corporations into a world governed by decentralized autonomous organizations that care about their communities and ecosystems.

The plan here is to subvert the Old Economic Order, by offering an alternative, utilizing basic technology and information services that have been widely unavailable without the umbrella force of corporate hegemony. By utilizing basic information services ourselves we may then dictate the terms of our engagements, nuanced and complicated as they are, as they should be in an enlightened society.

Until now these engagements have been stifled by the Old Economic Order which functions to preserve the wealth distribution of a prior epoch that has long since come and gone.

The ultimate goal here is to free the world's capital from the clutches of the Old Economic Order, which is currently controlled by a web of banking interests, their States and a tiny percentage of individuals.

Here, we have developed a comprehensive platform, an alternative which combines the many services we presently utilize through various corporate signifiers for social media, eg, financial institutions, and government, which auction our integrity through those few who are fully invested yet in the Old Economic Order. We have called this alternative "Common Planet."

Step 1: Create a Common Planet Account to Receive a New Voting Identity & Digital Currency Accounts:

- Complete a Common Planet application.
- Store voting identity, digital Credit accounts, and digital titles for existing property owned.

---

[7] Joe Brewer, *The Design Pathway for Regenerating Earth*, https://earth-regenerators.mn.co/posts/the-design-pathway-chapter-5

- Receive a new financial identity that is calculated in proportion to age and existing net assets.
- Receive a monthly Universal Basic Income (UBI).
- Download the app to interact on Common Planet for the purposes of:
    - Voting
    - Digital asset management
    - Communication

Unlike traditional leftist visions of revolution, where the social movement seizes State power and then installs new agents of the State, the emerging world of peer production is based on another vision: build an alternative economy outside the circuits of Game A and then develop its own functionalities and moral authority.

"The study of history", writes Thomas Piketty in his 2020 *Capital and Ideology*, "...has convinced me that it is possible to transcend today's capitalist system and to outline the contours of a new participatory socialism for the twenty-first century...what makes historical change possible is above all the existence of social and political mobilizations for change and concrete experimentation with alternative arrangements."

"We didn't plan our division of labor changes over the millennia. We don't change only when a hero makes us change. We don't change simply because some of us say we want a change. Changes didn't come because we somehow suddenly became smarter or more moral or more caring than our ancestors. Nor did they come solely because some of us desired them—or more accurately, said we desired them. Nor did we allow them simply because some of our economies later benefited from them. We change when we both have a strong need, and we have, or are near to having, new means to help us satisfy that need. Demand and supply, each push the other. We need both to change."[8]

If we continue to destroy our ecology it will ultimately lead to collapse and our extinction. The need for change has never been greater, and with modern technology capable of running the new currency system, we can finally implement change. The need and the tools are both here. Now is the time.

It's been 'the time' for change for over a century though. In the course of research, I came across so many articles and speeches that sound like they were written just yesterday. Recognizing the importance of the commons and

[8] Rawlins, *Shoulders of Giants*

the desire to build a 'Common Planet' isn't new. Here's the words of Samuel M. Jones again from his 1899 article:

> We are living in one of the most interesting and important epochs in the world's history, thus far — an age that has witnessed more of the marvels of material development than any or all of the ages that have preceded it… modern inventions and labor-saving machinery have increased the producing power of men twenty-, fifty-, and one hundredfold beyond what was believed to be within the possibilities 100 or even 50 years ago.
>
> The steps most likely to contribute to bringing about the better days and the better times for which we all long are to my mind those things that will unify the people, that will serve to weld them together in one common mass, those things that will help them to understand the oneness or solidarity of all society; and the things that are the greatest hindrance to this sort of development are those agencies that serve to separate the people into fragments, that keep alive the fires of hatred within their bosoms and tend to make them hate rather than to love one another. All these agencies are the enemies of progress and of liberty, and stand directly athwart the path of freedom.
>
> … that today we are ruled to a great extent in America by commerce and industry, that we are rapidly passing to a better and kindlier and a more rational system that will be the rule of the people; coming, indeed, to the time when business will be friendship and government will be love… these are the fraternal forces that are unifying our life, that are bringing us together as members of one great family having one common interest and one common destiny.[9]

Our goal is not so much to smash capitalism, as to make the commons the new, more compelling attractor for activities that create value. Rather than try to use private labor to produce value, which is then captured by privately owned corporations and sold in markets based on artificially created scarcity, the peer production economy proposes a new model: abundance based on an ethic of sufficiency. Instead of allocating surplus value through the market or hierarchical systems, the peer production economy creates value through open, voluntary contributions and "massive mutual coordination," as Michel Bauwens calls it. The goal is to create commons through social systems and the sharing of resources.

Yuval Harari makes this same point in a 2018 article: "All humans share some core experiences, values and interests, and that no human group is inherently superior to all others. Cooperation is therefore more sensible than

[9] Samuel M. Jones, "Golden-Rule Government"

conflict. All humans should work together to protect their common values and advance their common interests. And the best way to foster such cooperation is to ease the movement of ideas, goods, money and people across the globe."[10]

You are hereby invited to take down the old paradigms on this planet and birth an eco-harmonious, decentralized civilization that empowers all to be the wise, sovereign, joyful, loving creators they truly are.

The good news is that Common Planet can become a catalyst for transitioning into a new order without the usual calamity because today experts understand the process of self-organizing complex systems like never before in addition to having access to complex computer modeling and simulations.

Researcher John Boik outlines some of these other efforts in his concept paper: "Science-Driven Societal Transformation, Part II: Motivation and Strategy":

> The idea that societies must undergo bold change is gaining ground. There appears to be a public interest in transformation, as evidenced by groups such as Transition Towns, New Economy Coalition, Peer2Peer Foundation, Economy for the Common Good, Next System Project, and Wellbeing Economy Alliance. Some religious leaders, including Pope Francis, are adopting the language of transformation. Thus, there is reason to believe that enough public support is or would be available to initiate the proposed R&D program and, eventually, to conduct the first field trial. Likewise, as evidenced by tens of thousands of signatories to the warning letters of Ripple et al., and by groups such as Great Transition Initiative and Sustainability Transitions Research Network, there is reason to believe that enough interest in transformation exists within the global scientific community that, with adequate funding, work on the R&D program could move forward.[11]

The major design consideration of the next system is the present system. We must be able to transition into the new system from the present and that means the first iteration of this next system will not be a finished product. This is but another step in our evolution as a species, perhaps, for the first time ever into real Civilization.

---

[10] Yuval Harari, The Economist, https://www.economist.com/open-future/2018/09/26/we-need-a-post-liberal-order-now

[11] John Boik, pp. 17,18 https://principledsocietiesproject.org/RePEc/files/0011.pdf

> The biggest challenge in designing a viable Game B is understanding which legacy systems to disrupt and which to utilize. Successful macro game migrations pull the capacity of the last game cycle into the systems of the new game cycle. We want to produce an agricultural to mechanization style migration, and not a Rome to the Dark Ages style migration.
>
> The trick is actually producing advantages that make the old game obsolete, and doing so without causing a collapse in legacy systems.
>
> Game A isn't our enemy. It's the Game we came in on. It was a good game in that it created the modern world. It laid the groundwork for a one family game to emerge. It's tired, and has nothing more to give. We have to treat it with a degree of respect as we work to replace it.
>
> If Game B provides true exponential capacity advantages, which is essential to its success and our survival, the optimism, cooperation, and coordination it activates is what will keep collapse at bay while we manage the migration and begin building the global systems of a new age. Game B must be a game that, due to network effects, takes over the entire board.[12]

After sharing lots of great transition ideas in his 2009 book *Plan B 4.0*, Lester Brown urges us to move forward: "It is decision time. Like earlier civilizations that got into environmental trouble, we can decide to stay with business as usual and watch our modern economy decline and eventually collapse, or we can consciously move onto a new path, one that will sustain economic progress. In this situation, the failure to act is a de facto decision to stay on the decline-and-collapse path."[13]

"What you and I have to do," said Malcolm X, "is get involved." That's exactly what the great environmental scientist Donella Meadows did throughout her life. There is no destination sustainability or destination regenerative cultures — as some kind of end point we arrive at to live happily ever after — rather, the path towards human, community, ecosystems and planetary health and wellbeing is a continuous process of exploration, transformation and dilemma navigation. Donella Meadows reminded us in a posthumously published paper entitled "Dancing with Systems": "… there is plenty to do, of a different sort of "doing." The future can't be predicted, but it can be envisioned and brought lovingly into being. Systems can't be controlled, but they can be designed and redesigned. We can't surge forward with certainty into a world of no surprises, but we can expect surprises and learn from them and even profit from them. We can't impose our will upon a

---

12 Paul Daigle, GameB FB group

13 Lester R. Brown, *Plan B 4.0*, pp 264, 265, http://www.earth-policy.org/images/uploads/book_files/pb4book.pdf

system. We can listen to what the system tells us, and discover how its properties and our values can work together to bring forth something much better than could ever be produced by our will alone. We can't control systems or figure them out. But we can dance with them!"[14]

The Las Indias Cooperative Group, which is a real-world venture in establishing a phyle — a non-territorial networked economic support platform — tells us in their 2016 book the *Communard Manifesto* that "the new world will be born and affirmed inside the old."

> Profound changes in social and economic relationships—system changes—are not the product of revolutions and political changes. It happens the other way around: systemic political changes are the expression of new forms of social organizing, new values, and ways of working and living, that have reached enough maturity to be able to establish a broad social consensus. As of a certain point in development, a "competition between systems" is established. The new forms, until then valid only for a small minority, begin to seem to be the only ones capable of offering a better future for the large majority. Little by little, they expand their spectrum and their number, encompassing and transforming broader and broader social spaces, and become the center of the economy, reconfiguring the cultural, ideological, and legal basis of society from within.
>
> "As the technologies of abundance become cheaper, more accessible and smaller in scale, escape through building counter-institutions — Exodus — rather than attempting to conquer the institutional core of the old system becomes increasingly feasible"
>
> The appearance of new ways of producing based on new forms of communal property—like free software—and distributed communication architectures—linked directly to decommodification and the creation of abundance—put forth the notion that we are on the threshold of a new phase in which we will be able to change the nature of that competition between systems.
>
> But, above all, what justifies a new time for the development of communitarianism is an irreversible economic change that has been imposed gradually: the reduction of the optimal scales of production. This decline in the optimal productive scale explains the deep trends that have produced the current economic crises, and why the political and corporate responses are often times counterproductive. And any alternative is not centered on social class or the nation, but on community.[15]

---

[14] Donella Meadows, "Dancing with Systems", https://thesystemsthinker.com/dancing-with-systems/

[15] Las Indias, *The Communard Manifesto*, 2016, https://lasindias.com/, https://c4ss.org/content/45925

Technology and Tactics

"We shape our tools and afterwards our tools shape us." — Marshall McLuhan

I am not a programmer but there's lots of folks working on software capable of being modified quickly for the purposes of running the global currency and property protocols of this book. Some I've mentioned and I'll just list them here for those who are interested in exploring further.

The one I'm most excited about is Holochain. Holo is a distributed cloud hosting network. Peer-to-peer applications and transactions are possible with Holo, utilizing Holochain. Essentially, Holochain's open-source protocol allows for scalable peer-to-peer applications. These can take the form of financial, social media or collaboration applications, and the potential really is limitless.[16]

Another is the OASIS API, a global universal API that aims to connect everything to everything to eliminate walled gardens/silos. There are a number of open protocols/platforms/networks (such as Gab, Mastodon, Diaspora, WebFinger, SOLID, Holochain, CEPTR Pluggable Protocol, Ethereum, Fediverse, ActivityPub, XMPP & more!) that the OASIS API will support. The majority of these are aimed at building a truly decentralized distributed internet (Web 3.0) and this is also the aim of the OASIS API.

The Flow credit currency protocol could simply slot into this existing blueprint called 'sustainable finance' from the r3.0.org. Even their description mirrors ours: "r3.0 promotes Redesign for Resilience and Regeneration. As a global common good not-for-profit platform, r3.0 crowdsources open recommendations for necessary transformations across diverse fields and sectors, in response to the ecological and social collapses humanity is experiencing, in order to achieve a thriving, regenerative and distributive economy and society."[17]

Open Culture - Internet Archive - MetaCurrency Mattereum - Regrid - QGIS Mapeo - Envienta - Urban Footprint - DIVA GIS - Arc GIS - Reason Score My Hope for the World - Protocol Love - Thingverse - Bright ID - SourceCred - ValueFlows - Our World The Game - Logseq Obsidian - Magnova Peermaps - gun - fairapps - Sharebay

[16] Blockchain: A Holochain Perspective, https://blog.holochain.org/blockchain-a-holochain-perspective/

[17] R3.0, https://www.r3-0.org/blueprint-6-sustainable-finance/

Wikipedia and the Mozilla and Linux Foundations; there also are millions of programs, documents and other media distributed under "Digital Commons".

Let's discuss some tactics. Global evolution is not something we undertake lightly. All of us understand the need for urgency, the need to move quickly, however let's do it by thinking and planning first. This is what I've been thinking about the past few years. Those thoughts and ideas will be shared with the Foundation team when it's time.

One of the obvious primary tactics involves disrupting the existing financial order. It seems to me at this moment that the central banks of the world are ready to rein in some of the debt they've issued and cause a massive global downshift in the values of all assets. As they raise interest rates, private banks might be less likely to lend if values of assets go down. Less lending means less investment. More borrowers than anticipated might default. Shrinking bank capital from which to lend credit is also a factor. Anyway, that's their problem.

What I'm really worried about is their ability to push war. War inevitably shifts the focus and blame away from the banking system onto the political States, but don't fall for it, it is the banks who run the show, not politicians.

"If a thousand men were not to pay their tax bills this year, that would not be a violent and bloody measure, as it would be to pay them, and enable the State to commit violence and shed innocent blood. This is, in fact, the definition of a peaceable revolution, if any such is possible," advised Henry David Thoreau in *Civil Disobedience.*

Not paying our taxes or debts is certainly one approach but there's other ideas about how to change the game. Economist Michael Hudson thinks we need a global debt jubilee to avoid the coming global depression.[18] That's one way to do it. He's not the only one promoting this idea.

The Emancipation Party is another group that's advocating the same thing. Here's their plan:

> RESET THE DEBT
>
> The inevitability of implosion is built into our present monetary system. It has always been a matter of time. Soon–likely within ten years–some form of debt default (or, worse, debt monetization) would be upon us. If we allow

[18] Michael Hudson, https://www.washingtonpost.com/opinions/2020/03/21/debt-jubilee-is-only-way-avoid-depression/

this to happen, the results will be like 2008 writ large: the ruination of American citizens to the benefit of the money power.

The key to sweeping out the old system is thousands of years old: the Jubilee; the forgiveness of all debts. The Jubilee is a Biblical concept of Biblical proportions. In the Old Testament world, every 50th year was a jubilee year when all debts were forgiven. The year of Jubilee in both the Jewish and Christian traditions is a time of joy, the year of remission or universal pardon. Jubilee allowed the system to be reset so that hierarchies and obligations did not perpetuate themselves.

The Jubilee

In our modern Jubilee, all debt of citizens and of federal, state, and local governments will be discharged and declared null, void, and unenforceable. This full discharge includes both secured and unsecured debt, and any guarantees of such debt are also declared null and void. It will, in fact, be illegal to repay any previous debt, except that between two persons, in which case voluntary repayment will be permitted but not required. Cancellation of all debt applies to all lenders, domestic or international. It will be illegal for any American person or US legal entity to repay or to collect any international debt.

Because 97% of our money is debt money, a Jubilee will sweep away the existing monetary system all at once. Free Money will be put into circulation to replace it… With the chains of debt finance broken, we will experience a tremendous entrepreneurial renewal.

The Jubilee is an acceptance of responsibility. Rather than imposing our debts on the future, we (creditor and debtor) alike accept the consequence of our moral hazard today. The Jubilee will systematically remove the illusion of debt money. While debt will be possible after the Jubilee, it will not approach the debt frenzy of the present era. Those who have learned to live by the world of debt will have to produce real value, create goods that have integrity, and practice self-discipline to succeed in the post-Jubilee world.

We've all heard talk about the necessity of common sacrifice and a return to community. Through the Jubilee, we will put our money behind our words. This might sound naive or crazy, but we have good reason to believe that this strategy can be successful with only an ordinary dose of good luck. Why?

As the idea of a Jubilee begins to circulate, interest-rates will increase. Rising interest rates makes a Jubilee more attractive. This will cause more people to support the Jubilee which will force interest rates to increase even further! We call this positive-feedback loop, "the Ratchet."

THE RATCHET

Once the idea of a Jubilee begins to circulate, it will begin to influence the behavior of three different groups:

> 1. Some debtors will look at a Jubilee as an opportunity to get things for free. They will attempt to borrow money in the hope that they will never have to pay it back.
>
> 2. Some lenders will look at the potential of a Jubilee as an added risk. As a consequence, lenders will be more hesitant to extend debt and will try to protect themselves against Jubilee risk.
>
> 3. Finally, the big money interests that manage most of the wealth in the country will look at Jubilee and the rest of Free Money as a warning to stay away from any form of asset that will pay back in Federal Reserve Notes, specifically US Government Treasury bills.
>
> These three dynamics combine into one result: suddenly, lending money will look a lot more risky, so interest rates will rise. The higher interest rates go, the more attractive Jubilee gets (because repaying your debts gets more and more expensive). And as Jubilee gets more attractive, more lenders will start to worry about getting paid back – and they will raise interest rates even higher.
>
> It is precisely by playing with the self-interest of the existing system that we will be able to overcome it. We do not know how quickly this process will play out. This depends on the spread and perceived legitimacy of the ideas of the Emancipation party. But we believe that with as few as 4 million members (less than a third of the current Tea Party) we can drive the system to an "inflection point" and render do-able what might otherwise be impossible.[19]

Others like Jordan Hall have also been calling for a global debt jubilee, like he does here in this 2015 article.[20] Here he is in a more recent post about what comes after, with a message "For the critics: a rebuke. We are not designing an Nth generation messaging app or yet another new way to separate humanity from its soul (I'm looking at you Web2), we are endeavoring something extraordinary. We are trying to innovate an entirely new form of human coordination. And we are doing so in the degeneracy and tyranny of a dying civilization. We need all of the help we can get. If you can help, by all means do so. Otherwise, get the fuck out of the way."[21]

---

[19] http://emancipationparty.org/debt-jubilee/

[20] Jordan Hall, https://medium.com/emergent-culture/it-is-time-for-a-global-debt-jubilee-part-i-901cd0ec305d

[21] Jordan Hall, https://deepcode.substack.com/p/the-dao-moment

> All the dysfunction we're seeing in the world it's not new, it's been there forever… And one of two things is gonna happen: we're gonna see this and we're gonna go "well isn't that just the way it is?" Or, we're gonna go "enough is enough!"At what point do we break the cycle?... Pain is not insignificant. Pain based on history has been the greatest awakener that this world has ever seen because it's not until you experience a level of pain that you start asking yourself a question: "There has to be a better way." "This hurts too much." There has never been more potential waiting to be unleashed than there is in this moment right now. The two greatest moments in your life is the day you were born and the day you work out why. And I would suggest most of you are tiptoeing through life right now trying to get to death safely, rather than opening the door every day and jumping out of the plane and facing death head-on. Because here's what I know, at some point you're gonna die. Every single one of you. But there's one thing that lives forever, and you know what that is? It's legacy. And my question to you is what do you want your legacy to be? What do you want to be remembered for because right now you are writing in the history books your legacy. So you're either gonna wait to nearly die, or you can just live now. The choice is yours. And have you ever watched a good movie where there was just that surprise twist at the ending that you didn't see coming? Maybe that's going to be your life. Maybe there's about to be a massive plot twist and maybe that massive plot twist is a change in trajectory in your life and a change in the trajectory of every single person who knows you, but you need to find something that you're willing to die for and then you need to live for it.[22]

If this resonates with you, please join this deeper conversation about our journey and how you can participate in the deepest transformation of humanity with the resources you have available to you. We are the ones we've been waiting for. We are the change we seek.

F.E.A.R has two meanings: Forget Everything And Run or Face Everything And Rise. The choice is yours. "How long are you going to wait before you demand the best for yourself?" asked Epictetus.

"It's not man who is the scourge of the world, it's a single culture. One culture out of hundreds of thousands of cultures. Our culture.

And here's the best of the news I have to bring:

We don't have to change humankind in order to survive. We only have to change a single culture."[23]

I'll leave you with some words from the giant Martin Luther King Jr.: "When we look at modern man, we have to face the fact that modern man

---

[22] Kerwin Rae, video, https://www.facebook.com/watch/?v=726034332137041

[23] Daniel Quinn, *The Story of B*, 1996

suffers from a kind of poverty of the spirit, which stands in glaring contrast with a scientific and technological abundance. We've learned to fly the air like birds, we've learned to swim the seas like fish, yet we haven't learned to walk the Earth as brothers and sisters."[24] In his last speech before he was murdered: "I may not get there with you, but I want you to know tonight that we as a people will get to the Promised Land."

This has always been our destiny.
It's time to build a Common Planet.
Let us cultivate our garden.

[24] MLK 1960 speech, https://www.youtube.com/watch?v=kTC3cieV_NA

ABOUT THE AUTHOR

Remzi Bajrami is an anarchist Albanian (është Shqiptar anarkist) born in 1973, in Yugoslavia, in what is now North Macedonia, in a muslim village near the border of Albania. He moved to Connecticut, USA in 1979 with his mother and brother where they joined his father who had arrived 3 years earlier. He was raised and educated in rural CT, surrounded by muslim family and catholic friends who tried to assert their beliefs and authority over him, but he isn't the kind to automatically adopt opinions without questioning and thinking first. And, he isn't a coward or ever afraid to speak the truth and he insists others think for themselves too. He's a demanding, kind hearted, empathic, true friend to friends.
In short: human.

Today, he's a husband in love with a most remarkable woman. Together, they've raised three independent beautiful souls who still think their parents are idiots but in time will come to realize how much they are like their parents. They live in the USA but wish to live on a Common Planet.

Made in United States
North Haven, CT
03 September 2026

17987237R00147